AF245607

*Macnamara's Irish Colony and the
United States Taking of California in 1846*

Macnamara's Irish Colony and the United States Taking of California in 1846

by
JOHN FOX

McFarland & Company, Inc., Publishers
Jefferson, North Carolina, and London

Library of Congress Cataloguing-in-Publication Data

Fox, John, 1942–
    Macnamara's Irish colony and the United Sates taking of California in 1846 / by John Fox.
        p.   cm.
    Includes bibliographical references (p.   ) and index.
    ISBN 0-7864-0687-9 (library binding : 50# alkaline paper) ∞
    1. California—History—1846–1850.   2. California—History—To 1846.   3. California—Colonization—History—19th century.   4. Irish Americans—California—History—19th century.   5. Mexican War, 1846–1848—California.
6. Macnamara, Eugene, 19th century.   7. Missionaries—California—Biography.   8. Missionaries—Ireland—Biography.
9. San Joaquin Valley (Calif.)—History—19th century.
I. Title.
F864.F687   2000
979.4'03—dc21   99-16977
                                                    CIP

British Library Cataloguing-in-Publication data are available

Manufactured in the United States of America

McFarland & Company, Inc., Publishers
  Box 611, Jefferson, North Carolina 28640
    www.mcfarlandpub.com

For
Karl and Doris Gillette
"New Californians"
Thank you

Contents

List of Illustrations

Preface and Acknowledgments

As the crow flies, Eugene Macnamara traveled more than 40,000 miles in five years and literally halfway round the globe. He bit off more than he could chew. I feared doing the same in trying to follow his tracks, which are now 150 years cold, but, like early wagon-wheel ruts on the Sierra passes into California, still just discernible. Each country on Macnamara's journey could occupy a researcher's lifetime and each helps explain his adventure in California. Despite the flaws in my filling out this huge canvas, I feel the Macnamara story is worth an attempt to tell for the first time.

The Huge Canvas

He spent his best-known 46 days in California. The taking of California from Mexico by the United States in 1846 has been chronicled often by American scholars. My account, from Macnamara's standpoint and using new British and Mexican sources, adds the last major jigsaw piece which has always been missing from that American story.

Macnamara came from Ireland, which was administered by Britain as a colony. Today, with the rapid development of the independent Republic of Ireland into a leading, secular European nation, scholars are taking its story out of the hands of partisans. I have put Macnamara into his Irish context as scholars are beginning to understand it, not as sentiment or prejudice might wish it to be. The reality of early 19th century Irish rural life and religion was more earthy, complex and even less sectarian than a later "stained glass" filter showed.

Macnamara styled himself an "Apostolic Missioner," under the notably mission-minded Pope Gregory XVI (1831–1846). Early 19th century Irish missioners, within and beyond the growing British Empire, have to be understood against the background of the Papacy they served. At one point Macnamara dashed straight to Rome to complain about the dark side of the British Guiana mission. In fact, he worked under a series of dark clouds, from mission to mission, from Ireland to British Guiana, Britain's only South American colony, and from there to Mexico, almost at war with its North American neighbor.

Any mention of "British California" (as it nearly became), raises eyebrows of surprise right along Macnamara's trail—from Britain to California—despite the fact that California was charted as *New Albion* (New Britain) for 250 years after Francis Drake first landed near San Francisco Bay in 1579. Spanish Franciscan missioners went there in 1770 as part of Spain's defense strategy against Britain and Russia, who were suspected of designs on California as a back door into the Spanish empire. Seventy-five years later, the attempt to take California by "British agents," chief among them Eugene Macnamara, was a central *stated* reason for the U.S. preemptive strike in capturing that Department.

California historians, to steal Walter Colton's phrase, have "made the most of the blubber and the bones" of the whale of early California history. The Macnamara contract—to the Mexicans *El Proyecto Macnamara*—is the exception, despite the fact that it was publicly declared in 1847–8, under oath before the U.S. Senate, to have been the chief threat to the United States on the Pacific. The story was not picked over with the rest of the "blubber and bones" because its scant records made little sense. It also carried a dangerous charge in a split America between pro- and anti–Irish parties. All that could be said about Eugene Macnamara was summed up in 1888 by Hubert Bancroft, the Homer of California history, in seven pages.[1] Any commentator on Macnamara since then has had only those pages of considered evidence and judgment on which to draw. Only one researcher, Mary Karam, OP, in 1967, has written on the Irish colonizer. She discovered that the Macnamara documents from Governor Pico's Departmental archive, taken from Los Angeles to Washington by John Frémont in 1847, no longer exist. She also traced the Macnamara surname to County Clare, Ireland, where the Bishop of Killaloe confirmed to her that a Eugene Macnamara had been a curate there in 1837.[2]

Ignatius Murphy, late Vicar General of Killaloe, wrote a sensitive and frank history of the diocese, the third and final volume of which was published in 1995 just after his death.[3] It is a model for the objective handling of Irish religious history. Murphy noticed that Macnamara, after a brief career in the diocese, had ended up in British Guiana. Karam, thirty years before, knew nothing of the Guiana period. These small finds still added so little to Bancroft's account that, understandably, they did not register back in California.

I returned from three months research and travel in California in 1995, knowing only the Bancroft summary. During my time there, the editor of a

Central Valley periodical challenged me, as a Briton researching the early California Irish, to unearth the Macnamara story.[4] Months later, in the London Public Record Office, I came on a dispatch of 1845 from an Irish diplomat in Mexico which drew together the four elements of the Macnamara story—Ireland, British Guiana, Mexico and California—in as many lines. In Warwickshire, England, I found an 1846 view of Macnamara from Rear Admiral Seymour on the Pacific coast, including a private diary kept apart from the main papers and overlooked by researchers even as meticulous as Abraham Nasatir. The Seymour family has also preserved relics of the Admiral's time off Mexico and California, when Macnamara was his guest, the most notable being HMS *Collingwood*'s wardroom table around which the leading American, British and Mexican actors of 1846 gathered. Seymour's great great grandson, the late 8th Marquess of Hertford, kindly encouraged my work, and his son, the 9th Marquess, has continued that support. *Collingwood*'s painted figurehead still scrutinizes British sailors in Portsmouth Royal Naval Base, just as it inspected Macnamara, Frémont, Sloat and Seymour—and many British sailors—in 1846.

Historians of British Guiana (now the Republic of Guyana) knew a Eugene Macnamara from their records, but nothing of his subsequent adventures in Mexico and California. Californian historians knew nothing of Macnamara's time in British Guiana and, until Ignatius Murphy looked more closely, Irish archivists knew nothing of Macnamara's escapades in Guiana *or* California. The documents central to the story lay in Mexico City. In fact, the story has not been told, precisely because it spans half the globe and, in church law, Macnamara was a *clerus vagus*, a wandering cleric.

We have no portrait of Macnamara—etching, daguerrotype or written—save U.S. Consul Thomas Larkin's asides that he was "of very good appearance" and "dresses in Citizen [civilian] clothes." Patrick Connors, Jesuit missioner and archivist in Georgetown, Guyana, suspects that he was, in the language of rugby football, "a big front row forward, or maybe a wiry scrum half." He was certainly assertive, with a gift of persuasive conversation, confident in important company, with initiative enough to sail 8,000 miles to see the Pope when angry and to hector two presidents of Mexico into their duty to help him get his way. He was a maverick, in the original Texan sense of the word, the unbranded steer without an owner which lives with the herd on its own terms. I suspect he dried up spiritually and became disillusioned: the bitterness showed. He was suspended three times in three years by three successive bishops, and mistreated and maligned by the second of the three who was himself verging on mental collapse. Bitterness showed in Macnamara's attack on "American Methodist wolves," in his frustration "to the point of madness" in Honolulu, and in his scattergun accusations against fellow speculators in a mining business where he was out of his depth. Despite his abstaining from drink (and just possibly because of it), he seems to have been a restless, driven man, taking out his anger on the nearest moving targets and perhaps on himself. It may even have been the reason for his Proyecto.

The story of the Macnamara Project, I believe, is worth telling, despite or even because of its failure. A man who traveled so frenetically, was accused (uniquely in the history of Europe!) of being a Catholic Jesuit agent of Protestant Britain, who impressed a Roman Cardinal, Mexican Archbishop and two presidents, a British admiral, California deputies, British and American ambassadors, and French, British and American consuls, is worth at least closer examination. In the end he was defeated by events beyond his control. John Frémont, California "Pathfinder," admired him for the sheer grandeur of his failure. The British game of cricket was popular in 19th century British Ireland, played in schools and seminary colleges. Admiral Seymour's crewmen played cricket in the evenings on Mexican beaches. International Cricket Test Matches are still highlights of life in Georgetown, Guyana. The game provided the Victorians with a metaphor for life itself, where success might be measured, not merely in terms of "winning," but of "playing the game" and even of "losing grandly." It is beyond our judging how Macnamara—or Clancy, Hynes, Frémont and Seymour—really "played the game." We can only sift their recorded words and known actions, which make up "history." Failure and success are relative and usually out of sight.

If filmmakers can invite investment for the making of *Braveheart 2*, the story of William Paterson's failed and foolish 18th century colony of New Edinburgh, in the Panama jungle, they might do worse, next time around, than examine the Macnamara story for *Macnamara I*. Del Monte fruit, Gallo wines, even the Gold Lode are all elements of the salad bowl San Joaquin Valley which Macnamara contracted to settle—surely a better setting for colonists (and film crews) than the jungle.

Thanks

Had Macnamara had the international help I have had, he might now be marked by a statue in New Ennis, market center of the agribusiness ranches of the former San Joaquin Valley, long renamed New Clare in a tale of bogs to riches. I owe much to the Prime Warden and Wardens of the Worshipful Company of Goldsmiths in the City of London who gave me a Research Fellowship and time out to work in the hills of northern California in 1995. Martin Roberts and my Cherwell School colleagues encouraged, teased and put up with my tales afterwards. By definition, teachers are transmitters of the tribe's tales. Karl and Doris Gillette equipped me for the hills with advice, tent, coffee pot, gold pan, transport from Rent-a-Relic, and enthusiasm for their adopted home state: "Go for it!" Many have been thanked elsewhere for their kindness that year along main and side roads between the San Joaquin

Valley and the Cascades. Bill Anderson, editor of *The Dogtown Territorial Quarterly,* urged me to take on the Macnamara mystery and he and his historical advisors have helped me since. Richard and Frances Rohrbacher of Columbia, California, generously shared their own Macnamara findings with me. History in the Sierra Nevada is the property and work of local people, not an academic reservation. The late Joe King, in particular, made his home, his contacts and a lifetime's knowledge of the California Irish available to me with great warmth. Earl Schmidt of Palo Alto and Professor Robert R. Miller of Santa Barbara have also been most helpful.

Rachel Naughton and the trustees of the Cardinal Knox Centre, East Melbourne, Australia, provided and kindly allowed me to cite Bishop Hynes' Guiana diary. In Hawaii, the State Archive of Honolulu, the Bishop Museum and the RC Diocesan Archivist, Fr. Louis Yim, all helped in locating (and in Father Yim's case, trawling through) material. Sadly no biography exists of the Oceania busybody Robert Crichton Wyllie, one of Macnamara's key mentors. The loss of his papers remains an Hawaiian mystery. In Guyana Republic, Patrick Connors SJ rolled up sleeves between mission stints up river and trawled the filing cabinets and crypt of Georgetown RC Cathedral. "Bug, fire and water," in his words, have destroyed some records already. Patrick also offered valuable insights into the 19th century missioners. Time and gaps in the record put an odd black-or-white perspective on their behavior: they were either candidates for sainthood—or wretched. Unrecorded reality is always more grey.

Tom McCoog SJ of the Jesuit archive in London's Mount Street made me welcome and in turn put me onto Jesuit archivists in Maryland, New York and Fordham to whom I am also in debt. U.S. National Archivists in Maryland and the Archivist of Santa Barbara Mission also helped, as has Dr. William Franks of the Huntington Library, San Marino, Los Angeles, whose Trustees allowed me to publish the Macnamara circular and a crucial Larkin letter from the Stearns Collection, omitted from the Hammond volumes. The Bancroft Library staff, Berkeley, under Bonnie Hardwick, have welcomed me often and nothing has been too much trouble. I am grateful to their Trustees for permission to cite from several collections held there. Jane Garner, Head of Rare Books and Manuscripts, Benson Latin American Collection, University of Texas at Austin Library, gave help and permission to publish from the Gómez-Farías Papers, purchased in Mexico in 1921.

Interests and priorities have changed in Mexico since those days and even more since 1846. Carlos Enrique Ruíz Abreu and Erendira Peña Martínez, senior archivists of the Archivo General de la Nación, searched out, amid reorganization, the Macnamara file for 1845/6: it is published here for the first time, by permission of the Mexican Government. Director Hector Madrid Mulia was unable to locate the confirmation dossier of Macnamara's grant for 1847 in time for publication. His Excellency the Mexican Ambassador in

London and Marcella of the Embassy staff acted above and beyond any diplomatic duty and my thanks to them are very heartfelt. The Picpus Order archivist could not retrieve Abbé Maigret's letters from Honolulu in 1846 and knew of no list of the Irish students in Rue Picpus, Paris, when Macnamara was on Rue des Irlandais: Picpus archives are currently crated in storage.

In England, Warwickshire County Archive holds the Seymour Papers on loan. The late 8th Marquess of Hertford allowed me to cite the Admiral's papers and kindly provided the photograph of Frederick Lucas' portrait of Seymour; his son, the 9th Marquess, confirmed that permission. The commander of today's HMS *Collingwood*, a Portsmouth shore base, kindly provided additional information about the flagship. The warden, fellows and librarian of All Souls College Oxford allowed me to cite from Doyle and Bankhead letters held by the College. The Linley Library of the Royal Horticultural Society (formerly London Horticultural Society) gave me access to Theodor Hartweg's original diaries, most of which are in print. Her Majesty's Public Record Office in London, one of the most user-friendly archives in the world, permitted me to cite from Foreign Office, Colonial Office and Admiralty papers. The staffs of the British Library, British Newspaper Library and National Maritime Museum in London and most particularly of the Bodleian and Rhodes House Libraries, Oxford, have been unfailingly helpful.

In Ireland, Fr. Gerry Kenny and Martin Browne hosted me at the Killaloe diocesan archive in Ennis. I can only list my thanks to many others, including Martin O'Brien, Parish Priest of Borrisokane, Patrick Taafe, Parish Priest of Corofin, Sister M. Meaney, Archivist of the Presentation Order, John Fleming, Rector of the Irish College in Rome, Ignatius Fennessy, OFM, Archivist of the Irish Franciscans, Hugh Fenning, OP, of the Irish Dominicans, and Thomas O'Connor of Maynooth College. The Irish College, Paris, closed in 1939. In fact, every avenue explored in Ireland, with the exception of the diocese of Cork, proved open, courteous and helpful. Finally, after thanking my family for putting up with "Macnamara" for several years, I must thank Alan Fitzgibbon, whom I knew only through the Internet, but who helped and researched in Washington most generously. Macnamara would have enjoyed the Internet, although *virtual* reality would not have been enough for his restless spirit.

Reminder

Today, most Catholics and Protestants share and respect each other's tradition. Macnamara was from a polemical age, but one in which there was still human warmth between Catholic and Protestant. In Ireland, mixed religious marriage and mixed schooling were facts of life; sectarian bigotry was the exception, even when Catholicism was technically outlawed. The harsh 17th century penal laws had not been seriously enforced for a century before they were finally abolished in 1829. They had already been tempered forty years before. In the heat of the British Guiana Catholic schism, Bishop Hynes had the support of Protestant friends and stayed with an Anglican mission when he traveled up the Moruka River in 1844. Even Bishop Clancy, reluctantly, said some good of the Methodists. The Irish and the English have been neighbors and friends far longer than they have been enemies, as have Catholics and Protestants throughout most of Europe, a fact easily forgotten by their descendants abroad.

The 19th century Irish, while Celtic by race, were politically and legally British, the whole of Ireland being part of the Union, or United Kingdom. Since 1922 only the northeastern six counties of that island, two-thirds of the ancient province of Ulster, have belonged to the United Kingdom and are known as the Province of Northern Ireland. Three counties of Ulster stayed with the new Irish State of 1922, although, in good Irish fashion, part of "Southern Ireland," as the Republic is still familiarly known, extends farther north than Northern Ireland. The Irish of Macnamara's day were British Irish, and they called themselves "British" abroad: the term British included Irish, Scots, Welsh, English and, in the world of Mexican and Californian miners, the Cornish.

Mexico was the greatest landowner in the northern American continent. Mexican America stretched from the Yucatán peninsula to the Columbia River and from the Louisiana border across Coahuila-Texas, New Mexico, Arizona, Utah, Nevada and the Two Californias. Russian America was Alaska, but with a base as far south as Bodega in California. British America was what is now Canada. The United States of the North, as the Mexicans called the U.S.A., did not stretch "from sea to shining sea" but, after the Louisiana Purchase from Napoleon of France, only as far west as the Rockies. Washington felt hemmed in by British and Mexican territory, and even more so when Britain seemed to be taking over Mexican land. The year 1846 was only 70 years after the Declaration of Independence by the 13 colonies from Britain: a few just remembered that event. The British looked back on it as "Yankee treachery," which became a proverb. Many more, including serving officers, remembered clearly the burning of the White House by the British in 1812 during the Anglo-American war. History is a continuum of woven memories, not a row of segments. The ghosts of those two wars haunted Anglo-U.S. relations for decades, just as Napoleon long affected French-Anglo relations and two German wars have overshadowed 20th century Europe. The atmosphere in the theatre was already quite electric when Eugene Macnamara appeared on stage.

John Fox
Wheatley, Oxford. United Kingdom.
1999

One

Missioners, Merchants, Colonists and Continentalists

"Great scheming geniuses [or] tide-waiters of fortune"—*Emigrant and Colonial Gazette*, London, August 1848

On the morning of Tuesday, July 7, 1846, two hundred American marines and sailors landed out of the sea fog below the Custom House at Monterey, capital of Mexican Upper California. They paraded to hear their commander read in Spanish and English the formal proclamation of American rule.

The Eagle-and-Serpent tricolor of Mexico was not even on the Custom House flagpole to be struck: it had been missing for some weeks, along with the old cannon taken from the fort by the military *Comandante* to his field headquarters. Gun salutes from U.S. ships *Savannah* and *Cyane* acknowledged the raising of the Stars and Stripes and, for the first time, the sun burnt off a morning's coastal fog over American California. There was no resistance. In fact there were neither cannon, powder nor soldiers in the dilapidated fort onshore and the artillery captain left town pleading his lack of authority to surrender.

A hundred miles to the north, at Sonoma, beyond San Francisco Bay, American settler squatters had declared independence from Mexico under a homemade Bear-and-Lone-Star flag. Three hundred miles to the south, in Los Angeles, the California Departmental Assembly in extraordinary session, oblivious that its time was up, discussed and approved a single agenda item that morning—the Macnamara contract.

The Mexicans lost the Upper (*Alta*) of the Two (*Ambas*) Californias in exactly the way that, for years, observers had warned they would lose it: by neglect.

9

The U.S. Continentalists

The land was too vast, too distant from Mexico and too thinly populated, despite the attraction of its arable valleys and spreading word of its mineral wealth. Gold, silver and copper were being discovered right up to the American invasion. More important, a huge source of mercury (quicksilver), the essential amalgam agent for the extraction of gold and silver, had just been confirmed—in law to its owners and in yield at up to 40 percent. The Rothschilds in Europe controlled most of the mercury used in Mexican mines and the California strike broke that grip. Ironically, the find was accidental, in the one Mexican Department where no government prospecting had yet taken place. Political instability and lack of money had meant that the Departments (as the conservative centralists called them) or Provincial States (as the liberal federalists called them) of Coahuila (including breakaway Texas), Arizona, New Mexico and the Californias were afterthoughts, too far away and too expensive to be anything more than reluctant considerations for development or defense. They all needed people—*pobladores,* settlers, colonists or pioneers—to fill the lands. Others, not Mexicans, eventually exploited the Department assets.

Texas had been the first Mexican Department or Province to go. Settled by American and European colonists, including the Irish, even before the republican Lone Star flag was raised in 1835, Texas remained independent for ten years, but grew closer to the United States. It ripened for picking in 1845, after more and more settlers had poured in, and that year joined the United States of the North. Texas became another southern pro-slavery state: Mexico forbade slavery; the northern American States were against it; the free world outside bayed for its abolition. The capture of Mexican land and the introduction of slavery could increase the power of the U.S. pro-slavery states in Washington. Successive Mexican governments—they seemed to change by the year—lacked the wisdom and self-interest to swallow pride, cut loss, recognize Texan independence and negotiate a ready-made border against the United States. Popular feeling in Texas ruled out this option by the time Mexican troops were sent to the Rio Grande in April 1845, to attack when U.S. troops took over the new American State. A year later, Mexican soldiers did cross the Rio Grande and attack an American force within what Mexico argued was its border up to the Nueces River. The Americans argued that the land was American territory. President Polk, an expansionist, or "continentalist," welcomed the attack and declared war on May 13, 1846. It took time for news to travel. Two months later in Monterey Bay, the U.S. Naval Commander Pacific, John Sloat, knowing of the Rio Grande incident but unaware of the declaration of war, decided to risk claiming Upper California on July 7th.

He knew that in the California hinterland, John Frémont, a U.S. Army

Topographical Engineer, had linked up with the settler squatters occupying Sonoma in "the Popular Movement," later canonized as "the Bear Flag Revolt." Believing Frémont to be acting on White House orders (he was in fact acting on his own initiative, consistently for a son-in-law of Senator Benton, Polk's expansionist advisor), Sloat followed his apparent cue and raised the U.S. flag. It was not an easy decision. Four years before, Commodore Ap Catesby Jones had done the same thing, also believing that war with Mexico had begun. Jones lost his gamble and had been publicly humiliated: in 1842 the time was not ripe nor the pretext strong enough. By 1846 conditions were just right. Under the same orders as Jones, to take the Californian ports in the event of general hostilities, Sloat's overreach paid off. It also broke his health. He was surprised and angry to learn from Frémont, shortly afterwards, that the map maker had acted alone.

British Designs on California

Britain and France gave Sloat added pretext. European eyes had long lusted after California. General Paredes, military dictator in Mexico from January 1846 and staunchly anti–American, wanted a European monarchy for Mexico. Monarchist Britain was best placed to benefit since France had been virtually a republic for fifty years and British merchants, mining engineers and speculators already ran Mexico. British financiers held an option on 1,250,000 acres of Mexican Departmental public land as collateral for an accumulating loan-debt of twenty years; leading figures in the British Admiralty were keen to have San Francisco Bay as their base in the Pacific, denying it to France, Russia and the United States. Extreme British patriots in 1846 urged Lord Palmerston, a new and expansionist foreign minister who succeeded the cautious Lord Aberdeen that summer, to claim California by right of Sir Francis Drake's landing there in 1579. A shelf of publications since 1839 had broadcast the advantages to Britain of holding this Pacific paradise by colony and garrison. *The Times* in London added its voice to a crescendo of demand throughout 1845 and 1846. British national pride, dented within living memory in the Anglo-American war of 1812–1814, and even more badly dented in the Independence War forty years before that, was not to be damaged again by America's winning the race for the Pacific coast.

As apparent proof of British intent, fifteen war vessels, the largest Royal Navy fleet in peacetime, patrolled the Mexican, Californian and Oregon coasts through 1845-6. Up to that time only eight had ever even visited the region since 1820. Of this force of 360 guns (the Americans had 330 guns in the Pacific) two were capital battleships. HMS *America* was captained by the brother of Lord Aberdeen, British Foreign Secretary; his second-in-command was the son of Sir Robert Peel, British Prime Minister. HMS

Collingwood, the 80-gun flagship, under Sir George Seymour, a lord of the Admiralty Board, dominated everything afloat. Several sloops and frigates performed non-political tasks such as reconnaissance, hydrography and polar exploration. The United States and Britain were in dispute over where to divide the Oregon Territory, until then jointly occupied. As long as the dispute remained unresolved, a naval stand-off was inevitable. "Brag" they called it and war was likely. The issue was surprisingly peacefully resolved in mid-1846 by the British conceding land as far north as the Columbia River. It was as well: the draft treaty only reached Washington after the start of the Mexican war and the United States was not keen to fight two fronts. Britain, fearful of collecting even more far-flung imperial liabilities, did not want war with America. Additionally, its patience with Mexico had run out. France also haunted the British, who had feared the ghost of Napoleon since Waterloo. Other Pacific concerns competed with the Oregon: the Sandwich (Hawaiian) and Friendly (Tahitian) Isles both demanded a British presence to counter French and U.S. interference.

Throughout the California episode Rear Admiral Sir George Seymour, British Commander, Pacific, received no more up-to-date orders from London than a belated copy of a December 1844 instruction, forwarded by the British ambassador in Mexico one year later. Events moved faster than communications. The Admiral held to strict neutrality as his guide to behavior in the event of war between the U.S. and Mexico. He would, he insisted, answer a plea for help from California, only if that department declared independence from Mexico. Should there be a naval showdown, fighter though he was and still willing to "have a go," Seymour knew that he was too far from home to keep up a defense of California. He was drawing, he lamented, "in a lottery in which nothing remains but blanks."

Unpaid, unusual and apparently unnecessary diplomatic posts in California had been created by Britain, France and the United States after 1842. Despite its distance and supposed unimportance save as a tallow- and hide-trading coast in decline, California suddenly merited consuls. Each reported to his respective government on the activities of the others and on the general state of Californian intrigue. James Forbes, British Vice-Consul, like Thomas Larkin, the American consul, tempted the Californios to declare independence, but both felt it was inevitable that the U.S. should take over. Rumor, a potent force in California, had Forbes urging Governor Pío Pico to seek a British Protectorate by inviting the Royal Navy to land and raise the Union Flag. Rumor and distortion shaped Californian politics. Forbes *was* due to attend a Council (*Junta*) at Santa Barbara to debate independence from Mexico. The British Navy *did* have a vessel offshore, albeit a small frigate, HMS *Juno*, on reconnaissance. *Juno* also had on board a colonizer from British Ireland, Eugene Macnamara. The Santa Barbara *Junta* was canceled, but the grist had piled for the rumor mill. Mexicans and Americans alike read into the combination of Royal Navy, Irish colonizer and independence *Junta*, a serious British intent. Admiral Seymour was an experienced diplomat, as well as a fighting-deck veteran of Nelson's fleet, but his admitting of Eugene Macnamara to *Collingwood*'s wardroom in April 1846 and the assistance he gave him afterwards were perhaps the sole mistakes of a difficult tour.

Macnamara: Missioner, Colonizer, Speculator?

Word spread through California that Macnamara was a government agent sent to take California. That he was transported continuously for seven months by Royal Navy ships of such a powerful squadron on active service was taken as proof of his status. Between May and November 1846, Macnamara was either a guest of or on the ration strength of four Royal Navy vessels, one of them the giant flagship itself. Native Californios were greatly impressed, both by the presence of the legendary Royal Navy off their coastline and by Macnamara's apparent importance; the Americans were equally impressed, fearing a naval showdown with Britain. Macnamara fed belief in his importance with well-practiced name-dropping and self-inflation.

Seymour arrived at Monterey in mid–July 1846, and remained carefully neutral. The Department of California had not declared itself independent of Mexico and Sloat had raised the U.S. flag ashore. In a U.S.-Mexican war there was no more for a neutral British admiral to do once pleasantries were exchanged. Urgent tasks awaited him in the Pacific islands. Seymour had only to assure himself of the facts and make sure "the interests of British subjects" were safe. Eugene Macnamara, a thoroughly British subject, was probably less than safe in American territory. He boarded *Collingwood* on July 17th after a long ride from Los Angeles where he had completed negotiations for a huge colony of Irish farmers in California. Numbers and locations for the colony *haciendas* changed and expanded as negotiations progressed.

The Irishman took his place at *Collingwood*'s wardroom table and watched a virtual review of the cast involved in the American taking of California. *Collingwood* was a floating conference center moored for a week in the bay. British Vice-Consul James Forbes, Captain John Frémont, American Consul Thomas Larkin, commodores Sloat and Stockton all came aboard. Frémont later claimed before the U.S. Senate that Macnamara was the *reason* he had helped declare an independent, Texas-style California in June 1846, which he felt had paved the way for the American takeover. The "Bear Flag Republic" was a grand gesture with little substance; its flag motif included the Lone Star, like Texas, which it sought to imitate. Its Bear motif even failed to imitate a bear. It desperately needed a Macnamara to raise its status, even in hindsight.

Macnamara was a known Catholic cleric, although he did not wear habit, *soutaine* or clerical shovel-hat like his Mexican fellow-clergy. Recorded comment focused on his youth and on his intelligence, occasionally suggesting his intolerance. By July 1846, in Monterey, he was a British subject in need. In April, he had impressed Seymour with his manner and with the testimonials he brought with him. Macnamara had begun to exploit the empty, neglected Department of California, although late in the day. His colonists were acceptable to Mexico as Ireland was the only Catholic country in the British Empire and Mexicans would welcome its unique combination of Catholic British, although some did fear that the Irish were too close to the Americans and would prove to be more fifth column than loyal colony. Only Johann Sutter, the Swiss *empresario* (contractor) at the mouth of the Sacramento Valley, the other half of the huge Californian Central Valley, had the same distinction of being a European attempting a colony in California, but not even Sutter had applied to head a mass settlement. By comparison with Macnamara's contract, Sutter's 200-square-mile grant was small beer.

A Catholic priest in his early thirties, Macnamara styled himself "Apostolic Missioner," indicating he was under the Pope's direct authority or at least that of an "Apostolic Vicar," a bishop created by the Pope as a mission deputy. The Franciscans of the California frontier missions had used the same title until the missions were dissolved in 1833 by the Mexican government. Admiral Seymour thought him "intelligent and straightforward"; the French consul in California thought he had to be "a Jesuit"; Frémont thought Rome had sent him. Thirty years later, Hubert Bancroft sifted every surviving document from early California. He admitted that as British government records were closed, he could say no more about this "patriotic dreamer." In fact, Bancroft's contemporaries were already dismissing Macnamara as "apocryphal." The story of the missioner acting as speculators' frontman and agent for an expansionist British government was muddied and distorted after 1846. Bancroft, however, did suspect that the Macnamara threat was a "bugaboo," a bugbear, a distracting of scrutiny from those American expansionists who did well out of the taking of California, particularly John Frémont and relatives. "We know only that he was Irish, a priest and an Apostolic Missioner," stated Bancroft. That ended discussion for a century and a half. Even Frémont admitted that only "gleanings" from London confirmed the rumors of the time.[1]

Bancroft and Fremont were dead when the London records were finally opened. They revealed a vital clue to Macnamara's identity. Charles Bankhead, British Minister (ambassador) in Mexico City, wrote to Lord Aberdeen, Foreign Secretary, on May 30, 1845, reporting the existence of Macnamara and his colonizing project. In another letter written at the end of July, Bankhead outlined another plan, this time from the British Consul there, to colonize California, and, in passing, mentioned Macnamara again. Lord

Aberdeen certainly read the dispatches and called up the second letter, fresh from the Foreign Office in-tray, during discussions with the Mexican Ambassador in London that September. He never referred, however, to Macnamara in writing during his tenure of office. Bankhead was Irish and would have registered Macnamara's details accurately—Ireland is a small country. In fact, the British legation in Mexico City was virtually Irish at the time, as Bankhead's wife quipped to a family friend.[2] Ambassador Bankhead wrote that Macnamara had arrived in Mexico City late in 1844

> from Demerara, furnished with letters of introduction to the Archbishop of Mexico from the Bishop of that Colony, and many others to the British residents here. He is a native of the County of Clare, Ennis, I believe. I have every reason to be pleased with his acquaintance.[3]

Lost Tracks

Time and accident covered Macnamara's tracks, better than any conspiracy might have done. Church registers in Ennis only began twenty years after his birth. The scant records of the Irish College in Paris where he studied offer only a few names and dates. The parish priests who ordered Macnamara's first working years in their role as the new "squires" of the Irish countryside left some evidence. Records of the Irish Temperance Movement also showed his taking the Pledge, invaluable to him later in British Guiana, the most drink-sodden and depressing colonial mission in the British Empire, not far up the coast from France's Devil's Island. The colony saw a serious feud between rival Irish bishops during Macnamara's time there. Later, the Jesuit order took over the Catholic mission and the Macnamara years were consigned to an *obliteratio memoriae.* Even the Jesuit necrology or anniversary list, kept to perpetuate mission memories, omitted key early figures; a later house manuscript history of the period—the "Secret Diary"—was kept from young Jesuit novices. Macnamara's attitudes were shaped in Ireland and Guiana—toward the Americans, toward colonization, toward Protestants and toward his own status.

The British press made no mention of Macnamara in two years of reporting California events. The Catholic English-language newspaper, *The Tablet,* before losing Macnamara completely in Mexico, censored out his dramatic dash from Guiana to the Vatican in the summer of 1843. *The Catholic Directory* yearbook still reported his being in British Guiana as late as 1847, when he had already been in Mexico three years. Bishop William Clancy, Apostolic Vicar of Guiana, about whom Macnamara went to Rome to complain, died in Ireland, leaving no papers in the chaos of his deposition and flight. His rival and successor, Bishop John Hynes, the third bishop to suspend

Macnamara, left diaries and letters, but the key entries for January 1844–April 1845, when Macnamara left for Mexico, disappeared. Even the personal details on Macnamara's internal Mexican passport (*Carta di Seguridad*), a verbal photograph of height, eye color, age, characteristics, are missing from the hundreds of registered details of British nationals in 1845-6. As a cleric Macnamara was exempt from giving details.

In London, where finance houses were said to have used Macnamara as a front man, neither the private Spanish American [Bondholder] Association, nor its Mexican Committee, nor the known leading Bondholders left records, save passing asides. Thousands of miles away, in the Sandwich Islands (Hawaii), a leading Bondholder, Robert Crichton Wyllie, became that Kingdom's unlikely Foreign Secretary in 1846, just before Macnamara spent two months in Honolulu. Wyllie recorded everything for his autobiography, but the forty-volume archive was stolen, dumped or destroyed at his death in 1863. From Mexico in 1843 Wyllie had urged the London holders of Mexican bonds to take debt repayment in Californian land as a good business move in its own right. His report inspired Macnamara.

Two Macnamara dossiers (*expedientes*) of original papers from his negotiations with Mexican Central Government between 1845 and 1847, help authenticate the lost Californian clutch of Macnamara papers taken to Washington by John Frémont from Los Angeles in 1847. They discount any notion of American forgery and finally help make sense of the Macnamara affair. Since Bancroft's day, correspondences from Macnamara's Mexico and California have been published, most notably the letters of the first Bishop of the Californias, García Diego (1840–1846), and correspondence of Thomas Oliver Larkin, U.S. consul in Mexican California. Admiral Seymour's family also preserved intact the Admiral's papers with his detailed record of events on the Pacific coast in 1846, complete with observations on Macnamara.[4]

St. Patrick's on the Jumna River...

Whatever his other roles, Macnamara was on the crest of a church missionary wave, in the wake of the traders and troops of the new British Empire. The thought of newly discovered unbaptized millions spurred missionary zeal and even diverted churches from problems nearer home. There was competition for souls. "Limbo," the generous medieval notion of the "margin" bigger than the visible page, beyond the church's understanding, which might have relaxed the missionary frenzy, had disappeared. Mass baptism became a mark of success. As Protestant British and American missionaries evangelized along the routes of discovery, Pope Gregory XVI (1831–1846) also set out to evangelize a second New World in the void left by the collapse of the Catholic Spanish and French empires. The Pope created over seventy new missions or Apostolic Vicariates, run by bishops responsible to the Pope as Apostolic Vicars. The system also gave the Pope flexibility to acknowledge a territory for church purposes without taking political sides should the territory or its boundaries be disputed. New autonomous Bishoprics were also created. Colonial chaplains replaced the mission stations of the religious orders. Pope Gregory, mindful of past colonial excesses, Catholic no less than Protestant, demanded that slavery be fought and native dignity respected. In 1838 the Catholic Spanish governor of Cuba refused to allow publication of the Pope's encyclical against slavery.

One Apostolic Vicariate was London, capital of a growing Empire and of Protestant Great Britain where Catholics had finally been granted civic recognition in 1829. Another was Britain's sole south American possession, British Guiana. Yet another was the disputed territory of Texas, made a Vicariate in 1840, just as the first bishop was created for the new diocese of the Two Californias, marking a break with the missions, closed by Mexican law in 1833. Both heralded a new mission fervor at the very point where the old Spanish world overlapped with the new expansions of Europe and America. Offshore, the Pope also created the Vicariate of Oceania, covering the Pacific. Rome, through the Office for the Propagation of the Faith (*Propaganda Fide*), broke with "entrenched traditional allegiances," most notably Spain and the old religious orders. Financial support for the mission movement came from an Association for the Propagation of the Faith (APF) with branches throughout Europe, one of them in Ireland. The Hapsburgs in Austria, who saw themselves as the successors to the Holy Roman Empire, added support through their Leopold Institution. Prince Metternich, Austrian Chancellor, regarded Pope Gregory XVI as the solution to the collapse of world order and monarchy. Optimism was so high that rumor spread as far as California that the Pope himself was to set the tone by traveling, and his first call would be Ireland. In 1840 Mexico City was given its first Mexican archbishop after a twenty-year vacancy—when the Spanish left, the previous Primate exiled himself with them. While mistrusting republicans, this Pope did not quite trust monarchies either. As a cardinal he had seen Napoleon, the regal republican, kidnap and humble the Pope, and he vowed that the lay world, secular or even loyal Catholic, would never again rule the clerical church. Macnamara's journeys began in Ireland where the church mission structure had been acknowledged with Catholic Emancipation; he proceeded to the new Vicariate of Guiana, from where he went to the Archdiocese of Mexico and on to the new diocese of the Californias, returning through the new Vicariate of Oceania.

Catholic Emancipation in 1829 gave British Catholics the freedom to organize religion openly. Ireland, then part of Britain, had organized its religion openly anyway, even when outlawed. Irish clergy were best placed to answer the Pope's desire for "British subjects to be missionaries within the

British Imperial ambience." They became a recognized Irish export to the English-speaking world. They manned the Australian and English Vicariates. The Royal College of Maynooth, the Catholic seminary funded by the British government in return for an oath of loyalty to the Crown, supplied priests to India. Bishop John England of Carolina toured Ireland in the 1830s to get seminary volunteers for the American States. "Prior to Emancipation Irish priests were working abroad, but as yet in no organised or structured manner. Immediately after, [there took place] a tremendous burst of missionary activity." Gospel fervor sometimes displaced human sensitivity: in 1840 the Irish Vicar Apostolic of Tibet and India wrote to *Propaganda Fide* in Rome of the latest "glory for religion," his plan to build "a magnificent church opposite the famous Taj Mahal on the bank of the Jumna River." Mission was inevitably enmeshed with Empire building in "religious colonialism," no less and no more than it had been by the Dominican, Franciscan and Jesuit missionaries of Imperial Spain. Serving and ruling made uneasy bedfellows.[5]

...And on the Rio San Joaquin

In fact, Macnamara's final concession in the hinterland of California would have made more sense to a missionary pope or a Californian Franciscan than to an expansionist British government which had never expressed interest in more than San Francisco Bay as a naval base. In taking Hong Kong, Britain had no intention of taking the rest of China. Washington too, with its desire for San Francisco Bay above everything, should have been puzzled by the choice of the San Joaquin River for a strategic British colony. London speculators were also more interested in short-term potential than in long-term agricultural investment. A colony in the virgin San Joaquin Valley, dominated by Indians and mosquitoes, would have had to be a very long-term investment. Macnamara's contract, however, did make sense in terms of a renewal and expansion inland of California's defunct missions. The old "chain" of Spanish missions had never been more than a half-loop of links, confined to the coast and nowhere near the Indian hinterland under the Sierras. With a bishop and a newly constituted diocese to which Mexico had promised the revenue of the old mission fund, the time was ripe to re-establish the frontier mission in some new form, without Spanish religious orders, but with the support of foreign colonists. It was in the spirit of Pope Gregory's ideal. Macnamara combined the new Anglo-Saxon colony system with the spirit of the old Hispanic mission, simply by being British, Catholic and an "Apostolic Missioner." He was also well aware of California's mineral wealth, including its gold, by the time he arrived there.

An irritable if plausible man, Macnamara had the chip on his shoulder of the dispossessed. He was self-consciously part of a tide of Irish and Papal mission expansion, but three times suspended from a role in that expansion. He was also chronically short of money. Sharp, confident, courageous and probably ambitious, he mixed easily with governors, prelates, officers, merchants, diplomats and planters. His surviving letters abound with a confident, simplistic world view. He spoke and wrote French and Spanish with possibly some native Gaelic, as well as refined if verbose English. He was also on a well-worn path. Seventeenth century Irish settlers came to the Caribbean as Cromwell's prisoners or exiles. Monserrat was known as the Emerald Isle. The Irish also came to South America in the early 19th century as mercenary freedom fighters for the new republics being born out of the fragmented *Las Indias*.

English, Scots and Irish in Mexico

Irishmen made their way in thousands to South America in the early 1800s, "wild geese," but this time headed westwards to fight Spain alongside Simón Bolívar. Behind them in Ireland they left a population wounded from the failed rebellion of 1798, but expanding on limited land. The new South American republics, like their sister Republic of the North, knew the Irish desire for land and independence. They welcomed settlers, whose emigration relieved the Irish countryside of its burden, although it often took the youngest and brightest. Emigrant ships however continued to head for *North America*—a million Irish went between 1814 and 1845—and had gone there since the *Ark* and *Dove* tolerance ships first sailed for Maryland in 1628 from England and Ireland in the wake of the *Mayflower*. South America could not compete with the attraction of existing older communities in the north. Those Irish who came to California with the gold rush from 1849, 10 percent of the total immigration, came from families who had emigrated in the 1830s and 40s to the U.S. east coast or Canada and had acclimatized there for some years before going west. Admiral Seymour, returning from a private visit to New York in 1840, recorded seasonal Irish builders on board his passenger ship taking home great quantities of gold coin to their families.[6]

Mexico ruled a vast territory, larger than British North America (Canada) and the (then) United States of the North. Once the old Spanish exclusion zone on foreign trade was abolished by the new republic and the land renamed for the Aztec war god Mexitli, the British moved in as diplomats and merchants. The Irish British were already there, which explains how in the bragging games between Mexico City, London and Washington in 1845-6, the Latino Mexicans were represented in Anglo-Saxon London by Ambassador Tomaso Murphy, of unmistakable Celtic descent. In 1848 the breakaway Mexican province of Yucatán was similarly represented in

Washington by Juan Sierra O'Reilly. Don Hugo O'Connor had been Spanish governor of Texas, while the last Viceroy of New Spain, later Mexico, was Juan O'Donojú. The Catholic Irish, racially Celtic, but legally British (and generally styling themselves as such abroad), had no problem being accepted in Mexico where the law still ran that Protestantism was not compatible with the citizenship necessary for marriage, property and influence. In 1824 Britain recognized Mexico: this deterred Spain from attempting reconquest, save for one fiasco attempt in 1829. Treaty negotiations, however, took two years to complete. One of the stumbling blocks was religious intolerance. Britain disliked the Mexican ban on the Protestant religion in public; Mexico objected to British intolerance of Catholics. Catholic Emancipation in 1829, despite its limits, resolved one side of the issue; Mexico, however, only legalized toleration in 1860. Both nations agreed on the abolition of slavery, and that some decades before the United States.

The British gained a hold on Mexico. London speculators lent $33 million (£6½ million) to a bankrupt new state in a bond certificate float in 1823-4. Goldschmidt, Barclay and Barings became synonymous with South American loans. Mexico lacked banks and, for all its silver mines and mints, lacked cash currency. British merchant houses even controlled the mints as debt collateral. Mexico proved unable to repay the loan or interest, due to corruption, maladministration and overspending on the military. In 1837 the London debts were drastically renegotiated. Land, all that Mexico had, was offered as collateral on half the total. This major *refacción* of the debt meant Mexico promised the Bondholders higher interest on an increased principal; this helped soften the failure to pay the original interest on time. For the Mexicans, "restructuring" brought further advances of money borrowed on their land as a new (and abundant) collateral. English financiers gambled: the Mexicans could declare bankruptcy at any time, but land could not be towed away in distraint. If, however, the gamble succeeded, it was going to be hugely profitable: the 1837 agreement promised land in Mexican States—Sonora, Chihuahua, New Mexico, Coahuila-Texas and the Californias—in lieu of cash repayment. Bondholders agreed to a ten-year option on public lands (*tierrenos baldios*). The option was to expire in October 1847. Despite pressure from individual investors, no company was ever formed in London to raise funds to send colonists to Mexico, although Macnamara boasted that there was such a company.

A dozen British companies operated in Mexico City in the 1830s, twenty others spread out between the Gulf and the Pacific.[7] Over 70 percent of Mexico's imports came from Britain through these factor houses, some of them in blatant smuggling scams. The merchant houses were best situated to act as bankers to the Mexican government: they had capital and were on the spot to take advantage of negotiations. The stakes were high but the prize was immense. They reinvested little of their profit in the Mexican industrial or communications infrastructure. Mining was an exception, but even there in exporting silver, traders avoided payment of legitimate export dues on what was one of Mexico's few valuable assets. Long term, Mexican development was seriously set back by British private enterprise. "The beggar on the throne of gold," as they called Mexico, simply became poorer.

The wealth of Eustace (*Don Eustaquio*) Barron, a half-Spanish half-Irish dealer on the Pacific coast with a monopoly on mercury and gunpowder imports, was "almost legendary." His house in Tepic was a fortress and he controlled, through employment, the local population. He had been British consul out there since 1827, and from 1831 the British government allowed their consuls to engage in private trade. His partner, Alexander Forbes, acting-consul in 1846 during Barron's leave in England, had urged British colonization of California through a book on the subject in 1839. A diplomat with the confidence of the natives and information from Europe at his fingertips had a business advantage. "Barron practically controlled the economic life of the western Pacific coast." In Mexico City, Scotsman Euan Mackintosh (*Don Eugenio*) served as British consul. His wealth as a partner in Manning and Marshal, which became Manning and Mackintosh in 1845, gave him influence with General Santa Anna in particular and with other politicians as governments rolled over. Like Barron, Milmo and other merchants, Mackintosh married into a leading Mexican family, joining his money to their landed influence and connections.[8] "No Government could ignore Mackintosh and his money" or "his close relations with government figures." Mackintosh even helped broker the American-Mexican armistice in 1847. Thousands of leading families in Mexico admired Anglo-European styles. Merchants fed the new tastes and their wares were as much in demand as their finance. Presiding over business and social life in Mexico City was the British Legation.

To the Mexican mind the British Crown and British merchant enterprise were one and the same. Entrepreneurs were, in some cases, diplomats, lending to the government, negotiating on behalf of their own government, in regular contact with the Foreign Office and hinting of the influence they had in London and with the Royal Navy, which always had ships in the Mexican Gulf. In 1844 the Royal Navy reinforced its Pacific squadron. Merchants certainly used Navy vessels and, from 1841, the new Naval Auxiliary vessels of the Royal Mail Steam Packet Companies (West Indies and Pacific) to carry to Britain undeclared gold and silver in specie and ingot form, avoiding Mexican duty on precious metals. The Mexicans objected to the smuggling in 1846 and British ambassador Bankhead warned British merchants against transporting silver. Overall a dangerous confusion identified Britain with private British business interests. "British firms used the Mexican government's condition and the power conveyed by the name of the British Crown to prosper in a country where the overall economic situation was desolate."[9]

No wonder then, that when an Irish cleric arrived in 1846 on the Mexican Pacific coast bound for California with a plan for colonization, just a year before the London Bondholders' land option ran out, he was seen as a speculators' front-man in a land where doors opened easily to the Catholic clergy. His involvement with the Barron and Forbes Company in mining speculation served to confirm the links. He had letters from diplomats in Mexico; he boasted Crown and business links in London; he was conveyed up and down the Mexican and Californian coast by the Royal Navy. It all impressed Mexican and American onlookers. American and French consuls in California were convinced Macnamara was more politician than priest. The British always followed colonies with troops, missioners and finally annexation—it happened in the old 13 colonies, in India with the East India Company and in Canada with the Hudson's Bay Company. In 1839 colonists landed in New Zealand and forced the hand of a reluctant British government to take over the islands within weeks. Responsibility for the private concerns of merchants and speculators *was* sometimes assumed by the Navy of this merchant kingdom. Private lenders to the south American states spent an hour with the foreign secretary in 1836, asking him to "take more decided steps" and "appropriations" against those countries to obtain their money. In 1842 the Royal Navy had blockaded San Juan, Nicaragua, on behalf of the Central American Bondholders in London. Against such a background, Macnamara came to mean something to everyone: his own boastful self-assurance confirmed fears and buoyed hopes. "We considered him to be an influential person," confessed the former Californio military *comandante* eight years later.[10]

The Monroe Warning

In 1823 President Monroe had warned that no European power would be permitted to meddle in the Americas, either by force or by sending colonists. It was aimed at Spain and those conservative European monarchies of the Holy Alliance of 1815—Austria, Prussia and Russia—a loose linkage of nations pledged to uphold the Christian religion, which gave kings their "divine right" to rule. Republicanism, like Communism to a later generation, was seen as godless and anathema. It was anti-monarchist and therefore against the religious establishment. Paradoxically, the Pope (and more understandably the Turkish Sultan) was not a member of the Alliance. Catholic Austria put its financial and moral weight behind Pope Gregory XVI's mission expansion after 1831. Russia (and Britain and France, though not members of the Holy Alliance) still threatened the northwest Pacific coast well into the 1840s. Oregon and California, empty neglected parts of the great continent, seemed ripe for picking.

The Spanish threat to re-occupy the lost Americas had receded by the 1840s, but during 1846 monarchists in Mexico City, including the archbishop and president, discussed inviting a European, even a Spanish prince, to start a Mexican dynasty. British diplomats were involved in these discussions. Ideas about California went beyond the discussion stage. Prussian diplomats spoke openly in 1842 of purchasing the whole of California and colonizing it with Germans transported by the Danish Navy; the French toyed with a tract in the San Joaquin Valley.[11] The Russians had established and abandoned "New Archangel" at Bodega Bay. Switzerland, or more correctly the recreated Swiss *persona* of Captain Johann Sutter, established "Nueva Helvetia" in the Lower Sacramento valley. Five years later in 1844, a German, Theodor Cordua, named his Honcut ranch grant on the Upper Sacramento "Neue Mecklenburg." Neither Sutter's nor Cordua's settlements became the national colonies their owners had hoped for and the names did not stick. The Gold Rush population after 1849 finally overtook these earlier settlements and "nations within a nation" made no more sense in a large, settling population than would wagon trains in defensive circles.

Individuals had long advocated British colonies in California: Alexander Forbes of Tepic, in 1839; Sir Richard Pakenham, British Minister in Mexico, in 1841; Sir George Simpson of Hudson's Bay Company, in 1842; Robert Wyllie, vice-chairman of the Mexican Bondholders, in 1843; Euan Mackintosh, British Consul in Mexico City and agent for the London Bondholders, in 1845. Only El Proyecto Macnamara of 1845 created a favorable resonance in Mexican government ears and was seen through to legal completion. In London, however, when it was reported at the highest level, it fell on deaf, embarrassed ears. For Mexico it had the perfect balance of ingredients. Literally translated, the Hispanic *poblador*, colonist, means "populator." Mexico needed populating for its defence. "The richest country in the world without colonists is just the same as the driest desert of Africa," was the Mexican Council of Government's response to Macnamara in 1845.[12]

Successive American administrations offered to buy California. Washington wanted San Francisco Bay, with Monterey if possible, and President Polk offered $25 million in gold for them. No interest was shown in the eastern Californian hinterland. As foreign governments were rumored to be showing ever keener interest in California's coast, Washington worried. An aggressive belief in Manifest Destiny—a phrase first used in newspapers of 1845, meaning Fate's decree that the United States should advance west and hold the whole continent—replaced the original defensive Monroe warning. It was a secular version of Puritan predestinarianism brought over by the Pilgrim Fathers. President Polk came to the White House in 1845 declaring his aim of procuring the California coast for the United States. By then, settlers were entering California from the new southwestern fork of the Oregon trail.

Some took Mexican citizenship, but only in token subjection. Most came through Johann Sutter's New Switzerland, under the fort's Mexican flag, with no intention of ever changing their U.S. citizenship. From agents, newspapers and prospectuses, the word was that California had more to offer than the cold northwest, remarkable only for timber, pelts and fish. Even the Mormons set out for what they had heard to be an earthly paradise and called California their promised land.

Polk was kept informed throughout 1845 of designs by both Mexico and the California provincials to ask France or England for Protectorate status. All wanted the prized Pacific base. United States ambassadors in London and Mexico reported the same refrain. Polk also knew of the London Bondholders' mortgage on Mexican Departmental lands including California and of the spate of publications urging colonists to go to California. When therefore William Parrott, U.S. Confidential Agent in Mexico City, reported to his Secretary of State that a British agent, "a young Irish priest called McNamarrah," was parading full-blown colonization plans for California, Polk reacted.[13] Parrott's August letter came to him in September; by October he had drafted the annual December message to the nation as his warning to Europe.

While preparing the speech he told Senator Thomas Hart Benton (John Frémont's father-in-law) that "the United States would not willingly permit California to pass into the possession of any new colony planted by Great Britain or any foreign monarchy and in reasserting Mr. Monroe's doctrine I would have California and the fine Bay of San Francisco as much in view as Oregon." Both agreed that for a foreign power to colonize California would be as serious a threat as colonizing Cuba.[14] (Polk had offered Spain $100 million for Cuba.) Colonel Benton was so enthusiastic he even saw Destiny in passive mode: "California too had its destiny to fulfill, which was to be handed over to the United States." His map-making son-in-law echoed this: "the California coast is the boundary fixed by Nature to round off our national domain. From Mexico it was separated by Nature."[15]

That month, Secretary of State Buchanan shared the same sentiments with Thomas Oliver Larkin, U.S. Consul in California, warning of "colonization by foreign monarchies," designs on California by the British Hudson's Bay Company and active British financing of Mexican troops about to occupy California. "Emigration from the U.S., however," reassured Buchanan, "will soon make vasselage impossible." Neither Buchanan nor Polk nor any other American public figure ever referred to *American* migration into Mexican territory as *colonizing*, but rather as *emigrating* and *settling*. They too, however, were colonists, seen by the home government as a vanguard and as a fifth column. "What is a new state founded in the western desert of America if it be not a new colony?"[16]

Colonies: "Paper Empires" or "Tables Spread in the Wilderness"?

Hundreds of placenames across North and South America and the Pacific beyond mirrored their Old World pioneers' origins. Settlers prefixed their home names with "New," "Nova," "Nueva" or "Neu." Religious visionaries spoke of New Zions and New Jerusalems. California had been New Biscay; Mexico, New Spain; Canada, New France. New York had already been Dutch New Amsterdam. The British Isles spawned New England, Nova Scotia and New (South) Wales, but Ireland remained an exception, despite its emigrants. In fact, nowhere in the 19th century was a territory named after Ireland; an 1830s colony in Texas was called Hibernia with San Patricio its *pueblo*, and a wretched lava island in the Papua–New Guinea chain was named New Ireland only after Germany lost the Bismarck Archipelago in 1919. After 1845, the Famine and the acceleration of Irish emigration, many foreign localities were called after individual Irish towns, but nothing for Ireland itself. No hint survived as to what, if anything, Macnamara intended to call his 20,000 Irish square miles on the San Joaquin.

Coloniae, the ancient Roman settling of war veterans on lands abroad to hold an empire together with tested human cement, had also rid first century Italy of restless, potentially dangerous veterans and reduced a growing population. Nineteenth century Europe too had a growing population. Ireland's population expanded between 1750 and 1821 from possibly 2.3 million to over 6.8; by the eve of the 1845 Famine it was estimated at nearer 9 million. Ireland was also a republican thorn in the side of Great Britain. George III had welcomed refugees from the anti-monarchist French Revolution, including the ancient Catholic religious orders which had not been allowed in the British Isles since Queen Mary Tudor's time (1554–1558). Monarchists, even French and Catholic, were at least loyal to crowns. Not so, however, the Catholics of Ireland who had sported green sashes in the early 1790s in direct imitation of American and French republicans. Irish Protestant gentry and clergy joined with the Catholics in the early days, when Irishmen literally united and called themselves such. It climaxed in open armed revolt against the Crown, with French battleships in Irish harbors and French republican troops marching across central Ireland in 1798, while a Catholic peasant population was left leaderless and Protestant fellow Irish had second thoughts.

Young Latin American republics like Mexico or Gran Colombia (parts of which became Bolivia and Venezuela) were glad to offer public or waste land for colonizing in lieu of repayment of debt. Underpopulation, underdevelopment and the consequent vulnerability of large territories was Latin America's problem; overpopulation, crowded industrial cities, political unrest and the subdivision of limited arable land was Europe's problem. European speculators, dealing in South American loans, could make a further killing by taking land warrants in bulk in lieu of cash. Export and import tax concessions, monopolies and a guaranteed presence near the seat of government would follow, as well as possible mineral development, all underpinned by rent from colonists. Idealists too saw it as a chance to create Utopia. Robert Owen, the Welsh social commune theorist, accepted fifty leagues in Texas for a colony of common ownership in 1828. Mexico even agreed to waive its strict laws on religious practice. Shortly afterwards, Owen visited an Irish commune near Ennis, Eugene Macnamara's home, and was deeply impressed. Landowners in Ireland and Scotland in particular were anxious to clear their surplus populations, but in such a way on weekdays as to be able to face themselves and church on Sunday. Rural poor led to urban unrest. France had exploded in 1789 when the rural Jacobins swelled the urban malcontents of Paris; Ireland had gone the same way in 1798, although the poor had few cities to go to. Both uprisings were within living memory.

Edward Gibbon Wakefield first wrote in 1833 of colonization as "an art of vast importance to mankind" and captivated many with his ideas. He urged that free land grants in New South Wales be ended and that payment for land be pooled to cover emigrant passage money. He also condemned the transporting of criminals to Australia. Backed by the Duke of Wellington, he founded the National Colonisation Society and the South Australian Association which set up a colony on his principles in 1836. A New Zealand Association, Colonisation Company and Land Company followed in quick succession, the latter sending out a colony to New Zealand in 1839 which forced Britain within weeks to annex the islands, just ahead of the French. One-eleventh of the 20 million acres Wakefield accumulated in New Zealand was to be for native Maori use, and all of it was to be bought at a substantial, not a nominal price, lest the "bargain" lead to later recrimination.

Wakefield watched the United States expand westwards by emigration and colonization. He knew that the Irish poor needed to emigrate, but so often they ended in next-door England for want of passage money, "underselling English workmen for a hovel, rags and potatoes, content with wretchedness as the English labourer is not."[17] There was much land in America "open to be used by individuals with a title to the possession of it." Fix the land price, he urged, and limit each allocation to preserve its scarcity value and prevent people from being too far apart on vast ranches without community support. Young newly married couples without children were his ideal colonists; villages were his ideal size for a community.

Good social and economic reasons though there were at home for the sending away of people en masse, these "rejects" and "threats," once established in their new habitat, could be a force for the good of the motherland. Sheer weight of numbers was the way most observers expected American migrants to take California by 1847 or 1848, even had there been no war with Mexico or major gold discovery. It was the way America, in turn, feared that Britain, the most likely of all the European powers and an enemy within living memory, would try to take California.

Topo

The poverty of early 19th century Scotland and Ireland meant those peoples were the subject of many colonizing proposals. Such proposals were private because Britain had no state organized or subsidized emigration save for the two years 1825–1827 when some Irish were settled in Canada at government expense. At times the private projects were wild, such as the Churning Company's export of milkmaids to Argentina to make butter: they churned a butter mountain before discovering that the Argentineans disliked butter. It was common for a priest or minister, with the trust of the community and a modicum of education, to approach or be approached by politicians or entrepreneurs. In 1843, a Dominican priest, Anthony Fahy, was made chaplain to the small Irish colony on La Plata, in Argentina: by 1848 a colony of 1,500 lived there. In 1842 the apostolic vicar of the London District wrote to the archbishop of Dublin saying that Rome wanted an Irish Apostolic Prefect (non-episcopal prelate) to travel with Irish and English emigrants to Bolivia: Bolivia was paying. An early example of a British colony in South America was the Scots colony of Topo near Caracas, recruited by a Presbyterian minister.[18] Caracas was in the district of Venezuela (Little Venice) which then formed a part of Gran Colombia.

Charles Herring, William Graham, John Diston Powles and the Goldschmidt family, leading merchant speculators, were officially known in Columbia as "old friends and faithful servants." (Disraeli called Powles "the great loan-monger.") They published newspapers to push opinion, fashion and taste the British way. They imported education in the form of Joseph Lancaster's school system, known as well in Latin America as it was in County Clare. In 1823 the Colombian government turned to the merchants for loans; the Mexicans too turned to the same names as well as to Barclays and Barings. John Diston Powles was for years vice-chairman of the Mexican Bondholder sub-committee of the South American Association in London, a partner with Euan Mackintosh in Manning and Mackintosh and a partner in Herring, Graham and Powles. At the same time, Columbia and Mexico legislated to encourage and recruit European immigrants to the wastelands. Colonists came to Texas and included Irish settlers. Columbia offered 320 acres and accelerated citizenship to any colonist. Several French, Swiss and British finance houses took up the offer.

Herring, Graham and Powles contracted one-third of a million acres for settlement, agreeing to cover initial expenses, to bar any public display of Protestantism, and to settle a mix of Europeans so that no land grant became a "nation within a nation." The Colombian Agricultural Joint Stock Company in London raised the working capital. A first colony was founded in 1826, in Trujillo Province, under an Irish ex-soldier; it was named "Gibraltar" because of its strategic position. He planned to recruit 300 colonists and may have planned to recruit from Ireland.

Topo was the second concession to the Colombian Agricultural Company, but sited in the intensively and long-farmed province of Caracas, on the last and worst of the untilled waste. A Scots Presbyterian minister took out nearly 200 colonists from Aberdeen and Inverness. They stayed several months, their wants met by the local Colombian Company agent, but they felt tricked: the soil was toxic. Then the London Stock Exchange collapsed and shares of the CAC became worthless. There was no money to support the colonists and the CAC cut its losses. "Gibraltar" had no settlers on its good soil; Topo was supporting 200 on fouled, unwatered soil. Joseph Lancaster interceded with Bolívar; others asked London to help. Bolívar made a donation and a Westminster Parliamentary committee questioned John Diston Powles on suspicion of fraud. The colonists eventually escaped to Canada with the help of the British ambassador in Caracas. Powles emerged unscathed and continued to speculate in Latin America. He was as keen to establish similar colonies in California in 1845-6 and was still tendering for colonist schemes in Venezuela in 1863.

Macnamara's Role

In 1846, Eugene Macnamara was just another European *empresario* contracting land for settlers in Latin America where the new republics needed "populators" and development money. While shopkeeper Britain was expanding its "store chain," its island government encouraged (but neither organized nor paid for) emigration to populate its own possessions. British imperial expansion was inextricable from "Ireland's spiritual Empire" and "Irish ecclesiastical imperialism."[19] Macnamara too was an Irish missioner. By the end of the 1840s the Irish mission direction had slewed towards Australia, Britain, the United States and Canada rather than the less familiar, more remote Vicariates of, for example, Tibet and British Guiana, despite initial enthusiasms.

While Britain, Ireland and the Papacy were finding a new and unexpectedly intertwined spiritual destiny, the United States was also claiming its own "destiny" to expand across to the Pacific. Mexico's destiny was equally manifest: to give way and allow California to be the United States Pacific coastline. As Polk delivered his address in December 1845, Eugene Macnamara was about to move, with Mexican government support, to choose land for his Irish colony in California. Washington and Westminster governments knew of Macnamara specifically by name.

British, Irish, influenced by entrepreneurs, but neither their nor his own government's agent, Macnamara was essentially part of the Irish missionary expansion. It was his bad luck to choose to "go for broke" in the most sensitive place possible in the Americas of 1846, and in the process stealing a march on John Diston Powles, Robert Wyllie and Euan Mackintosh, the merchant speculator giants of the day. California, its missions suppressed, stripped and ruined, was as ripe for a new missionary approach as it was for an American takeover, British expansion or even for mining speculation. The Pope had given it a new diocesan structure and there was no looking backward to the missions, a Spanish legacy only seventy years old which had barely survived the end of Spainish rule. The missioners' spiritual and educational work on the frontier had not penetrated interior California. What inspired Macnamara to come to Mexico and propose his plan in the first place remains unclear, but despite the right instincts, he was too late. Events overtook him.

As the Mexican Council of Government discussed his proposal in September 1845, the first potato blight of a five-year run was reported in Ireland: the Famine began. A year later, the U.S.-Mexican war broke out around Macnamara: California was its first casualty. Two years later this new American territory produced the gold in the quantity which some had long suspected existed: from 1849 "the world rushed in" and populated California. The void which had invited the Macnamara project was filled.

In 1851, Admiral Seymour, who had transported Macnamara up and down the Pacific coastline, browsed through his private diary for 1846 and paused on the spare back pages. In July 1846, on board HMS *Collingwood* bound from California for the Sandwich Islands, he had copied in précis a letter which Macnamara had shown him from Juan Bandini, an old Mexican colonizer, about mineral prospects in California. "These anticipations," Seymour added to the old diary in a postscript, "were realised within two years to an extent no one, Bandini included, could have imagined. It has become a rich and populous country in consequence."[20]

No one who met Eugene Macnamara in 1846 knew his colorful background or what drove him into the whirlwind of his Proyecto. Americans who remembered anything about him saw a perfect stereotype from Spanish Black Legend—conspiring Papal cleric, backward European monarchist, leader of Irish immigration under a corrupt Latino government—thwarted in the end by Protestant republican virtue and resolve. The rest simply forgot him.

Two

The Outcast.
Ireland 1814–1841

We know that some are tough old terrors, frozen fogeys
   who believe
God blundered when he fashioned Eve,
But others secretly admit,
They think her Nature's choicest bit!
—(*The Midnight Court*, Brian Merriman, c. 1780, County
   Clare)

On arrival in Mexico City, late in 1844, Eugene Macnamara told the British ambassador that he was a native of Ennis, the chief town of County Clare in western Ireland. The ambassador, also Irish, reported the details to London. "Macnamara" with its variant spellings from the Gaelic was a family name particular to the County, and found across the social and religious divide. "Eugene" was a European romance variant of the Irish "Eoain," the Scots "Euan" and the Welsh "Owain," in turn anglicized into "Owen." In Mexico and California of the mid-1840s he was repeatedly described as "young." Since he must have been about 18 when he began studying for the priesthood at the Irish College in Paris in 1832, he would have been born around 1814. Priests came from the families of comfortable farmers or successful townsmen to Catholics, the upwardly mobile middle class; but to the Establishment these were origins which were still humble.

Ennis and County Clare

Ennis grew and prospered in the 18th century, putting behind it the revenge inflicted by Cromwell's troopers in 1650 for the Irish rebellion. Like nearby Quin, known from its ancestral burials as Quin of the Macnamaras,

30

Ennis had been a Franciscan town. The English took the roofs from the friaries in both places and desecrated the tombs, adding to a thousand similar ruins across Ireland two more warnings to the population. The friars were the gentler side of the Anglo-Norman colonizing in the south and west of Ireland in the 13th and 14th centuries. Simple Franciscan houses with their thin roughstone towers marked Ireland's more distant settlements: in later Spanish America where they were known as "missions" they also gave rise to towns around them. After their dissolution, in Ireland as in Hispanic America, the ruins became hallowed ground.

The law took many rights from Catholics, including those of bearing arms, owning land, having a horse worth more than £5 and living in walled towns. Refugee Catholic merchants made their way from walled Limerick to Ennis. As a result, the Catholic middle class of Ennis prospered, although under theoretically serious civil disabilities. Several Macnamara families were merchants, teachers, men of small property and lawyers. Catholics worshipped in a tiny oratory down Chapel Lane in the early 19th century, where Eugene Macnamara would have been baptized, but no records survive. Ennis was well provided with schools from the end of the 18th century; Catholic joined Protestant in the classroom in varying proportions. Joseph Lancaster set up a school there in 1812, on his way to establish "Lancasterian" schools in South America and Mexico. His religiously "neutral" education was feared by some for its "indifferentism" which might create drift from the churches, but day pupils were shaped more by home than by school catechisms. Macnamara may have attended Stephen O'Halloran's Classical School which, in 1829 was said to have educated most of the Catholic clergy of Clare before their seminary years.[1]

Ennis and Clare County were the setting for Macnamara's impressionable years. The land had not witnessed the abortive 1798 rebellion nor had it been on the route of the failed French liberation army. While Clare was not directly burdened with recent bad memories, it shared a folk memory common to the Irish. There had been brutal reprisals nearby in 1798, in Limerick and Tipperary. The majority Catholic population increasingly called itself "Catholic Ireland" and politicians played the same card. The 17th century penal laws of religion imposed on Catholics (and nominally on Protestant nonconformists) were largely softened by repeal in 1792. Despite the mythology of later years, Catholic and Protestant had lived side by side in relative harmony throughout much of Ireland, as on a sensitive scale balance. It found political expression in the totally mixed religions of the United Irishmen, founded in Belfast in 1791. Mixed marriages and mixed schooling were facts of life. Protestants had held lands on behalf of Catholics (and perjured themselves in the process) as a way round laws which many Protestants, as well as Catholics, saw as unjust and outdated. The more spiritual-minded among the Anglican clergy exercised a restrained religious monopoly in a population not of their church. Divided more by symbolic "small differences" than by a gulf, "the people were nobler and gentler than their laws." In Ennis a leading Protestant landowner chaired the committee planning a new Catholic church on prominent ground donated by a Protestant landowner to replace the huddle in Chapel Lane. Both were active supporters of O'Connell and the Catholic Emancipation movement.[2]

After 1815 and the end of the war with Napoleon, it was in the air that entry to the Westminster Parliament and voting rights would be conceded to Catholics. Apart from service commissions and degrees at Oxford, Cambridge and Trinity Dublin, Westminster was the last legal disability, centering on a test oath of Protestant allegiance and the taking of a Protestant sacrament. Catholic Emancipation became as inevitable as Slave Emancipation: a strong groundswell supported them as linked issues. Limited Irish independence or repeal of the 1801 Union with Westminster would be a subsequent goal—a form of Irish emancipation. For some years Daniel O'Connell had traveled the Clare court circuit as a lawyer and in the process held meetings for Emancipation. He founded a Catholic Association which included Protestant landowners, among them William O'Brien, Member of Parliament for Ennis. The Association levied a "Catholic Rent" of one penny for the Emancipation campaign and when London heard that Clare was almost in arms for Emancipation, the Association was outlawed. O'Connell promptly founded the *New* Catholic Association and in 1828 stood for election to Westminster as Member for Clare. He was returned unopposed—a Protestant candidate stood down—but was refused entry to Parliament when he refused the oath. The British Government, on the advice of the Duke of Wellington, granted Catholic Emancipation in 1829 to head off unrest. Wellington, it appeared, also knew of an Irish Army of 40,000 in Charleston, Carolina, organized by the local Irish bishop, John England, ready "for the invasion of Ireland should Emancipation be withheld."[3]

Sixty thousand people cheered and chaired O'Connell through the streets of Ennis after the test by-election in 1828. Out on the Clare coast at Doonbeg, a big-hearted, big-framed parish priest, Michael Comyn, notorious for his political bluntness and revered for his championing of ordinary people, hugged voters and threw whiskey punch parties for his fellow clergy to celebrate. Comyn boasted that his coastal folk were "gentry" and told an English gentleman who called them "peasants," "they will be wearing good cloth clothes when you are in the workhouses." These Catholic priests, no longer shadowy outlaws in the wings, became the educated local figures of influence whom their own race could follow. Emancipation confirmed their new role in Ireland, displacing the squire, the established church minister and at times the politician, physician, policeman and provider of welfare. This versatility (at times amounting to a confusion of role) also made them good frontier missioners abroad. In Ireland they came to live modestly well, better than a comfortable farmer. "Squireens" were an expanding social class. In fact, all

Map of Ireland

Irishmen—politicians, patriots and emigrants—came to be identified as Catholic. This change of attitude as respectability increased, along with an increasingly centralized and assertive Catholic church after 1850, magnified the "small differences" between majority Catholic and minority Protestant Irish. Famine also brought bitter recriminations.

The young Macnamara would have known, even smelled the Clare potato crop failures in 1822 and in 1831. Irish nostrils never forgot the smell of blight, a familiar horror over centuries. When the archbishop of Canterbury raised funds in London to help, one Clare parish priest wrote to him of "my gratitude and love to my Protestant brethren." In 1830 while the new town church was still in the building stage, the Franciscans returned to Ennis. Friar James Macnamara built a church near to the shell of the medieval friary, but he was challenged by the diocesan priests for distracting from their appeal for the town church: in those days secular diocesan clergy challenged religious, priests challenged bishops and the people had to decide which side they took. Going to Rome about a local quarrel was not uncommon. By the time of Emancipation in 1829, the number of candidate priests volunteering for Killaloe diocese was increasing, although the number of parishes remained static. The population had also been increasing rapidly for decades. A priest's life had its attractions in 1830, especially in the absence of other options. It brought respect, social importance, education, security and even travel. For the secular clergy, who took no vows of stability, poverty, chastity or obedience, and were bound to celibacy only by church law, vocation sat uneasily with ambition and lifestyle. A new phenomenon appeared, a surplus of curates, young priests apprenticed to a parish priest while queueing for their own parish. Where a curate might once have waited two years for a parish, it was now possible to be a curate for years. Curates had few rights in a world where bishops had only recently come out of the woodwork and were frequently away on the Dublin-Rome circuit, and where parish priests held the power in the church. Rome was still far away.

The influence of the priesthood grew more overt. By the end of the 19th century the Catholic church controlled much of Irish (and Irish emigrant) life. Respect from the people sometimes degenerated into obsequiousness. After the solemn affirmation of clerical authority by the Synod of Thurles in 1852, there was less room for a healthy irreverence in peripheral religious matters or for the religion of Nature which farmers understood. The clergy lacked fool jesters like Brian Merriman of Feakle, 12 miles from Ennis, who had written *The Midnight Court* in 1787, an irreverent, bawdy and strangely spiritual complaint in Gaelic of the Irishman's lack of sexual enthusiasm at a time of population decline. The "Court" listened at midnight to women's evidence of men's ignorance about sex. Go to Mass to find a man, pray to lure a man and fast to appear attractive to a man, the judges advised. Men who had to go to a hedge prostitute serving all "Clare, Ennis and Quin" knew nothing of romance. The priest's "handsome fee" for the "fuss and racket" of marriage was another obstacle. Merriman advocated free love: the baby of Bethlehem was a perfectly respectable illegitimate birth. The celibate clergy "living in the lap of luxury, well dressed, well treated and well fed," either disliked women or "graced their beds." The hedge teacher of Feakle threw their Scripture back at them: "Lust, said Paul, not a wife, was something man should shun for life." Change in the celibacy rule, he reminded, only needed a nudge from a Papal Bull. Red-blooded literate young men in Clare in 1832 knew *The Midnight Court*, notorious in its time.[4]

Twelve miles south of Ennis a unique cooperative community was founded in 1830, based partly on the Paraguayan Jesuit missions of 1750 and on Robert Owen's socialist "villages of unity and cooperation" in England and Scotland. It lasted only two years—not unusual for such idealistic experiments—but it attracted attention beyond Ireland. Ralahine was a cooperative farm where all was held in common, children were brought up communally and a strict code forbade gambling, alcohol, nicknames, tobacco and religious compulsion. The talents of each were to be used for all. Everyone had to do some field labor and Gaelic was the common tongue. A rota committee ran the scheme; "now that our interest and our duty are the same we have no need of a Steward." *The Times* of London called it "A city on a hill." Members were also forbidden to waste time attending O'Connell's (or any other politician's) mass meetings at Ennis. The Bible was not used in school and religious disputes were taboo. "Both Protestant and Catholic clergy were favourable to the system, once they understood it." Robert Owen himself visited Ralahine, just after being offered land in Mexican Texas for a similar colony; William Thompson from Cork handed over his estate for the "new system" of ownership and production, about which he had also written. An intelligent young man in Ennis, about to train to serve his community, would have known of Ralahine and the ripples it caused, before he left for Paris.[5]

Paris

The expatriate Irish College on the Rue des Irlandais, Paris, was one of a chain of thirty continental Irish academies between Prague and Lisbon. Men originally studied in these places for many professions which the law forbade them at home, but increasingly they became seminaries for student priests "on the Irish mission." For two centuries France was second home to thousands of Irish, but after 1789 France was neither royal nor Catholic. An Irish College priest attended Louis XVI at the guillotine. Killaloe diocese continued to send young men to France and they returned to the nickname of *"Abbé"* from colleagues. In March 1832, the beginning of the second semester-term, Eugene Macnamara from Ennis arrived at the Irish College in Paris with William O'Shea from Killaloe town. They joined four other students from the diocese in the 60-strong community. Clare men had status in the wake of O'Connell's recent victory. The College stood on the left bank of the Seine, between the Pantheon and the Luxembourg gardens and a short walk from the Sorbonne University which students attended. Their course lasted about five years and students needed French to follow the outside lectures. Two French teachers on the small Irish College staff gave support tutorials and students spent summers at the College villa in Ivry. There was ample opportunity to learn the language well. On the nearby Île de France stood Notre

Dame cathedral, a scarred, stripped reminder of the Revolution in 1789 which had toppled the French crown and the church with it. Victor Hugo had just put it back on the map with Quasimodo, in his novel *Notre Dame de Paris*. Paris churchmen polarized, in the wake of successive revolutions, between monarchist, authoritarian conservatives and modernizers who felt that lessons had to be learned by the church, even from anticlericals and republicans.[6] Seminaries also polarized.

In 1828 a new and illiberal rector came with a complete new staff. Patrick McSweeney was a former teacher from Carlow College in Ireland, known for his combative approach to Protestantism. In 1827, he offered to take on in public dispute six evangelical Protestants at a time, calling them "non-commissioned apostles." A six-day disputation followed, chaired by Daniel O'Connell himself, which led directly to McSweeney's Paris promotion.[7] In 1831, Pope Gregory XVI was elected and the Catholic mission to the wider world became as much a perspective of Irish life as the horizon itself. John England, Bishop of Charleston, South Carolina, who had helped draw up the Irish American army to force Emancipation, visited the College in Paris while Macnamara was there. He preached in the College in October 1832 when McSweeney received an honorary degree. John England was on route to Rome and would have been revered by the students as a folk hero and a patriot. He probably suggested quite openly that they consider the American mission.

McSweeney, a champion of the Church Belligerent, believed he had to forge priests tough and sharp, like himself, for the wider hostile world ahead of them. A new and regimented generation of clergy was growing up which no longer looked to its own initiatives, but increasingly to the nod of a newly assertive mother-church in Rome. Emancipation meant there was also ground to be made up, assertively. Britain, on the other hand, may have emancipated Catholics, but it drew the line at the Pope. Catholics guarded their independence of the State in religion by obedience to the Pope, but never overcame the inherent contradiction that the Pope too was a territorial monarch until the end of the Papal States in 1870. The confusion irritated Protestants at Westminster and in colonies like Guiana. Catholics were emancipated, but no reconciliation was forged between London and the Rome Papacy. In 1832, the year Macnamara joined the College, the British government refused the College for the second time any share of damages paid to Britain for losses on French soil during the Revolution and Napoleonic war. London deemed the College to be a French foundation, not British. The refusal fueled existing Catholic clerical suspicion of their Tory rulers. McSweeney went on to rule his students with iron rigor for over two decades. During the 1848 Paris uprising they struck back by joining the demonstrations, wearing tricolor cockades on their *soutaines* and painting across the College walls, "*À bas le tyrant McSweeney!*" A visiting archbishop in 1850 called them "Rough old fellows. Poor Ireland has much to fear from its future ministers."

Students studied in a large ground floor hall, where they also prayed morning and evening. Rooms above one side of the hall looked onto apartment windows on the Rue Postes where, reputedly, the world displayed itself in the flesh. Students drank openly in *cabarets*—drinking shops, but they sounded better than *shebeens*. Out in the fermenting city, Lammenais, Montalembert and Lacordaire, esteemed clergy and academics, had tried to rethink the Catholic world-view in the light of the secular and anti-religious French Revolution. They wanted to find what was authentic in the new movement, just as Christian humanists had learned, with papal approval, from the classical pagan world three hundred years earlier. The tags of "liberal," "republican" and "democrat" they argued, could enrich the label "Catholic" and "Christian." Government and church should be separate, not in unhealthy embrace. Less liberal thinkers found it hard to accept after the burning of the Paris archbishop's home by the mob in 1830. In August 1832, the Pope issued a powerful encyclical condemning "indifferentism." There was only one true religion; government and church had a duty to uphold that truth together. Democracy and free speech had no place in an orderly society.[8] The coin had another face, that of narrow zealotry and credulity. Two of the three Paris modernizers left the church while the third recanted. It would certainly have been the talk of the student priests and their lecturers in the year Macnamara arrived. There was also a King in Paris, if only a "Citizen King," who allowed Napoleon's statue to be restored to the Vendôme in 1833. In the spring of 1834 the National Guard put down a Paris worker's uprising. Word of it, if not the gunfire, spread through the city. The re-establishment of all the traditional authorities was the order of the day: Macnamara was molded between two opposing cultures.

It was said that continental training created broader-minded men than the more parochial colleges in Ireland, but that may have been a partisan conceit. Maynooth was known for its narrow, restrictive rigor. In 1830 a student of the Paris college thought the fabric neglected and the students "poorly educated and rough." In 1837 an Irish priest in France told the Archdeacon of Dublin that the French clergy were more zealous and less worldly than the Irish clergy.[9] One of Macnamara's fellow arrivals in Paris in 1832, James Moloney, died there in the summer of 1834. The four Killaloe students already there were ordained and left at the end of their course in summer 1834. Pat Moloney from Killaloe, who arrived in the summer of 1832, a term after Macnamara, was hospitalized *per une alienation mentale*. In the later 1830s several students "left for town" (*sorti en ville*).

They may have gone to Rue Picpus, across the Seine, where the Missionary Order of the Sacred Hearts trained French and Irish students. Some Irish College students completed studies there without joining the order. The Picpus Fathers served in the Sandwich Islands, based at Honolulu, from where Patrick Short, formerly of the Irish College and a teacher at Rue Picpus, had only recently landed in California after being expelled by the King of the Sandwich Islands. First news of this came to the staff and sixty students of the Rue Picpus in 1832 through another expelled missioner, who had left Patrick Short in the care of the Californian Franciscan missions. Short became a teacher at William Hartnell's Monterey ranch school as well as a friend of Padre Durán, the California mission Prefect. These developments would have been known to the wider Irish student fraternity in Paris.[10]

Eugene Macnamara was "*sent* home to Ireland" at the end of August 1834 after only five semesters of study. Others "*returned* home" or "*left* for town," usually after five years and ordination. When they did go it was in June, occasionally July. It is likely that Macnamara went to a religious house like Picpus, because no other college for secular clergy in Ireland or in Rome registered his name on its roll. Being "*sent*" away may indicate some sanction by Patrick McSweeney. That same month, August 1834, the former administrator of the College, John Hussey, accused McSweeney of maladministration and had himself been barred from entering the College.[11] When Macnamara was eventually ordained for Killaloe diocese in 1837, wherever it happened, he was fluent enough to be able to preach and hear confessions in French and could still do so a decade later. In 1837, however, French was not much use among the Gaelic-speaking people of Doonbeg and Kilkee on the southwest coast of the Clare peninsula where he was posted.

Doonbeg and Kilkee

Owen Macnamara, as he was first known in 1837, joined two other curates with the larger-than-life "squireen" and parish priest of Kilkee, Michael Comyn. The young, enthusiastic, perhaps "rough" *Abbé*, fresh from the latest thinking abroad, came down to earth as "Mr." Macnamara, most junior of curates, in the bulrush and limestone fields around the shelterless bay of Doonmore and along the coast road to Kilkee. Whatever Macnamara's College rector and even Pope Gregory himself said about Protestants and absolute Catholic truth, Michael Comyn thought more broadly and pragmatically. He had pledged money towards a new Church of Ireland church at Kilkee and earned the support and respect of local Protestants for his own attempts at a new Catholic chapel there. Rome's aggressive theology and new sense of mission could not be allowed to disrupt hard-learned Irish habits of living together. The habit continued to the Famine when Comyn and the Church of Ireland rector manned a soup kitchen and campaigned together for government relief.[12]

The parish stretched the seven miles from Doonbeg village to the seaside resort of Kilkee and east to Lisdeen, but Comyn lived in a large family house at Balthard Point on the bay by Doonbeg. One window of Balthard

House looked straight out to the Arran Isles.[13] Before and after Comyn's mother's death in 1834, the house was known for its hospitality, its library and its long noisy parties. Mrs. Comyn complained that her son was "not to be reasoned with when fits of folly come on him." He was nicknamed *Taoiseach* (prime minister) of the area because of his open house and his role as "priest, ruler and judge" among a "turf digging, seaweed eating, fish catching, amphibious population, as bad fishermen as farmers, content on the lowest possible scale of existence." Charles Lever, the Victorian novelist, wove two works of fiction around Comyn, describing in passing his house, parish and character.[14] In a feudal exchange of respect, Comyn spent his energy on the people who looked to him—demanding support for their coracle fishing, seizure of absentee landlords' land, compulsory development of local clay-fields, a railway, and a proper harbor for Doonmore Bay. He opposed the Poor Law and its ominous new workhouses. Ennis was the nearest "house of indus-try," twenty miles away: it might as well have been in England. The gaunt barrack buildings built across Ireland on a common template made people fear the bad times even more. Tact was not Comyn's strong point. He hosted Father Mathew, the Irish "Apostle of Temperance," after a successful Tem-perance drive in Kilkee, with a celebration dinner at which drink flowed.

Mass attendance in 1830s western Ireland was not the total muster of later years. Perhaps one-fifth of Comyn's 6,600 parishioners attended on Sun-day. Lack of clothes, sheer distance, ill-health, lack of space in chapel, out-side worship in winter, all affected attendance. The Irish church still had much of the medieval about it, including the old minimal requirement of attendance once a year. It was also a Catholic Christianity close to Nature, pragmatic, earthy, irreverent and with an ingredient of superstition which attached itself as much to priests as to ancient wells. The devotions and pieties which came in from Italy and France in later years had not yet arrived; even the continental "Father" for the priests and the "Roman" collar were still novel and by no means widely adopted. Clergy dressed on a range between "ultra-clerical" and "*à la mode*"—titles and dress mattered more in the politics of revolutionary Europe, in polarized cities like Paris and Rome.

Besides Doonbeg chapel itself, dating to 1813, there were chapels at Lis-deen (1800), beyond Kilkee, and an almost complete chapel at Kilkee when Macnamara arrived in 1837. It is not known whether he lived over the chapel at Doonbeg, often the place for a curate, or in Michael Comyn's house, or even in his own small cabin as far away as Lisdeen. Given Comyn's hospi-tality and his mother's references to previous curates, it is likely that Mac-namara lodged in Balthard House, at least for some of his time. Its books would have been a comfort. The chapel of Doonbeg was only a mile or so inland, spartan and doubling as meeting hall. Irish chapels were simple, func-tional shelters, not the florid and gilded gothick of later decades. Marriage, baptism and often mass were conducted in homes where, until the rules were tightened in 1852, the booted and spurred priest was glad of a hospitable meal and a rough malt whiskey afterwards.

To the outsider it was the back of beyond. The reed and peatbog bottoms supporting a cow or two seemed hostile, but they gave thatch and fuel to the inhabitants. In the spring and summer the bogs advertised their underlying wealth with a thousand flowers, including rhododendron and masses of yellow iris. Fields of fertile stones hid a world of underground rivers and springs. An average smallholding had about six acres of indifferent land.[15] Beyond the beaches and the cliffs buttressing Ireland was a moody Atlantic ocean which changed unpredictably from blue to grey to gold as the weather and light of day painted it—enough to make a man restless and curious and to provide a vast mirror for the more reflective. The horizon had its legends. Newspapers told of America beyond, but a span of 3,000 miles was hard for coracle people to envisage. Ships had been wrecked along the coastline from time to time, from the Armada vessel in 1588 at Spanish Point just north, to the Limerick emigrant ship at Doonbeg in 1836. To emigrate was to toy with destiny, yet an old dream beckoned from beyond the horizon, of youth, gold and the afterlife. The local appetite for tobacco fed the dreaming and priests took it in snuff form.

Macnamara saw and may have tried to alleviate poverty in his two years at Doonbeg. The Irish rural poor had few cities for refuge. Occasional distress collections were held in chapel, but cash was not the medium of rural aid. While cash went on church buildings, noted the Poor Law inquirers, there was much community support for the poor, the sick, the old and children. Potatoes and milk mattered more than cash. On the other hand, the new spate of church building was beginning to distract from relief of the poor and was worrying Protestants as they watched the revival of a powerful religious organization held suspect for centuries.[16] Macnamara was there in the summer of 1839 when Comyn attacked the workhouse system during Poor Law elections, insisting his "peasants" were "gentry." He was prosecuted for threatening a magistrate and, typically, shared snuff with his accuser during the hearing.

Curates on increasingly long apprenticeships in Ireland were shaped by parish priests who might inspire or embitter. Comyn must have impressed Macnamara. At times he even replaced him, preaching in Gaelic to the people after the curates, educated away from their roots in Europe or Maynooth, had delivered in English. There would have been banter about the uselessness of seminary training for the bogs of West Clare. The curates must have missed their books and the youthful company of college. They met as a body every May at Castleconnel, lodging locally and in communal retreat at the church for nearly a week. Parish priests had their own separate retreat. All clergy had to attend a two-day deanery conference every year, which included an examination of competence. It was important to have social events to reduce isolation and for mutual support. The religious orders had communities; secular clergy did not and a solitary life could weigh. Curates had no rights, even to an agreed stipend, only an arbitrary £10–20 and a garret somewhere in the parish. The power formation of Bishops, Rome and parish priests excluded curates. If Macnamara visited his family home in Ennis 20 miles away he would have met James Gleeson, the curate who left for the West Indies mission in 1838. Clare was far-flung but not isolated: the British Empire, the Catholic mission network and emigration to America saw to that. There were real alternatives to being a long-toothed curate or parish priest in Clare.

The little blue gold-embossed handbook, *The (Complete) Catholic Directory,* was a novelty in 1836 and gave the clergy the annual satisfaction of seeing their names and status broadcast across Ireland and the English-speaking world. William Battersby produced it to help the mission movement. Macnamara was *Eugene,* not *Owen,* in the 1839 edition (covering 1838), which also summarized the previous year's news from the missions. Bishop John England claimed his diocese in South Carolina had lost 50,000 Catholics for "want of priests." The exaggerated figure, "calculated" back two centuries, assumed all Irish emigrants were Catholic, although much of the pre–Famine emigration was Protestant. It impressed young priests to volunteer. Bishop Clancy, former controversial assistant to John England, was in Rome, "laying before the sovereign Pontiff an account of his past mission in Charleston and receiving new vigour to plant the standard of the cross in British Guiana." Clancy had a reputation for rhetoric and love of comfort. He also spent more time in the finer climates and circles of Rome, Vienna, London and Dublin than in Guiana. In the fall of 1838 Clancy was reported to have sailed for British Guiana with six priests from Irish dioceses. Four students from Carlow also signed up for the Guiana mission. Mission bishops were the new heroes, spiritual trailblazers on a par with the secular colonizers, traders and explorers. Esoteric place names colored mission reports back to Europe, as esoteric as the growing red map of British colonies around the world and the simple maps offered by the travel and emigration agents in Irish market towns.

Borrisokane

The Catholic Directory depended on respondents' returns for its information. Macnamara did not feature at all in its 1840 edition (the information deadline was November 1839), but he was curate in Borrisokane, County Tipperary, sixty miles from the Clare coast, by March 1840 when he attended a Temperance rally. Curates had no right of stability: bishops could move them as a punishment or as promotion, but Macnamara's predecessor moved to be his uncle's curate in what seems to have been a routine shift. To be sent to a less wealthy parish was a mark of disapproval and Bishop Kennedy of Killaloe was known for disapproving. It seems that Borrisokane was a growing parish, which Doonbeg-Kilkee was not. No replacement for Macnamara was reported in Doonbeg, leaving just two curates with Michael Comyn. Macnamara was not demoted. Borrisokane, according to Samuel Lewis's *Topographical Dictionary*, had "many new houses, 2,635 inhabitants in town, much improvement" and a "commodious and handsome RC chapel" had just been erected, suggesting something of a boomtown. It was also in more arable, better timbered land. The Silvermines Mountain just to the south hid gold and silver, then being actively mined. Doonbeg village had 213 people who gathered seaweed, quarried flagstones, made flannel and frieze, but in a stagnating area, despite and even because of the seasonal popularity of Kilkee resort seven miles away. Seasons also attracted beggars in droves, leaving them and the local population isolated in winter.

It could have been a late Fall move in 1839, just before the time limit for information to *The Catholic Directory*. Macnamara's new parish priest, James Birmingham, recorded his own and Macnamara's taking the Temperance pledge in March 1840 during Fr. Mathew's all–Ireland crusade. Birmingham sat down in March and April to produce the first book on Fr. Mathew's work. As he scribbled for distant publishers in London, Dublin and New York, parish work probably fell on his sole curate. Macnamara would have recognized his values as like those of Michael Comyn, pragmatic and tolerant.

On Shrove Tuesday, March 1, 1840, Theobald Mathew administered the alcohol abstinence pledge to 8,000 people in the center of Borrisokane. He had been in Birr the previous two days, when cavalry, infantry and police had to restrain "an immense influx from adjacent parishes and from counties far remote," gathering to see him on the Sunday. This "mild, unassuming, but extraordinary man" arrived "late Monday night and unexpectedly" at Birmingham's door in "plain dress, nothing *à la mode* and nothing ultraclerical." Borrisokane's new chapel, at the bottom end of town on the Birr road, was large enough for a good size population. Like Comyn and Birmingham, Mathew won the respect and affection of many Protestants, including Orangemen further north. In Borrisokane, "each moment Fr. Mathew was moving away, numbers hurried in from surrounding parishes. Some Protestants took the pledge and thus help forget the unhappy differences that have so long kept us asunder, as it ought to be, to be hailed with joy by those who wish to see narrow bigotry and religious discord at an end." It was a far cry from Patrick McSweeney's taunt of "non-commissioned Apostles" and the later boast of Archbishop Cullen of Dublin that he had never shared a meal with a Protestant. Moderates of good will would find much in common; fundamentalists and bigots could provoke and alienate at any time, but even Theobald Mathew and Michael Comyn were on their guard against the zealots and evangelicals who had characterized the decade 1820–30 with attempts to convert the Catholic peasantry in a "second Reformation."

Friar Mathew gave small medals to clergy who took the pledge—gold to a bishop and silver to a priest. Birmingham listed 20 Temperance clergy, including himself and Eugene Macnamara.[17] Mathew moved on to Nenagh the following day, Ash Wednesday, March 2nd, where he administered the pledge to 20,000 people. At the end of the year he appeared in Michael Comyn's parish. The "foul stigma" and "habitual intemperance of drink" marked out Ireland and to some extent its clergy. The Irish Catholic clerical drink was whiskey, which had less class but more punch than the wine of the established clergy. Alcohol was a serious social issue in 19th century Ireland and its control through the Temperance Movement coincided with O'Connell's mass political meetings for repeal of the Union with Britain and an Ireland with its own Parliament where emancipated Catholics would vote and stand at elections, as they now could at Westminster. Fr. Mathew stayed clear of politics, but the coinciding of his crusade with O'Connell's gave Irish political crowds a new reputation for orderliness. The Irish penchant for violence and rebellion disturbed English Catholics, who were from another class and race.

A new Catholic periodical appeared in London in 1840, *The Tablet*, a tabloid smaller than *The Times,* but with a coverage to match, and emphasizing the Irish, English and colonial Catholic world, Papal Rome, Latin America and the United States. It was edited by Frederick Lucas, a former Quaker with an eye for fair play. His newspaper was fed by correspondents, some more impartial than others. Church disputes were aired in Lucas's letter and news columns. Protestant writers contributed to the weekly paper in its earlier years, before the church it served hardened around it. "Drawing room Catholics" in England had little in common, save their label, with Irish immigrant "cellar dwellers," or with politicians like O'Connell who rocked the boat. O'Connell might have stood for the civil rights of Catholics, Irish and slaves, but conservative English Catholics were used to a lower and very privileged profile and they feared he would revive the anti–Catholic mobs. The specter of successive American, French and Irish revolutions against Crowns and established churches still haunted upper class memories, whatever their religion. They also opposed O'Connell's case for repeal of the Union with England. In the colonies and the United States, which *The Tablet* covered, Irish Catholic emigrés were not universally welcomed. Lucas became the champion of Catholic grievance and the trumpeter of Catholic achievement.[18]

Macnamara would have noticed the omission of his name from *The Directory* of 1840 (covering 1839), but he would have read in *The Tablet* and in the wide range of Irish newspapers of Bishop England, Bishop Clancy and O'Connell. Lucas published O'Connell's angry rebuke to the Methodists of Manchester for their bigotry towards Irish Catholics. He printed Bishop

Clancy's reports of his own hard work in the jungle of British Guiana, his ordination of yet more Irish priests for that mission, and his successes in converting that colony. The godly numbers game was being played, spiritual "success" was a statistic and Clancy became the model Irish missioner. *The Catholic Directory* reported his preferred styling, as "Titular Bishop of Oriense, Vicar Apostolic of British Guiana, Count of the Holy Roman Empire and Parish Priest of Georgetown," a fine heraldic achievement for a farmer's son from west Cork. Prince Metternich honored missioners like Clancy in support of the new self-assertion by the Papal authority. *The Directory* also reported Clancy's numerous journeys home to appeal for funds and recruits. He occupied platforms with O'Connell and others in the early days of the Catholic Institute of Great Britain, one of several societies founded in the head rush after Emancipation. Clancy was a polished writer and speaker. He wrote fulsome reports for *The Tablet* on missions, on American attitudes, on the clergy in London, and was frequently found on glittering platforms in London and Dublin.

Bishop Clancy's Rise

William Clancy had been ordained at 21 after only three years at Maynooth and spent six years as a country curate in Cork, his home county.[19] A priest ordained early could earn his keep through customary offerings from the faithful on his administering the sacraments. In 1829 he returned as a teacher to Carlow College where he had been a pupil. A younger brother, Francis, studied medicine at Edinburgh, joining the bishop later in British Guiana. Dr. John England, also a Corkman, toured Europe in the early 1830s recruiting for his American mission in South Carolina. When Rome ordered John England to Haiti as a papal negotiator, Charleston needed an assistant bishop. Clancy was chosen from a shortlist which included McSweeney of the Paris college. "I almost regret that Clancy has accepted," warned a Dublin priest. "He is too young and too fat to encounter that climate."

Clancy received his brief from Rome in November 1834, but took three months to reply, asking for expenses and for 16 students from Carlow College, who could then earn customary offerings after immediate early ordination. He spent much of his life searching for money. Writing to Rome, he whined (in Latin), "Everyone in Ireland knows that my going out to the American region is to make an exchange, not for the better, but mostly for the worse." It took him a year to get to Charleston, which scuppered Bishop England's negotiations in Haiti. Clancy had himself ordained Bishop in Ireland; Bishop England wanted the public event to take place in the mission of Charleston itself. Clancy continued to fight the noose, complaining about 12 pages of recriminations from Bishop England, "to me, now his equal and formerly his friend." Anywhere else but Charleston, he begged of Rome. "If there is any other place where the knowledge of philosophy and theology and the faculty of preaching in English would rebound to the glory of God [let me go there]. If however the Holy Father insists I shall go with an heavy heart. I cannot forget the great sacrifice I have made for God, the Roman Curia and the Bishop of Charleston in freely exchanging my homeland, tranquillity, family and sufficient means of support for a foreign country, hardships, long journeys and poverty."

Clancy hid behind lack of money, poor eyesight, lack of papal letters and a pending "future transfer request" to delay his coming to America. Bishop England had his own brother in Cork lend Clancy whatever money he might need, but drew the line at the 16 students: "I have students enough." He may have known Clancy's enthusiasm for money. However habitually Clancy manipulated, he rarely deceived people for long.

He finally arrived in Charleston—to a warm welcome—at the end of 1835. Bishop England explained Clancy's delay as "due to the discharge of his duties and a heavy, protracted sickness from which, thank God, he has fully recovered." Clancy responded graciously, "I did not come in search of gold or power—there is less of either in this wilderness of a diocese than in any other portion of Christendom. America has, with few exceptions, exhibited an enviable example of religious toleration, refuge of the persecuted and afflicted." He was to change his tune about America and Eugene Macnamara would soon hear the revised version.

In April 1836, four months after arrival, Clancy begged Rome to release him from South Carolina as there was not enough work for two bishops. Rome rebuked him, but he persisted, claiming that Bishop England would let him go if another would take him. "I would prefer any diocese in America or Great Britain to my present connexion with Charleston. It is rather too bad that I should be sent on a voyage of discovery through the old and the new world." To his credit, Clancy rose to the crisis of a cholera epidemic, begging unity, tolerance and courage from all denominations as "all part of one social family." Bishop England wrote to the Pope in 1837, "Clancy is the best of men and we are the best of friends, but I do not want to keep him unhappy. He is very distinguished for his character, zeal and piety, but in one year he has wrecked that whole constitutional system of church government which has taken me years to perfect."

Rome finally ordered Clancy to British Guiana in the summer of 1837 and nominated John Hynes, Dominican friar in Rome and former parish priest of Georgetown, Guiana, as Bishop England's new assistant bishop in Charleston. Hynes too was a Cork man and sometimes gave Clancy hospitality at the Dominican house on the river in Cork. One night Clancy entered Hynes' room alone and opened a sealed Papal brief to Bishop England. When England received the letter with the broken seal, he assumed Hynes and

Clancy were conspiring and refused Hynes as his assistant. Clancy then had the gall to ask Rome for Hynes as *his* vicar general in Guiana where Hynes had spent eight years placing the Catholic mission on the map. The governor of Guiana had given a church site on public land and Catholic and Protestant alike had supported Hynes.

Meanwhile, in spite of Rome's orders, Clancy lecture-toured Ireland and mainland Europe—an attractive, profitable circuit for a man after money and repute. He attacked the United States for its intolerance and bigotry so vehemently that the bishop of Cincinnati visited Ireland and publicly condemned Clancy's views. Clancy replied brazenly, "I have publicly dissuaded and will continue to dissuade Catholic Irishmen from emigrating to the USA until they learn that a great change has taken place in the Protestant Republican mind of the Union. The publication of these doubts from the altars of Ireland may help keep many of our people from encountering such physical moral and mental desolations in a country where the Catholics are only 1 million and the Protestants fully 120 million." By the end of 1838 Clancy was in Guiana, writing reports to the Society for the Propagation of the Faith, using Hynes' old letters and figures as his source. He inflated the number of Guiana Catholics, just as the colonial authorities deflated them.

The Reluctant Recruit

Bishop Clancy was given much coverage again by *The Tablet* during 1840 and 1841 when he returned from Guiana on yet another collecting and recruiting drive, which included visiting Rome, Austria, England and Ireland. He appeared on a platform with O'Connell, "called from the swamps of Guiana and Charleston to address such a reunion of so much that is good and repectable in Great Britain." In England, he thanked student priests for their warm welcome, "however accustomed I am to congratulatory addresses in the USA, Ireland, Haiti and other countries." In London he claimed, during an after-dinner speech, to have abandoned an appointment 200 miles away in order "to represent the Colonial department" after traveling thousands of miles in South America and the Caribbean. He brought to the guest of honor, a politician well-disposed towards Catholics, gratitude "from the lips of the red man in the primordial forests of Guiana, and from the prisons of the sable sons and daughters of Africa."[20]

In 1841, Eugene Macnamara left Borrisokane parish. The Catholic *Limerick Reporter* announced on March 12th,

> Removed from Borrisokane, Tipperary, to Corofin, Clare, the Rev. Eugene Macnamara, a most truly Christian minister.

On the following day, the hostile, Establishment *Limerick Chronicle* reported, in the same column as the suicide of a Killaloe student priest at Maynooth and near the full text of an anti–Catholic lecture by a Protestant cleric,

Rev. E. Macnamara is removed from Borrisokane to Corofin.

Corofin parish was run by Stephen Walsh, a fire-eater, who lived in a fine regency home by the river on the road curving up into the narrow town. Corofin village was much smaller than Borrisokane, a side-road backwater by comparison. It could have been a curate's financial punishment; working with Stephen Walsh may have been a social punishment too—he was a "provincial Boanerges" who enjoyed frightening his people by constant harping on Hell. The posting may even have been a fiction to preempt speculation. Macnamara may never have reached Corofin or, if he did, he did not stay there long. Bishop Kennedy suspended him for "proven seduction," presumably at Borrisokane, and informed Rome.[21] Drink problems were more prominent than sexual such among the clergy, but they were sometimes accused of soliciting during confession or of fathering an illegitimate child. Between peccadillo and scandal lay a spectrum. Kennedy evidently provided Macnamara with an *exeat*, as church law then permitted, to leave without any particular destination or Bishop to take him. He became a wandering, unattached cleric, an "ecclesiastical tourist," of which there were a surprising number.

Macnamara and Bishop William Clancy may have met in London. Clancy came back to London from Rome late in March 1841 and was gracing platforms and dinner tables there up to the end of May, when he went to Ireland. He was good at redefining reality and here was another money-making recruit. Clancy planned to force the hand of the colonial administration to pay for twice as many clergy in Guiana as the four they were already paying for. In church law, Clancy was the parish priest of Georgetown, Guiana, and the other priests were his curates. As in Irish parishes, the curates were totally dependent on the good will of the parish priest. The latter decided how the parish income would be apportioned between himself and the curate(s). Clancy hoped to receive a higher lump sum from the colony to cover himself and an increased number of curates; as parish priest he would decide how the lump sum was divided and his curates would receive a nominal pittance. Macnamara was in need of a role and in need of a living. No longer welcome at home, he was somehow recruited for Guiana, where Irish missioners were not afraid to go to "save the existing flock from paganism and heresy and from those ravening wolves in sheep's clothing," namely the Protestant, predominantly Methodist, missioners.[22]

A vivid example of Bishop Clancy's ruthless recruiting was recorded that summer. He wanted to found a convent in Georgetown, Guiana, with hard-working nuns who would contribute to his reputation and to local education. His cousin, Abigail Cantillon, was a nun of the Presentation Order in the

North Presentation Convent, Cork city. She had helped found a new house out at Midleton, but something made her superiors uneasy and she was recalled to Cork city in 1840. Possibly Cantillon was unsettled (or unsettling) as there was tension among the nuns as to whether they should be an outward going active order or more contemplative. The superior of North Presentation was Mary England, sister to Bishop John England, who happened to be in Ireland in 1841 at the same time as Dr. Clancy, his former reluctant assistant in Charleston. Clancy came to Cork from London and Rome with permission to recruit nuns, including cousin Cantillon. Rome stipulated that he must obtain the consent of the convent superior and the local bishop before taking anyone. On June 10, 1841, Clancy appeared at the convent for the Superior's response, but Mary England refused to release Cantillon. The feeling was that she would be "liable to an infringement of her vows and rules" in Guiana, but Clancy was only told that she could not be spared. He accepted the disappointment piously as "God's will."

A week later "Bishop Clancy came to our convent between eight and nine in the morning and called for his cousin. The Rev. Mother England also went to see him and prayed him to breakfast with her brother, Dr. England, who was then in the community room, but he declined. The Rev. Mother took leave. Immediately afterwards, he conducted Sister Cantillon out of the convent, without the permission or knowledge of the [Bishop of Cork] or her Superior, and handed her into a covered vehicle which was in readiness for them at the convent gate."[23] Cantillon, in turn, recruited other nuns from Port Laoise and Carlow. They assembled in Dublin at a half-way house convent, ready to sail with Bishop Clancy in the early autumn.

Meanwhile, at the end of May, Eugene Macnamara and others boarded a vessel on the River Thames. Clancy was in London still and may have seen them off.

> Rev. William Nightingale, formerly of London District, Rev. Eugene Macnamara of the Diocese of Killaloe, Ireland, and a Capuchin friar of Spain, Juan Baptista Esquinigo, have sailed per the ship *Rambler* direct from London to Georgetown, on Tuesday 25th May 1841. Bishop Clancy will ordain two priests for the same Vicariate during Pentecost week in Carlow College, who will sail from Dublin. The Bishop hopes to be accompanied by nuns.[24]

The flowers were just coloring the bog in West Clare and the yellow gorse was softening the limestone fields as Macnamara sailed. He never saw Clare again, but its people and their plight stayed with him, too many on too little impoverished land. He must have known Thomas McMahon, the Kilkee laborer, who told the Poor Law Enquiry in 1835, "We are worse than the slaves in the colonies and we give up the ghost at 58 or 60." A decade later and literally halfway round the world, Macnamara was still dogged by the memory.

Three

Mission and Misadventure. British Guiana, 1841–1884

A scandal to the Church, a disgrace and an injury to the cause of religion everywhere—(President of Carlow College, Ireland, on Bishop Clancy of Guiana, 1844)

The whole story of the quarrel would fill a very bulky portfolio—(*Demerara Royal Gazette*, September 3, 1844)

On July 3, 1841, the 500-ton brig *Rambler*, thirty-six days out from London, entered the mouth of the Demerara estuary, turned into the wind and crabbed slowly across to her berth at the Georgetown wharves. For the first-time visitor it was a dismal sight, not even offset by the two dozen familiar ensigns of European and American ships straining their cables. The sea turned muddy brown as it heaved and pitched against the outflowing river. The town and flat green landscape sat below sea level. Beyond the wharf front and the market ran the old Dutch town of Staebrok, renamed Georgetown by the British. The rubbish and effluent of 25,000 people lingered on tidal mud flats, under the mooring wharves and in a swamp under the old Dutch fort. There the mosquito bred and passed on "yellow jack" and malarial "colony fever" to the residents. The nose picked up the open yard cooking and the undrained ditches of Georgetown before the eyes made out its detail.

Unease in Georgetown

The ship tied up at the wharves at the north end of town, where the main streets or dams met the river. The duty port medical officer—it could even have been Bishop Clancy's brother—came on board. Portuguese immigrants were making up for the loss of slave labor, but they brought disease

Map of British Guiana.

and poor hygiene. *Rambler*'s more acceptable passengers would have been glad to feel their land legs for the first time in five weeks. They would also have perspired in the sapping humidity of Guiana. Crowds watched the unloading: a ship meant news, fresh goods, a link with the outside world—and occasional labor for hopefuls around the quayside. Guiana was in a severe economic depression, because of the freeing of slaves. "Commercial and agricultural distress is unprecedented," wrote the U.S. consul that summer.[1] Exports of coffee and cotton were down by half, sugar, rum and molasses down by one-third and plantations were being sold or squatted. Only half the workforce was still on the plantations. Josiah Booker's Wharf was quiet in a way it had never been in 1820 in the first days of the colony. The enlightened Booker had emancipated his sugar cane slaves six years before the law required it, but he paid a price.

Ashore, beyond the hucksters and beggars, white painted houses on stilts with verandahs overlooking gardens of bougainvillea and cabbage palms made up for the approach. Compensation for the freeing of slaves had been lavished on houses. Houseboys would have helped Macnamara and Nightingale with the baggage down the broad, fashionable Brickdam—literally a brick dam which served as a road—to Christ Church, recently enlarged. Next door lay the presbytery, also recently re-built by Bishop Clancy. William Bates, Franciscan and vicar general to Clancy, welcomed them, but they were uneasy. Nightingale wrote to Charles Weld, a London lawyer, at the end of July, "Our salute on gaining the Bishop's residence was a hearty welcome [from Bates] and a brotherly reception. We soon gained the church, but we became incredulous as to the Bishop's residence. Then, we saw that what we took for an outbuilding was our abode, rough and plain, secure above by a slated roof, but not proof in the walls against wind or rain."[2] Macnamara and Nightingale were both seasoned curates and moved easily into the familiar routine of sick calls, poor school, prison and hospital visiting, taking Sunday services and serving outlying plantations. Macnamara went out as far as the Essequibo River where he baptized his first Guiana child on July 11th. An adult professed faith before him in Georgetown on October 20th. There were few Catholics among the freed slaves, or "labourers" as the church registers called them, but a couple of thousand among the white Europeans, their numbers swollen by the Portuguese, many of whom crowded the plantation dispensaries and the town hospitals. Many never made it to the fields, preferring the cash and tumble of Georgetown life. Settler Catholics did not entirely welcome the new arrivals.

Routines changed when Bishop Clancy arrived with three nuns, two postulants and a lay sister on October 5th, by the brig *Sandbach*, 42 days out from Dublin. Clancy made sure *The Tablet* was informed by return of mail. "Nuns of the Presentation Order took immediate possession of a large and commodious building." He told *The Catholic Directory*, in time for the new 1842 edition, that the nuns were "the first of the Order ever established on the great continent of South America." They were, he said, running six free schools, although people preferred a "pay school." The "large and commodious building" was in reality Clancy's grand presbytery; there was simply no convent, despite his promises to the nuns. He wrote to *The Madras Catholic Expositor* in India, run by a colleague, reporting that the nuns had "a large and commodious dwelling near the Catholic church," but again failed to say it was his own house. Governor Sir Henry Light was more blunt. "Dr. Clancy and the nuns lived in the same house; the nuns and novices quarrelled with the Superior and with each other and most quitted the establishment."[3]

Bates, Macnamara and Nightingale could not all live in the "outbuilding," nor could they live with the bishop and six females. Privacy in an all-wooden house was impossible and Presentation nuns were already in tension about their role. Bates ordered Nightingale out to the so-called Arabian (Caribbean) Coast, beyond the Essequibo, before Bishop Clancy returned. In December, Bates himself was posted as pastor to New Amsterdam, a small settlement down the estuary of the Berbice River. Most of Guiana's 98,000 population lived on the low-lying coastal belt where the plantations flourished on a rich silt under 90 inches of annual rainfall. Nightingale was miserable out among the heavy-drinking planters, the curse of Guiana. Medical Officer Hancock, from a quarter century's experience, put most illness down to "alcohol debauchery" and lack of exercise. Polluted water in a dehydrating climate was also a serious problem. "The habit of intemperance to which Europeans seem particularly tempted in the tropics [produces] three fifths of the deaths in a year," wrote one Protestant missioner. Anthony Trollope, who saw nothing but good in Guiana, claimed "yellow fever is not half as bad as a fellow with a brandy bottle." A planter recorded that "drinking, fighting and rioting are indulged [on major holidays] to an extent known nowhere in Europe, out of Ireland." Four of Macnamara's colleagues, half the clergy in fact, including Bishop Clancy, became serious alcohol addicts. Guiana was a test of a Fr. Mathew silver medal holder and Nightingale had taken the pledge, like Macnamara. They carried medals in the first place because the Irish Catholic clergy had a drink problem. In Guiana, although sarsparilla was advertised prominently, only the smaller Protestant missions like the Methodists seriously promoted temperance.[4]

"I was ordered immediately to this coast [although] the Bishop still calls me his chaplain and says that is what I will always be," Nightingale wrote to Charles Weld in October 1841. He fretted about the immorality and profligacy of the planters on whose hospitality he depended. They, in turn, benefitted from a missioner on plantation: it helped keep the workers on site. In January 1842, months of unrest and desertion culminated in employers being forced to improve working conditions. It was an uncomfortable time for a newcomer like Nightingale. "Total abstinence agrees with me very much. Here nothing is done without the bottle. It is an insult not to partake. I have often been obliged to produce my silver medal in vindication. It separates me entirely from the constant convivial parties. A man knows himself best when he is alone." He found this knowledge in sea and sky, and during days of fever in the hammock. "My books are my sole companion and my snuffbox my constant solace."[5]

To the Colonial Office and Governor Light, Bishop Clancy was a parish priest, perhaps an immigrant chaplain, but certainly not a bishop by Papal appointment. Britain recognized Catholics and their religious needs, but not the Pope, save as an Italian ruler and bishop of Rome. Papal prelates, titles or ranks could not be acknowledged on British soil. Curiously, the Colonial Office also administered Ireland, in the United Kingdom homeland itself. Irish priests serving in the colonies therefore held the Colonial Office in some disrespect, yet from a Protestant state Clancy received a colonial stipend for two priests, including himself as parish priest, at Georgetown and for two at New Amsterdam. He chose what to pay his curates out of the allocation. A constant source of friction between the Catholic Vicar Apostolic of Guiana and the Colonial Office was the estimate of numbers and needs of Catholics in the colony, particularly the Portuguese immigrants, overstated by Clancy at 8,000 and understated by Light at 4,600. Clancy could have built many bridges, but instead, flaunted his dignity and titles in line with Rome's reassertion of clerical authority. He first asked for four priests to be funded, extra to the existing four, but was refused. Despite this, by the end of 1841, Clancy had doubled the clergy and made sure the press in England knew, as if to force the Governor's hand. Bates was pastor at New Amsterdam; John Cullen served an Indian mission upriver with a Spanish friar, Thomas Morgan looked after the Indian and penal settlements on the Essequibo, and Nightingale languished on the Arabian Coast beyond. John McDonnell assisted Bates, Eugene Macnamara assisted Clancy in Georgetown and Joseph Kelly arrived in November 1841 as "teacher and catechist."

The Prison Incident

Mass and Vespers were celebrated on plantations Jalousie and Versailles by the Georgetown clergy every other Sunday. They also visited two other plantations and islands in the estuary. In town, the crowded Colonial Jail, five garrison stations with Irish soldiers, and the main church also required a priest. The Catholic tradition of ritual observances needed intensive manpower to provide mass, confession and other sacraments for all who wanted them.

Early each Wednesday, Macnamara visited the jail a block away from the church. It was a functional building with 80 cells and over 1,200 male prisoners. They worked treadmills and morning chapel may have been light relief. It may also have become a security problem as more prisoners, particularly Portuguese, took advantage of the concession in overcrowded conditions. Unrest and depression meant a rise in prison populations across Georgetown, in the main jail, in the female jail and in the debtor's clink. The end of 1841 was a particularly tense time. Early on December 15th Macnamara returned to his lapboard shelter against the presbytery and wrote to Bishop Clancy on the other side of the wall.[6]

My Lord, I beg leave to bring to your notice a circumstance which has occurred this morning regarding my duty as a clergyman. [As] for a long time past I attended this morning at the Jail to celebrate mass for the Catholic prisoners. When about to commence divine service I was publicly obstructed by the jailer who in a loud and blustering manner and with anger depicted in his countenance told me I should not celebrate mass. I reasoned with him and said that Wednesday was the day appointed for the visit of a Catholic clergyman. His answer was that he had received orders from the sheriff not to admit me. Of course I had no alternative but to yield. However in order not to deprive the poor Catholic prisoners of their religious rites I performed divine service in one of their cells. I beg to observe that the jailer delivered his message in the most ungracious manner. He seemed to derive pleasure from the duty imposed on him. Instead of acquainting me privately with the sheriff's orders, he did so in the most public manner and in the presence of all the prisoners. I anxiously await your Lordship's will to know what I am to do under these circumstances. I remain, My Lord,

Your obedient servant and subject.

Clancy was already sore at Governor Light's rejecting his call for extra funds. Fever, drink and possibly gout were also beginning to tell on him. "As a painful duty" he immediately sent a copy of Macnamara's letter to Governor Light. "The gratuitous service of one of my curates has been given in the jail on Wednesday mornings between six and seven o'clock. Under the former jailer, Mr. Horan, every facility for public worship was kindly and promptly afforded." The pitch then rose an octave, possibly with another glass; the lines of the draft version crowded each other out. Money was a Clancy motif.

I need scarcely inform Your Excellency that in England Roman Catholic chaplains are appointed with a fixed salary in many of the prisons and that

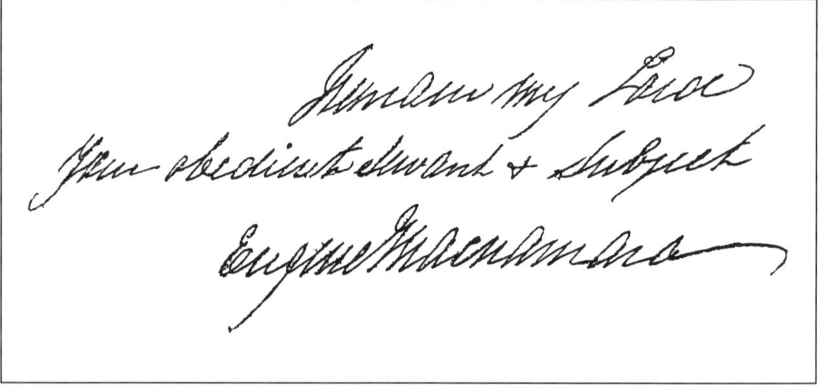

Macnamara's signature on a letter to Bishop Clancy, December 1841 (*Georgetown Catholic Cathedral Archive*).

where gratuitous attendance is secured by the Catholic Bishop, so far from the sheriff or jailer *daring to obstruct a priest* [Clancy's emphasis] in the exercise of his public devotions, that to my own personal knowledge in the prisons of Cork, Carlow and Dublin reasonable facilities are afforded by every high and subordinate functionary. In connexion may I beg as a favour, perhaps I ought to say in the stronger but no less respectful language of a Christian Bishop that I demand as a right, redress for this wanton and unprovoked act of intolerance or incipient persecution [before I make] complaint to the Colonial Office in London. Your Excellency's faithful servant in Christ.

As well as pontificating, Clancy enjoyed "pontificals"—walking-out purple, lace, skullcap and biretta; liturgical vestments complete with mitre, crozier and attendant candlebearer. Like the pompous phrases he adopted, the dress helped confer on Clancy the "respectability" he craved. He once issued a reprimand to the acting colony secretary, "as a recognised Catholic prelate and a Nobleman, which I am by creation of a European King, to a mere layman not my equal in spiritual or temporal rank." On January 2, 1842, Clancy invested two nuns with the habit during a solemn High Mass, with Macnamara as deacon and Joseph Kelly as sub-deacon. Clancy made sure *The Tablet* knew that "the cathedral was crowded with colonists of the highest respectibility and of different creeds."[7]

Nightingale was not cut out for the Arabian Coast. He sailed for New York in December 1841, leaving Clancy, Macnamara and Kelly in Georgetown. Charles Weld handed Nightingale's letters to *The Tablet,* of which he was a trustee. They were duly published in March 1842, but the edition did not reach Guiana until late April or early May. Clancy meanwhile had written for *The Tablet* at the beginning of March 1842 to puff his success.[8] "Judge Firebrace's conversion in my presence more than amply compensates for all I have endured during eight years in the swamps and forests of Charleston and Guiana." In fact, he had engineered to spend a total of six out of those eight years in Europe, far from the swamps and forests of either diocese. As he wrote, Thomas Morgan and one of the nuns quit Guiana. *The Tablet* containing Nightingale's letters arrived just as Clancy embarked on a health cruise to Nevis, "ordered by my physician to sail among the healthy islands and to bathe in the salt waters after several recent fevers." Clancy returned to the attack after his 2,000-mile round trip.[9]

Nightingale, he claimed, was on £100 annual salary and had passage money paid from London. If Nightingale were so destitute, Clancy asked, how was it he had "a very fashionable pony?" If he was a temperance medal holder from Fr. Mathew, "my co-worker in the apostolate," how was his house full of "bottles as candleholders—had he drunk them?" Bates, McDonnell and Cullen, Clancy added, wondered the same: revealingly, Nightingale's shipmate and fellow medalist, Eugene Macnamara, was not mentioned. The cracks in Clancy's facade were widening. After Nightingale left, John

McDonnell requested home leave for six months on health grounds, which may have been drink-related, as he certainly had a problem by 1844. McDonnell left at the start of August 1842 and was due back at the end of January 1843, but needed an extension until the end of April. Clancy too requested leave of the Governor for himself, "for the benefit of health," from 31 August 1842.[10] The Governor knew there were other reasons, but Clancy was expected back at the end of February 1843. Macnamara and Joseph Kelly covered for Georgetown, Macnamara receiving some 26 adult converts up to February 1843, and baptizing 108 children up to April. Apart from the humidity, the insects, the frogs' chorus at night and at times the incessant rain, boredom may have been a more serious problem than work or even drink. Kelly signed off his last Baptism in the register in March 1843 with *"Deo Gratias!"* (Thank God). Sailors and missioners feared Demerara, but both were drawn there by profession.

Anglican Governor Light needed the wisdom of Solomon to preside over the competing missions of Guiana. Nextdoor lay Catholic Venezuela, from where Indians had made their way up river in 1830 for safety on British territory, after their Franciscan missioners had been massacred. They pledged loyalty to the British Crown in exchange for protection. Before he went to the Moruka mission in 1844, John Cullen first worked in a former Spanish mission on the Cayumi River and the Governor saluted its history: "Its worth may be estimated when it is known that upwards of 30,000 Indians had been brought into a quasi-civilisation by the Spanish missionaries." When a Methodist missioner approached Light for permission to demolish a Spanish wayside cross (despite its fairly central place in Scripture), Light turned him down. When a freelance missioner approached him "for a licence to teach the Doctrine of the New Jerusalem and to be general catechist of the Indians," Light dismissed him as "labouring under religious delusions."[11] The Governor reported sectarian bad feeling between the Presbyterians and Church of England, but generally the free churches made good headway among the freed slave communities, the Methodists in particular, financed entirely by collections from their congregations. British evangelicals and nonconformists had led the campaign against slavery. The Methodists also related well to the establishment Church of England.

The same was not said of Bishop Clancy, who asked tartly of Lord Stanley, the colonial secretary, in May 1842, if his proposed extra stipend was being denied "by a few bigotted Tory planters." The colonial secretary endorsed in pencil "rather an intemperate letter."[12] Governor Light, however, felt that some extra help for the Portuguese "would have been good reason for the Portuguese government to espouse emigration from Madeira had it been advisable to continue it." The implication was clearly that if the Portuguese stopped coming, there could be no case for extra Catholic clergy. They did stop coming and many returned home. Clancy complained to Lord

Stanley of "parsimony" and insisted he had been promised the extra stipend. He threatened to tell the Portuguese to go home and to "advise the civil and religious authorities of Malta, France and Madeira that all Catholic emigrants are likely to have their religious rights eroded or destroyed by [prejudiced property holders]," signing himself Bishop, Apostolic Vicar and Count of the Holy Roman Empire.[13] A fool jester and some deep reflection was needed in the Bishop's household.

Bishop Clancy's Demise

Bishop Clancy was ambitious for ease. The inner and the outer man gradually separated, partly due to drink. He had cut a sad 36-year-old on arriving in Guiana, constantly invoking his rights. When, in May and June 1842, he sailed to St. Kitts and the sulphur waters of neighboring Nevis, he took with him Anna O'Regan from the convent. Bath Village, near Charlestown on Nevis, hosted the wealthy of the Caribbean with gout and other complaints. St. Kitts welcomed him and he effused about the future of the island church, promised a donation and promptly left, ignoring an appointment with the lieutenant governor. News returned to Guiana, before he did, that he and O'Regan had stayed in the same house on Nevis. It was held against him, yet they went again in December 1844. Governor Light reported routinely to London, "Dr Clancy and Mrs O'Regan went on the plea of ill-health to the islands and resided at the same house for some weeks in Nevis. On return, Clancy found his flock scandalised at the intimacy and a petition was signed and addressed to Rome for his removal."

Governor Light's misgivings over Clancy were not new. "Clancy came [in 1838] with great pretensions—he refused at first to produce his credentials, but read them [out] in his Chapel, then afterwards presented them to me. I objected to an innovation, namely Midnight Mass fearing that the host and other Papal ceremonies in the streets might form part of Dr Clancy's system. His correspondence with me was in the tone of supremacy over all civil authority."[14] Even at a formal dinner with the Governor, Clancy had ridden a roughshod horse. A toast "to the Church" was proposed, to which Clancy and the Anglican archdeacon both rose to respond. Clancy suggested a bishop was senior to an archdeacon, which sent a ripple of anger through the gathering and the guests walked out. Light had noted Clancy's extravagance in enlarging the church and building himself a "large and commodious house. He refused to account for the money and created discontent. His priests received what he chose to give them out of the Colonial grants. There were constant quarrels, dismissals, intrigues, mutual recriminations which have ended in the appeal to Rome and still greater scandal."

Just before leaving for Europe, Clancy constructed an alibi through *The*

Tablet, warning darkly of a growing clamor from "schismatical, lower class, European, nominal Catholics," the sort who would steal the plate from the church. He left William Bates as vicar general in charge of Georgetown parish and Macnamara as his assistant. Bates "associated with a lady of some attraction," explained Governor Light, "and the pair appeared to live together as man and wife, he pleading instruction to convert the lady in his suite to the RC faith." Late in October 1842, Clancy put into Ford's Hotel at 13–14 Manchester Square in the aristocratic heart of London's West End. Ford's was a Catholic hotel, hosting "clergy and nobility" and advertising "best viands and wines" in *The Tablet*. It was to be Clancy's base for six months' official leave.

Sir Henry Light assumed Bishop Clancy was going to Rome in the autumn of 1842 to counter parishioners' complaints. Clancy was still in the British Isles in February 1843 when his six months leave expired. In London he again asked government funds for extra priests, this time for Irish soldiers in the Guiana force. The War Office refused a garrison chaplain and chapel. It became personal. After receiving a letter from the War Secretary styling him as "Reverend," he peeved that there was "no such person in London," and demanded the title of either "Bishop" or "Right Rev Dr" the War Office apologized and Clancy accepted, still complaining of "the strange identification of the high title of a bishop with that of a mere deacon."[15] He consoled himself with the Catholic spotlight, sending regular contributions from his hotel to *The Tablet* on various topics. *The Tablet*'s regular "Roman News" column reported his arrival in Rome for Lent 1843, his preaching at the Jesuit church and his appearing under Bernini's bronze *baldochino* with eleven other bishops in attendance around the Papal throne on Easter Sunday. Roman customary offerings could sustain him for a time.

Craftily, Clancy waited until he was in Rome before writing to Stanley on April 24th. His leave had expired two months previously, but he told the colonial secretary (not Governor Light) that he was on *nine* months leave for ill-health, due to expire on June 1st. He requested a six-month extension until the end of 1843, which would allow him at least half salary. "I am apprehensive that business connected with the ecclesiatical department of my Vicariate will detain me in Rome for a few months. [I am also] very seriously attacked by local fevers [Rome was surrounded by malarial marsh] and sore throat since my arrival." Stanley was not fooled, and replied "some mistake must have arisen," offering "six months extension on the expiry of the *six* months granted, [but] the half salary shall be received only on the return of the absent functionary to the Colony." Bishop Clancy had until the end of August 1843.

Immigration to Guiana

With the emancipation of slaves in 1834, the freed slaves took paid labor, but preferred to dig their own allotments or "provision lands." The labor intensive farming of coffee, cotton and especially sugar declined. Guiana needed an estimated 5,000 new laborers each year to make up for the drift from the plantations since 1834, but it could not be met. Alcohol consumption and the prison population were the only real signs of growth in the colony. It was hard to induce anyone to emigrate to Guiana. The proposed transport of willing Sierra Leonians in 1843 ended in ships returning from West Africa virtually empty. If talk of "the graveyard of Europe" was exaggerated, so too was one planter's description of Guiana—"as healthy as Rutland county" in the heart of England. Of nearly 7,000 Portuguese, one-third had returned home by the end of 1842 and mortality was high among the rest. The Portuguese also brought a folk religion quite alien to the British. "Being all rigid Catholics they are interfered with in their [work] by the number of saints days which are strictly observed by them." Port Medical Officer Henry Dalton felt that they were in the main "the refuse of the town of Funchal [Madeira] and its neighbourhood [where] they have three times emptied their jails to fill British Guiana with their occupants." The Guiana administration withdrew the bounty on Portuguese immigrants in 1842, placing the $30 on each U.S. immigrant instead. No more than 150 American citizens lived in Guiana and scrap metal was its main export to the United States. Immigration was topic of the year in 1842, as it had been every year since 1838.

Clancy pressed for Irish immigrants and advertised Guiana on his tour of Ireland in 1840–1. He ran his own immigration model, bringing his doctor brother, his nun cousin and his priest nephew to join him. He had seen, he said, Irish canal diggers in Southern Carolina and Irish cotton workers in Savannah, climates far worse than Guiana. Forty, in fact, came to Guiana in 1836 to work on the coffee estates. The Colonial Office proposed that young offenders be sent to join them and even planned an agency in Constantinople to recruit Bulgarian peasants. The few Irish workers who did come made a bad impression. All sentiment among Irish planters for their own countrymen evaporated when they employed them. The owner of Plantation Donneybrook "imported 30 Irishmen from Connaught [1839–1840] and would pay anyone handsomely who would take them off his hands. They never miss their evening grog and such a set of wild ruffians never appeared in these regions before. They are enough to scare the Indians from the settlement altogether and they are accounted but savages inferior to the Africans." As late as 1848, after a failed uprising in Ireland, "Demerara and Berbice" were being advertised as "*the* place for the Irish. If Paddy would keep from drink he would be a comparative gentleman in the West Indies, better than idleness, pikemaking and starvation in the Emerald isle." The British government, it was calculated, would need spend only one million pounds to export a quarter of a million Irishmen to Guiana at £4 passage money each. Two weeks later, the same journal published a warning against "Irresponsible Colonisation."[16]

There were wilder schemes. In September 1842, one Correa de Costa advertised that he intended to bring 500 British socialists to create Coburg colony (named for Prince Albert), for the cultivation of grapes, tobacco and coffee, assisted by millions of native Indians. Nothing happened. Bernhardt Ries planned Cartabo, a German colony up the Essequibo, but only an advance party arrived. Clancy supported it briefly as a means for recruiting clergy. There was a feeling that the planters for whom immigrant labor was being promoted should also pay immigrants' costs. In 1845, the Tropical Emigration Society of London asked Lord Stanley if they could settle 1,525 members up the Essequibo. They would need four years to break in a third of the land, but feared that "the RC priesthood would look with jealousy on such a large and united body of English Protestants on the Essequibo." Only five months before, the Venezuelan government had turned down the same Society on grounds of exaggerated publicity and demand for a lavish subsidy of £10 per head. Behind both applications lurked John Diston Powles, of Topo notoriety. Irish migrants were also trickling into next-door Venezuela, "to lay their bones" in remote unhealthy mining areas. John Cullen, the Guiana missioner up river, was in touch with the archbishop of Venezuela, the Venezuelan ambassador in London and his own brother Edward, a doctor in Ireland. A family member had served under Bolívar. Edward visited John in Guiana several times and became an eccentric expert on Central America, claiming in 1851 to have found the ideal flat route for a Panama canal after two years in the jungle. At the peak of the Irish Famine in 1847 both Cullens were asking Venezuela to take paupers from the west of Ireland.[17]

Macnamara Goes to the Pope

John McDonnell must have discussed events in Guiana while on sick leave in Ireland. "Reports are contradictory," mused *The Catholic Directory*. On return, in May 1843, he stayed with Macnamara in Georgetown rather than go back to New Amsterdam where Bates and the Bishop's nephew had both been banished in disgrace. Macnamara had carried the Georgetown parish for two years on what the Governor himself called a "a pittance," living in a shanty and with Clancy there for just nine out of twenty-four months. He had also covered for Bates as the vicar general kicked over the traces. The two young priests decided on drastic action.

> Last Sunday after Mass, the Rev Mr Macnamara, Catholic pastor of Georgetown, and the Rev Mr McDonnell of Berbice, announced to the congregation from the altar their intention of immediately proceeding to Rome to lay before His Holiness the Pope the degraded and unhappy state of this Vicariate.[18]

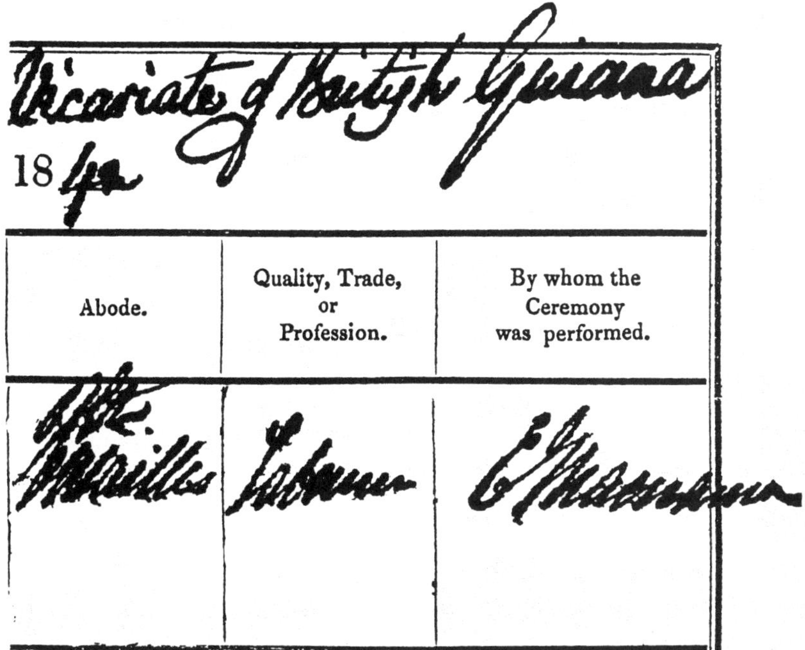

Baptism Register entry by Macnamara on Plantation Versailles, 1842 (*Georgetown Catholic Cathedral Archive*).

The congregation met afterwards to pledge support. A general meeting of all Catholics was proposed for noon at the church on the following Sunday. A petition of complaint was drawn up, signed by what Governor Light called "a large and respectable body of RC's" which included judges, doctors, planters and John Taggart, consul for Portugal and long-time friend of John Hynes, the former parish priest of Georgetown living in Rome. The complaints included Clancy's drinking, embezzlement and undue intimacy with the convent; the lifestyles of his vicar general, William Bates (who died shortly afterwards) and of his nephew W.J. Clancy were added. "The priesthood being numerous," Light later reported, "funds were wanting for their payment, limited by Bishop Clancy to a mere subsistence—complaints were made [but] Dr Clancy refused audits and as large sums have passed through his hands he has subjected himself to charges of misappropriation."[19]

On June 3rd the two priests boarded the barque *Mary* from the Demerara wharves and headed for Liverpool, their only company for five weeks being the crew and barrels of sugar, molasses and rum. Joseph Kelly took the *Rebecca Turney* for Belfast. Consul Taggart sent a letter to John Hynes in Rome by the next mail ship and Macnamara and McDonnell arrived in Liverpool around July 10th, from where they made for Ford's Hotel in London, en route to Rome. Mr. Ford gave them news of Clancy. Across from the Hotel in the corner of Manchester Square lay the French Embassy, leased in the town house of Lord Seymour, Marquess of Hertford. Seymour's brother, Sir George Seymour, was an admiral. Off the northeast corner of the square lay the Spanish Chapel where Simon Bolívar once worshipped. *The Tablet* was available for guests, along with *The Times*, but unusually the current Ford's guest list was withheld by *The Tablet*, as was its regular "Roman News" column.

In Rome, John Hynes, now a bishop but with no diocese, knew that Cardinal Franzoni, Prefect of the Office for the Propagation of the Faith (*Propaganda Fide*), had demanded Clancy's resignation and promise not to leave Europe. Ecclesiastical Rome had its national sub-cultures of the influential and the informed, the intelligence hub of the Catholic world. Irish clergy and missioners were near the center of that hub. Around the rim lay other clergy, eccentrics, scholars, those out to dry, those with their own means and those who just liked being near the hub. A living could be eked out as a convent chaplain and through customary offerings. Clancy, living at the Twelve Apostles convent, was already a talking point among the Rome Irish, "running about with Donovan [a former Maynooth professor] without his episcopals." Donovan and Clancy, both on alcohol and with too little to do, fed misinformation to *The Tablet* and "would have the world believe that the greatest men in Rome are the Pope, Cardinal Acton and Dr Clancy." As Irish dignitaries took the cool of the evening on the city hills after hot, humid Roman days, they could not help but spot the two black sheep. "This evening Donovan passed pretending not to see me…. In the evening walked by the Villa Borghese, met or rather saw Dr Clancy in his disguise."[20]

Hynes received from Taggart a Demerara paper reporting that the two priests were on their way to Rome "to represent the degraded state of that Vicariate to the Holy See." The article and Taggart's letter were translated for Cardinal Franzoni. Hynes duly wrote to Macnamara and McDonnell at Ford's on July 16th, suggesting they delay their coming to Rome while Clancy's case pended. In early August the Pope appointed John Hynes Apostolic Administrator of Guiana, upon which Clancy, who had resigned months before, made for England and took the mailboat *City of Glasgow* from Southampton on August 16th. "The idea of Clancy's making for Demerara is not at all improbable. I regret now placing any impediment in the way of McDonnell and Macnamara's coming to Rome. Strange however that they have not written. Clancy has hoaxed Propaganda. His object was not to hurry to London to discuss the question of his salary with Lord Stanley, but to hasten off with some papers connected with the mission, either to screen himself or to turn them to account."[21] Clancy, in fact, had to get back to Guiana by the start of September if he were to obtain the arrears of half-salary for his extended leave. Money called.

In 1843 a man could still tell one story in Rome, another in London, a third in Guiana and not be found out for months. Clancy announced his sailing, through *The Tablet*, "in consequence of the death of several priests and the abandonment of their mission by several others leaving only one clergyman, and to reclaim property from schismatics." He told his brother Francis, lately back from Guiana, that "he repaired to the colony with all speed to protect the ladies of the convent against future aggressions from [Bishop Hynes] and his miscreant agents [Macnamara and McDonnell]." Clancy told Thomas Griffiths, Apostolic Vicar of London, just as he sailed, that he had resigned "on grounds of health and of poor sight," but was going to Guiana to prepare for his successor ("if such be appointed"), order his own legal affairs, give the nuns a chance to return home and finally, to sort out the confusion left by the death of William Bates "of a broken heart in consequence of lay persecution and the flight of two priests named Macnamara and McDonnell." He further told *The Tablet*, without irony, that he was paving the way for "a supply of clergymen from Rome." En route to Georgetown via Barbados, Clancy persuaded William Rogers, a priest whom Governor Light remembered as "a simple minded good man," to leave Barbados (without permission) to help in Guiana. Rogers had been dismissed by Clancy in 1839, but had once been proposed as apostolic vicar of Jamaica. Now he was made Clancy's vicar general and secretary.[22]

Macnamara and McDonnell arrived in Rome early on September 3rd and confirmed that Clancy was halfway to Guiana. Hynes read their report and petition that morning, "a deplorable account of the state of the church in Demerara," and promptly informed *Propaganda Fide*, who asked to see them the next day. It gave them time to recover from the journey, presumably under Hynes' roof in the Dominican house of Santa Maria, near the Pantheon. That evening, the three took *passeggiata* in the cool, taking in the vast St. Peter's Basilica on the side of the Vatican Hill. No doubt Hynes introduced familiar faces from the Irish Roman scene, among them Thomas Mullock, superior of the Irish Franciscans and former Warden of the friary in Ennis when Macnamara was younger: Hynes knew him well. The following morning "they were very graciously received" by Cardinal Franzoni. He listened to Macnamara's account and informed them officially of Hynes' appointment to Guiana "so that now the matter must be made public." Macnamara wrote to Judge Firebrace to inform him and McDonnell wrote to Dr. Clifton, both leading Guiana Catholics, Clancy's boasted converts and complainants about him to Rome. In the evening, Hynes took the two missioners in a carriage "to see some of the churches and the ruins" of the Forum and Colosseum and to meet the prior of San Clemente, the Irish Dominican house nearby.[23]

They relaxed for another three days before the return journey overland to England. On Friday, September 8th, Hynes wrote many letters—to Governor

Light, Bishop Clancy, the convent superior Abigail Cantillon, the apostolic vicar of London, and formal ones for the two priests confirming their roles: Macnamara was to be pastor of Georgetown and vicar administrator of Guiana, McDonnell pastor of New Amsterdam. The following evening they left by public stagecoach. Hynes then had second thoughts about his letters to Clancy and to Cantillon: the tone was intemperate. He wrote to Macnamara at Ford's in London, ordering him not to use the (unsealed) letters he held, but to use new (sealed) ones he was sending him under the same cover. Hynes' intention was to follow as soon as possible. On October 1st, Macnamara and McDonnell took the 1,600-ton Southampton mail steamer, *City of Glasgow*, described as "like a princely mansion"—it had carried Clancy on its previous mail relay. They landed on the Georgetown wharf on the morning of November 10th. John Cullen arrived that evening from up river "to receive from them any commands from Dr Hynes."[24] When Macnamara went to Rome, Cullen "was called [by Governor Light] to Georgetown where he remained until the return of Dr. Clancy in September last." They must all have lodged privately with parishioners because the Presbytery and Church were occupied territory.

Bishop Clancy had been there since September 12th, still styling himself apostolic vicar. A majority of local Catholics supported him; a more sophisticated minority, including Irish and English planters, judges and doctors, bit their tongues and waited. Clancy advertised "a free church" open to all in the colony—perhaps to boost collections, perhaps to underline his status. On his first Sunday he accused Dr. Clifton from the altar of having read a lesson from the sanctuary during mass in his absence, contrary to church law. In fact, John Cullen had asked Clifton to help out in a simple ritual matter. Clifton, "from Protestant Cambridge," was one of Clancy's most prestigious converts. He rose in his pew. Clancy left the altar, strode down the church, took Clifton by the collar and called the police, charging disturbance of the congregation. The magistrate dismissed the case. Dr. Clifton countercharged for assault and Clancy was bailed on £20 to appear, but the charge was dropped. A week after the event Clancy read out from the altar a litany of accusations and justifications.

On September 30th John Taggart writing as "*Catholicus*," denounced Clancy in *The Royal Gazette* for his lies, his "mephitic family" and for being "the calamity of this Vicariate." Taggart described the Clifton incident as "a mountebank performance in the church itself" warning that his captive audience had had enough. Many wanted nothing more to do with Clancy, "including most of the ladies." It brought "no credit to you as a man nor lustre to your mitre" and a "fearful vengeance" of public revelations loomed. He urged peace and charity pending "the arrival of the formal decisions of the Pope. [But] it is not in human nature to submit without complaint or retort to continued unmerited insult." In retaliation, one of Clancy's supporters set about Taggart in the street with a horse whip and appeared in court. Dr. Clifton received the Rome letter from McDonnell in October confirming Clancy's dismissal and had it published in the *Gazette*. Clancy published a strong refutation.

Confrontation

Macnamara and McDonnell disembarked at Georgetown into a highly charged atmosphere. They delivered Hynes' letter to Governor Light at the new Public Buildings on Brickdam where Light had temporary residence, "stating that [Hynes] was Bishop and Apostolic Visitor" and Macnamara his deputy. Delivering to Clancy and the convent further down Brickdam was another matter. "Dr Clancy laughed at the letters and when the priests, having taken two or three partisan witnesses, delivered the letters in person to Dr Clancy, he, a burly bigfisted Irishman, walked forth with a shillelagh to drive them from his premises. The letters, however, appeared in the newspapers. Both letters were very undignified and very offensive, impolitic and premature."[25]

Macnamara had orders to deliver sealed revised letters to Clancy and Cantillon. He was to suppress the original unsealed letters, which presumably he had read. It may have been in the heat of real anger that he led the way to the offices of two colony newspapers just as they were composing the Saturday editions. The press in a backwater colony thrived on scandal, gossip and *opera bouffe*. Such excitement relieved the boredom which cloaked Guiana. Macnamara had also watched Clancy use the media. He offered the *Royal Gazette* and the *Guiana Herald* the original, unrevised letters from Hynes to Clancy and Cantillon, insisting they were "authentic copies" of what he had given to Clancy. It may have been revenge, the lancing of two years' bitterness, compounded by weariness after a long voyage. He knew Hynes' orders, yet the unsealed letters were all he had left to publicize, since Clancy now had the sealed ones. He may have genuinely thought they were the same in content if not in style and he did have authority as the bishop's deputy. Hynes had enjoined on Macnamara and McDonnell in writing to "announce to your congregations that the jurisdiction of Dr Clancy has ceased," yet the heralds could not even get into a church; Georgetown church and Presbytery were under Clancy's lock and key while the bishop's nephew held the church at New Amsterdam. The press was a far more efficient way of announcing the complex facts of the case than a public meeting, which was the only other alternative.

Macnamara wrote a covering letter for the newspapers as "pastor of Georgetown," with McDonnell as "pastor of Berbice." He admitted it was "unusual for pastors of the Roman Church to adopt the press as their medium of communication with their flocks." He described his Rome meetings,

Clancy's resignation, Hynes' appointment and Clancy's disobedient return to Guiana "after two attempts to escape privately from Rome and the Papal States." Had he not returned, there would be "congratulations for you and for us." Rome feared that "no irregularity was too great for him to be guilty of." He attacked Bishop Clancy's behavior as "sacrilege," "sinful," "illicit" and "contumacious" and described how Clancy refused to accept the letters from Hynes. "We are reluctantly obliged to publish them for your information." Publication meant that the rest of the colony also enjoyed the spectacle. "The scoffers are amused and the serious grieved."[26]

Hynes had regretted and withdrawn his first letter to Clancy, but it came back to haunt him in print. "You proceeded where prudence would have shunned, where your presence can only be productive of mischief, without surrendering the documents and monies belonging to your late Vicariate, leaving me without a shilling to meet the wants of a ruined mission. $25,000 or upwards of funds, grants and contributions are still in your hands. All these you may hand to the Rev. Eugene Macnamara who is authorised by me to demand and receive them. One point more, of great delicacy. You have been in the habit of residing within the precincts of a convent established in Georgetown, causing thereby great scandal and bringing grievous reproach upon the Presentation Order. As the guardian of the desolate and scandalised church of Guiana, I forbid your lordship's entering, living and sleeping in that establishment on any pretext whatsoever and should you be domiciled therein at present I insist upon your retiring without a moment's delay. I cannot permit you to exercise any function of Catholic ministry publicly or privately."

Abigail Cantillon, Clancy's cousin, received shorter shrift. "For the little edification which you have hitherto given to the people of Guiana, you are all to depart." She eventually went to Rome to clear her name and spent the rest of her days in Midleton Presentation Convent, Ireland. The North Cork convent, from which she had eloped with Clancy, refused to have her back.

Clancy put down the shillelagh, took up the pen and wrote to the *Royal Gazette* on November 14th. "I never authorised the publication of a document so manifestly illegal, ungentlemanly and uncanonical. A priest named Eugene Macnamara threw two sealed letters into the gallery of my dwelling house into which I could not consistently with propriety permit him to enter owing to a recent knowledge of his character. He had been publicly deprived of jurisdiction in the parish church of Georgetown by my late Vicar General [William Bates] and was previously suspended in Ireland by Bishop Kennedy of Killaloe for a transgression. I reserve further answer until the arrival of Bishop Hynes in this colony when I shall prove the allegation contained therein and those of the clerical traitors who call themselves his friends to be baseless and wicked fabrications of depraved and ungrateful men."

Implosion

Meanwhile, Bishop Hynes was stuck in London without permission to enter Guiana. His Roman papers were delayed, but even for Lord Stanley to accept them officially would imply recognizing the Pope's authority on British soil. Clancy was in post and on the state stipend. Stanley was courteous, promising to talk it over and admitting that some face-saving principle had to be devised in view of "the enormous practical inconvenience of a Protestant Government maintaining a Catholic Church establishment without any Concordat with the Papal Authority."[27] Hynes heard, probably from Taggart, that the letters sent to Firebrace and Clifton by Macnamara and McDonnell from Rome in September had reached Guiana. "Dr Clancy with the most unblushing falsehood denies that he has been deprived." Clancy wrote to the vicar general of Dublin and Hynes saw the letter in December, "breathing the most direful vengeance against me. He called the three priests [McDonnell, Macnamara and Cullen] who gave evidence in a court case, 'Judases'; he called Taggart 'an unbaptised pagan' and threatens in the case of my approaching the colony with the two scoundrel priests Macnamara and McDonnell for the invasion of his rights' that he was prepared to give us such a reception as we should remember to the end of time. This passage he underlines."

In London, *The Tablet* broke its silence. "We have refrained from publishing. We believe Dr Clancy resigned in the early part of this year and had no jurisdiction in British Guiana since February last. We are shocked by Clancy's letter of September in Georgetown proclaiming his authority." Only in August 1844, when Hynes was securely back in Guiana, did Frederick Lucas tell of how Clancy had broken his promise and returned to Georgetown "to augment scandal, a restless, turbulent and unscrupulous enemy" giving "our iniquitous government" a pretext to interfere in church affairs. Stanley was either "madman or knave" to continue allowing Clancy to be paid. In an earlier edition *The Tablet* noted that Stanley's treatment of Hynes merely reflected his treatment of Ireland.[28]

Clancy "interdicted" Macnamara and McDonnell, already suspended in June 1843 by Bates, when they left for Rome. In turn they "denied Dr Clancy's authority, supported by a large and respectable body of Catholics. Macnamara remained in Georgetown, McDonnell went to New Amsterdam. In Georgetown a room was hired as a Chapel where mass was performed by Macnamara, while his colleague was able to get possession of the chapel at New Amsterdam. A party of Catholics there broke open a door at midnight, siezed William Joseph Clancy, a priest nephew of Dr Clancy and confined him for the night in a police station."[29]

The Catholic mission was imploding. Since Macnamara's publishing of Hynes' orders, nephew Clancy had not officiated at New Amsterdam. Local people "could not countenance his immoral and vicious conduct by attending his ministration of divine service." The discontented included a magistrate and the Port Master of Berbice, who, complained Clancy, "threatened to lay hands on me and throw me out the window. They collected an indiscriminate mob that night at 8.30 on December 25th and forced in the locked door and windows. By such burglarious conduct and sacrilegious housebreaking they proposed my final ejectment." He spent Christmas night in prison and was bound over for £70 to keep the peace. Light knew him already as "a notorious and beastly drunkard, oftener found in the grog shop than in his chapel, who was turned off [La Jalousie] estate, by the Jerningham family, for drunkenness and sent by Dr Clancy to New Amsterdam. [He was] oftener in drunken revels in the negro houses than giving spiritual aid in the sanctuary." A governor's inquiry followed because nephew Clancy was on public salary. Bishop Clancy began a court case against the "burglars" of December; "against himself legal proceedings are also instituted by the Rev Mr Macnamara for defamation." The nuns too, it was said, complained to Rome of Bishop Clancy's "incontinence and scandalous indecency." Light, in fairness, reserved judgment, as a man of the world. "I should say good eating and *poteen* were more to his taste than a woman of his own age and that, however, drawing towards 50 he is considered a sober man, though like many of his class he seems to have a strong head on which liquor would not take much effect." Clancy was barely 40.[30]

Light received petitions early in 1844 "from Berbice and Georgetown in favour of Messrs Macnamara and McDonnell, praying that the half salary unpaid to Dr Clancy and his nephew the priest at Berbice be paid to the rival

First Roman Catholic Cathedral.

The First Catholic Church and Presbytery, Brickdam, Georgetown, British Guiana (*Rodway*).

priests who are now officiating to their respective partisans. These petitions have been attended with success."[31] In April 1844, Clancy fired a gun and threw stones at passing Catholics from the shadows of the Presbytery gallery. It was generally agreed, with relief, that his eyesight was failing. He denied later he had ever used firearms on "clerical gatebreakers" or others, although he *had* offered to fight—challenging them in both French and English.

Both Clancys objected to Light's inquiry, calling it lay interference. In London, Stanley noted dryly, "The Church has no power of unlocking the Public Chest when the Legislature chooses to close it!" Fifty-three petitioners called for nephew Clancy's dismissal. The portmaster of Berbice spoke of his being drunk at his child's baptism; a planter found him "naked in the river at night searching for oysters. He even drank the rum in which we had preserved some snakes." Another found him, after release from jail, having "thrown off his coat, bound his head with a handkerchief and danced to the music of a clarinet played by a negro." He broke into yet another planter's bedroom and attacked the owner with a lead-tipped bludgeon, spiked with nails, after failing to get drink from a servant.

Bishop Clancy, however, had "never seen him intoxicated" and denied that the court at Berbice had jurisidiction over a priest in dispute with parishioners. He asked for time to contact character witnesses in New York. Governor Light wearied of the "courseness, rancour and virulence. The conduct of the partisans opposed to Dr. Clancy has been scandalous and outrageous; that of Dr Clancy undignified. In the 19th century of our Redemption it makes religion a mockery and our Redeemer a by word." He censured Hynes' "undignified imprudence" and felt that "all the parties should be removed or at least not be paid. It has been a great oversight to allow such persons to come on a mission of adventure." In March he stripped nephew Clancy, and in June Bishop Clancy, of the colonial stipend. Brazenly, the nephew demanded it back and the Bishop warned melodramatically that it was "not expedient or wise under the existing circumstances of Catholicism in my portion of British South America," citing the episcopal oath in Latin and various ancient authorities against civil interference. Light cut through the pathos and bathos to confront Clancy: was he or not "at this time authorised to perform the services and rites of the Catholic Church?" By return, Clancy replied tartly, "I am."[32]

While visiting Ireland in December 1843, Hynes received letters from Macnamara, Cullen and Rogers as well as copies of the Demerara newspapers, which he forwarded to Rome, with his own copy of the revised, sealed letter "which Macnamara had suppressed." Angrily he wrote back "to Mr Macnamara withdrawing faculties from him, with the exception of permission to say mass for a month" and ordered John Cullen to minister in Georgetown.[33]

Hynes Returns

Rival supporters flew their respective colors as Bishop Hynes stepped onto the Georgetown wharf in July 1844. Whatever the impasse over Papal documentation with the Colonial Office, Hynes was patently *sent* by Rome whereas Clancy had *fled* Rome. As Hynes closed in on Clancy, the latter petitioned Stanley with 700 signatures for renewal of his salary, warning that Hynes was pro-slavery. The five remaining Presentation nuns also sent a memorial to Queen Victoria for Clancy's salary to be resumed, for the sake of "the negro and coloured children." Light was a fair man: "the convent has given rise to scandal, but in a country like this, scandal may be without foundation." At the end of July 1844, although unpaid, Clancy was still in possession of house and church, with "a numerous congregation greatly in his favour." A mere 40 or 50 persons attended Hynes' public meeting on July 18th, "planters, stockkeepers, clerks, master mechanics, Doctor Clifton, Judge Firebrace and Judge Norton."[34] Macnamara was not among them.

In August the colony legislature recognized Hynes, in "a most ludicrous scene." Hynes' messenger brought the Papal letter (*bulla*) of appointment to the colony council as evidence, but neither governor nor attorney general could receive it as it was a Papal document. Two council members, one an old Presbyterian friend of the Catholic community, "took the Bull by the horns," read it, proposed recognition for Hynes and "reconsigned the terrible animal" to its keepers. Laughter was badly needed in Guiana. Clancy fired a last shot at Macnamara, "a suspended fugitive so intrinsically weak and wicked as not to be even recognised by [Hynes] himself."[35] In September 1844 Hynes petitioned for the use of troops to repossess the church and house: Clancy was "profaning the temple of God with unlawful ministrations." Light pointed out that "the public order is not so imperilled, even by so bold, determined and cunning an enemy as Clancy, as to warrant my using bayonet and artillery."

A strategem was devised. Hynes went away, diplomatically, to visit Cullen at a new mission. On November 15th, observers saw Bishop Clancy go from the house to the church and one went to the house to ask for him on urgent business. The servant called Clancy, who came, leaving the church door open. The rest of Hynes supporters rushed and occupied the church. Clancy struck John Taggart "with a massive bludgeon" and had to be forcibly disarmed before loosing a second blow. A court adjudicated that the Catholic Committee now held the church lawfully as trustees and ordered Clancy to hand over the keys to the sheriff. On December 8th, a week after Clancy had surrendered the keys and sailed again with Anna O'Regan to Nevis, Hynes held his first mass in the church. The Clancys and the nuns maintained a separate congregation next door for another 18 months. Hynes rededicated Christ Church to Church of the Resurrection, as if to exorcise, but Light found the devil the same. "Hynes' pretensions, founded on the titular dignity which the see of Rome has unfortunately conferred on him, are little less than those which the Pope himself might be expected to assume were he in British Guiana." It was hard for an establishment Protestant to be objective or to distinguish the Irish from the Catholic, the Catholic from that English hate-figure the Pope, the farmer-clergy of one church from the gentry-clergy of another. "So many of the Roman Catholic priests, Irish and foreign, are of such low station and manners and of very inferior education [that if the Bishop] is allowed to disperse an aggregate grant for salaries the colony will swarm with clergy of the above description."[36]

The schism was a terrible waste of energy. Bridges between Catholic and Protestant were damaged. Quiet achievement was eclipsed by noisy failure. The lives of 86,000 newly freed slaves in an economic depression, those of the planter employers with dwindling income and land value, and those of the children of former slaves and of colored immigrants were no better for the feud. Everyone agreed it had done religion much harm. Its root causes lay not just in human clay, but also in the constant, perhaps understandable, paranoia of some Irish Catholics about the English Protestant establishment; they saw bigotry everywhere and in so doing, helped fan and perpetuate a bigotry which was still very real, if increasingly masked. An Irish sectarian-ism was growing, which had been less visible in an older Catholic generation for whom tolerance in adversity and a less aggressive stance had been an Irish strength. Ironically this came *after* Emancipation. It was reinforced by Rome's new authoritarianism. At least Hynes made a courtesy stay with the Angli-cans on his way to John Cullen's mission and had his Protestant friends and supporters, but he was still crossing the Colonial Office as late as 1847 when that department finally made him apologize, on pain of being banned from Guiana, for accusing it of supporting Clancy through anti–Catholic malice. Clancy and the world in which they both lived affected Hynes badly. Eugene Macnamara was poisoned too.

Last Days in Guiana: The Poison Pen

Macnamara may have missed the siezure of the church in November 1844. Suspended by Hynes on December 30, 1843, he only received the let-ter in mid–February 1844. A week before sailing to Guiana in May 1844, Hynes wrote to his nephew that he had "but three priests in the Vicariate, one of whom is under suspension *but notwithstanding* [Hynes' emphasis] still continues to officiate." According to the governor, Macnamara was paid to the end of August 1844. He obeyed an order from Hynes in July to stand down after ministering for eight months to the Georgetown parish from hired rooms on Main Street. He was certainly not present at Hynes' first public meeting on July 18, 1844. In September Hynes told *The Tablet* how "the three priests previously here, McDonnell, Macnamara and Cullen, receiving colonial stipends in full possession of their ecclesiasical faculties, have submitted to my authority, Macnamara having since at my command, resigned the colonial stipend. I have canonically released [him] from [his] obligation to this Vicariate."[37]

Macnamara was in the shadows, but not necessarily in serious disgrace. Hynes judged that Macnamara had gone too far in publishing the letters, but acknowledged his qualities by giving him a letter of introduction to the Primate of Mexico. Many in the community gave Macnamara similar letters for other contacts in Mexico. Hynes had a rented house on Brickdam: he or some other leading light gave Macnamara a roof. Hynes openly sympathized with Macnamara when they were both targeted by vicious public letters from Europe during 1844. In *The Tablet* Hynes spoke of how Macnamara and McDonnell had been "cruelly assailed"; in the *The Royal Gazette* he advertised to find who else had received these poison letters in this "wicked conspiracy to defame" and asked for the envelopes as evidence.[38]

Francis Clancy, "Late physician to the convent of Guiana and Acting Health Officer for the Port of Demerara," had received from his brother the Demerara newspapers of November 1843 with Macnamara's and Hynes' printed letters. Francis Clancy, then in Rome, showed the newspapers to Cardinal Franzoni, in translation, evoking Franzoni's "astonishment and regret." In January 1844, Clancy M.D. wrote to Hynes, defending his brother's reputation. Hynes ignored the voluminous diatribe.[39] Bishop Clancy, according to his brother, spent all his money enlarging "the spacious and beautful convent with its enclosures, outbuilding and schools, added the new gallery and embellished the church with paintings, paid the travel expenses of the nuns, furnished their convent and schools and supported them for the first 12 or 18 months after their arrival." If he lived in the same house as nuns, so did other famous missioners: tradesmen were still building when they arrived. "Would it have been proper to have left defenceless females without some protection against the midnight robber or revel intruder?" Hynes view of the nuns, he insisted, had been distorted by Macnamara, who had been

> banished his native diocese of Clare for conduct which not even your Imprudence will induce me to name unless challenged to the proof, that flagitious conduct rare, thank God, among our spotless Irish priesthood. It was laid before Propaganda in a letter from his former bishop and I leave it in the obscurity in which it was perpetrated.
>
> But of his conduct towards the religious ladies of Georgetown I cannot be silent. For months this Killaloe delinquent was employing his demoniacal arts to induce one of the ladies to elope with him from the convent. To facilitate his plan, he tried every means in his power to interrupt all communication between the religious and myself their Physician, but such was the horror created in the minds of the whole community by this

unprincipled wretch that for seven months they abstained from the sacraments and declared their intention to die without the consolations of religion rather than be contaminated by his ministry. To cover his delinquency now commenced a series of vindictive outrages on the part of this wolf in sheep's clothing, furious at the loss of his prey. The delicate morality of the old Offender shrunk like the sensitive plant from the contact of virginal purity. The atmosphere of the convent was not sufficiently pure for his ethereal spirit to breathe. The schools whose fair fame he whispered away became deserted, nor was it till justice and self defence compelled the friends of the convent to lift the veil and expose the monster that a reaction took place [against] the ostracised priest of Clare and his guilty associate McDonnell, the outcast student of Maynooth. [It was] a scene unparalleled in the annals of human turpitude.

Francis Clancy attacked the "Hydra" of church lay democracy, Taggart's "adulterous offspring by different mothers" and his conspiracy with Hynes. He extolled Bishop Clancy and the nuns as "exiles from home and country braving the terrors of a tropical climate, its swamps, morasses and yellow fever, to diffuse the blessings of religion and useful education among the children of the Colonist, the negro and the uncivilised Indian." When they took the colonial stipend from his brother in June 1844, Frances Clancy fought with gloves off.

Now "Honorary Secretary to the Paris Medical Society" he sent to Lord Stanley in August a copy of his January letter to Hynes. In a covering note he described "Rev.?" (*sic*) Macnamara as "a reckless and abandoned ecclesiastic who had to fly from his native diocese, Clare, for proven seduction while McDonnell had to seek a foreign mission to screen the early infamy of his collegiate career." McDonnell was also disciplined by Bishop Clancy for "gross and indecent conduct in the house of a respectable planter." Hynes was at fault in asking the Governor "to recognise such convicted reprobates as ministers of religion, thus sending them forth on a society to carry ruin and desolation into the midst of families." Bishop Clancy had gone back to Guiana "with all possible speed, to protect the ladies of the convent from [Hynes] and his miscreant agents." Clancy M.D. had both letters printed in France and distributed in Ireland and Guiana during September 1844.

McDonnell was in good company. Fr. Mathew, the Irish temperance "apostle," had also been forced to leave Maynooth—for having student friends in his room. Enclosed seminaries were inevitably often narrow and petty. The accusation against Macnamara could have been fabrication, a wrong word or action in the great wooden house during Clancy's absence abroad, especially when the superior was Clancy's relative. At least he could get out and about; enclosure and lack of exercise afflicted mission nuns such as those in the heat and day-long rains of Guiana. Solitude too had its impact on a priest, even a non-drinker, especially if the frog chorus or mosquitoes prevented sleep night after night. *The Tablet* was well thumbed and repeatedly read. Priests also could be overbearing and make enemies of nuns. Above all, Georgetown loved a scandal. The governor said the colony made up scandal. The Clancys even cast scandal into different molds to suit the moment. In fact, the Clancy family were so strongly represented that Cantillon, the bishop, the doctor and William Joseph were the least likely "victims" of a Macnamara acting solo. Hynes acknowledged that Macnamara had been unjustly accused and Bishop Clancy did presumably know his Killaloe background when he recruited him in 1841.

Macnamara needed a fresh start and Hynes needed fresh personnel. There was no rancor in the manner of Macnamara's leaving Guiana, as there was with John McDonnell in 1845 and with Bishop Clancy in 1846. Armed with "many letters" of introduction, Macnamara passed the presbytery occupied by the Clancys and made his way through the market at the end of Brickdam to the wharves where he probably boarded a mail packet for the Gulf. He had learned from the wild and the wise about colonies, immigration and the failings of the Irish in the tropics. He knew the effectiveness of initiative and going to the top in a crisis. He had seen the rivalry of mixed denominations on the mission and recognized the strength of the Methodists. He had imbibed anti–American sentiments and a sense of clerical authority from Bishop Clancy and knew something of the Colonial Land and Emigration Committee in London, whose attention was then on the Caribbean during its economic depression. Macnamara would have been glad to leave Georgetown, where normality had begun to lose its meaning. As the wharves of the Demerara receded at the end of a lengthening stern wake, he may even have muttered, like Joseph Kelly before him, *Deo Gratias!*"

Four

The Maverick.
Mexico 1844–1845

Evidently in the exercise of his special functions, he had
selected California as the field for his labors, a great field
and a noble ambition.—(John Charles Frémont on Macnamara. *Memoirs,* 1886)

Macnamara entered Mexico around the end of November 1844, probably through the deep-water port of Vera Cruz. Along with Tampico, Vera
Cruz was on the Royal Mail steamer route through the Caribbean and Gulf
of Mexico. Twice monthly, Demerara post and passengers could go to and
from the Mexican ports by the packet. The mail steamer *Forth,* for instance,
left Southampton on September 26, 1844, arrived in Demerara on November 12th and docked at Vera Cruz on November 30th. It may have carried
Macnamara. From the port of entry it would have been a four-day journey
to Mexico City. The road led through Jalapa with its British factories and
under the twin cathedral towers of Puebla pointing dramatically to the nearby
volcano peaks of Popocatepetl and his female companion. The capital itself,
at 7,000 feet, was halfway to the summit of its own snowcapped volcano.
After the heavy subtropical flats of Guiana, Macnamara would have noticed
the thinning air no less than the snow as the road rose. Travelers took the
road in company and with a mule train, or on the ten-mule public coach with
a military escort.[1]

Mexican law demanded that within a month of entry a foreigner take
out a *Carta di Seguridad* or passport through the national consulate. On January 2, 1845, Macnamara called at the British Consulate in the capital. Euan
Mackintosh, a powerful and wealthy Scots partner in Manning and Mar-
shall, (soon to be Manning and Mackintosh), combined wide commercial
dealings with the office of consul into a commercial listening post. Mexicans

and others could not easily distinguish British national interests from British private ones, as long as diplomats like Mackintosh and, on the Pacific coast, Eustace Barron of Barron and Forbes mixed government diplomacy with business. Mackintosh, "the biggest speculator in Mexico," also acted for the British holders of Mexican loan bonds who were owed $60 million (£12m) by the Mexican government. It was more tempting to speculate in loans than to invest.[2]

There was a long queue at the Consulate that first working day after Christmas. Macnamara, halfway along a line of 43 applicants for passports, received a *Carta* with his name and nationality.[3] Through clerical privilege, no further detail was registered, nor did he have to pay the 11 *reals* for the half-page document. Paper in Mexico was in chronic short supply ever since the Spanish had left and none was wasted. When Mexico changed its federalist title, "United States of Mexico," to the simple centralist "Republic" in 1841, a line was drawn through the title on existing printed *Cartas* and the new title added in longhand.

It took another five months for the British ambassador (minister) in Mexico, Charles Bankhead, to report Macnamara's arrival to the foreign secretary in London, Lord Aberdeen.

> About six months ago a Roman Catholic priest arrived here from Demerara furnished with letters of introduction to the Archbishop of Mexico from the Bishop of that colony, and many others to the British residents here. Mr Macnamara called upon me. I have had every reason to be pleased with his acquaintance. He is a native of the County of Clare, Ennis, I believe.[4]

Why Mexico?

John Frémont concluded that Macnamara's title of Apostolic Missioner explained his arrival in Mexican California as a general Papal warrant to "select the field for his labours." It was, however, no more than an old courtesy title for an Irish missioner in Guiana or a Spanish missioner in California. By itself, it explained little.

The (Irish) Catholic Directory first mentioned Mexico and California only in 1847, but *The Tablet* and *The Times* reported routinely on Texas, Mexican Bond prices and other items from the region. The Guiana clergy welcomed the latest copies of both and made full, sometimes ruthless use of *The Tablet*'s pages. Clancy, in 1842, called it, fulsomely, "an invaluable journal, a most interesting channel of British and Irish Roman Catholic intelligence between the Old and the New worlds." Macnamara knew the Franciscan mission in Ennis and the work of the Franciscans in Spanish America would have been generally, if imprecisely, known. The Temperance preacher in Ireland, Theobald Mathew, was also a (Capuchin) Franciscan. Macnamara sailed to

Guiana with a Spanish friar and Franciscan William Bates was the first to welcome them to Georgetown. In his Paris days, Macnamara had also known the Picpus missioners and their link with Mexican California.

Bishop Hynes may have known Archbishop Posada of Mexico from Rome, where Posada went in 1840 to receive the archbishop's *pallium* or scarf of office. A conservative monarchist, Posada had spent a short exile in New Orleans during the liberal Gómez-Farías regime in 1833-4. He read and spoke English and may have met Bishop England there. Hynes, besides noting in his correspondence a Mexican monk at the Irish Dominican house of San Clemente in Rome, also mentioned John Urquhart of the Irish Dominicans, an ecclesiastical rolling stone who, according to British Consular registers, stayed in Mexico City in 1843—the Dominicans had once run the missions of Lower California and President Santa Anna had recently allowed them back into Mexico. Papal Rome was the center of a wide communications network, particularly through the religious orders. Once out in Central America, clergy of various nations maintained contact. The new Royal Mail Steamship Line which linked the Caribbean islands to Guiana, Venezuela, Mexico and the United States created a communications revolution. If John Cullen from the Guiana hinterland was in contact with the archbishop of Caracas, it should not be surprising that Hynes was in touch with Mexico City.

The firm of Manning and Mackintosh, dominant in Mexican financial circles, delivered goods to the church in Guiana en route for Mexico. The firm of Lizardi, dominant in London-Mexican and Bondholder circles, used the steam packets for transporting goods and silver to England. Representatives shared ships with the Irish clergy of Guiana on their many voyages. A vessel of as few as 20 passengers would see some strong contacts grow during a forty-day voyage across the Atlantic. The fact that Macnamara carried "many other letters" from leading figures in Guiana to leading figures in Mexico confirms that the British expatriate network across the Gulf of Mexico was complex. Timber came from New Orleans to Georgetown; Murphy of Baltimore and New York, bookseller and general cargo agent, advertised in *The Catholic Directory* as well as the *Demerara Royal Gazette*. A Charles Taggart ran a company in Mexican Puebla and a William Taggart ran the Pacific Steamship Company from Austin Friars Street, London's "little Mexico," both possibly related to John Taggart of Guiana. One Dr. Bankhead served at the Colonial Hospital in Georgetown, when Macnamara was on its governing board of five in 1843; he may have been the Irish Joseph Bankhead who qualified in Glasgow in 1832, possibly related to Charles Bankhead, the Irish-born British ambassador in Mexico.

In the slump after the abolition of slavery, some plantation managers went north to the United States, as did some clergy. A West Indies Naval Squadron and the Army garrisons of the Caribbean also meant constant

Map of Mexico

circulation of contacts, news and gossip. Communications may have been slow, but they were continuous. Disintegrating Mexico was world news. Rebel Texas, up on the northern Gulf, with its naval force, and the secession of Yucatán in 1840 would have been points of conversation. Mention of Mexico and Texas led to talk of California. If questions of immigration or colonization were raised, a resident of Guiana, where they had tried every immigration possible, would always have something to say.

The Ireland Macnamara left for France in 1832 was already seeing handbills in market towns and villages for colonists to Mexican Texas. O'Connell did not want them to go; he feared Texas would secede by sheer number of American settlers and become another pro-slavery state, dragging its Irish residents along with it. Instead, he wanted freed slave colonies placed as a buffer between the southern U.S. slave states and the rest of the free Catholic world.[5] O'Connell, nicknamed "The Liberator," saw hypocrisy in the United States' formally declaring that all are equal and free, while still permitting slavery, and war with Mexico, he felt, would only serve to expand slavery. The British had pounced on the inconsistency in 1776 when they first saw the Declaration of Independence. In 1837 the Pope roundly condemned slavery and most of the Catholic world followed his lead. In the year Macnamara entered Mexico, *Forbes Colonial Magazine* produced articles on the Guiana labor problem, on the wealth of Mexico and on British enterprise in South America. It would have been hard for Macnamara not to be aware of what was going on, so near at hand.

The Colony Scheme

The first indication of Macnamara's plans for a colony on Mexican soil, *el Proyecto Macnamara,* came at the end of May 1845 in Bankhead's initial report to London.

> Mr Macnamara mentioned to me some time since [his arriving] that he intended to present a Petition to the President for permission to bring two or three hundred Irish families from Ireland to California and to ask of [the Mexican] Congress a Grant of Land on the Bay of San Francisco. He feels assured he could procure a large number of married persons (small farmers) who would become useful Colonists and furnish additional strength to the country. He has received assurances of support from the Archbishop and Señor Cuevas [Foreign Minister] is likewise favourable to his scheme. He can however entertain no hope of an advance of money from Mexico, but he seems to think that if an additional grant of land was given in lieu thereof, he could raise money upon that portion in London sufficient, with some aid from the Emigration Committee, to bring over his colonists to California.
>
> I of course could afford him no assistance officially, but upon Señor Cuevas asking me my opinion of Mr Macnamara personally, I had no hesitation in speaking of him as I thought he deserved. I shall receive further information on the subject which I shall submit by the next Packet.[6]

It seems that Macnamara conceived the idea *after* his arrival in Mexico, possibly in talks with Archbishop Posada about the new wasteland diocese of Las Californias, founded in 1840 in place of the dissolved Franciscan missions. California desperately needed people. Macnamara also met commercial speculators in Mexico and must have known of the mineral discoveries and prospects in California. By the end of May 1845 the project was hatched and probably on the president's desk, but it was only the latest of many schemes.

When Bankhead next reported on its progress to Lord Aberdeen at the end of July 1845, he appended another proposal, this time from Consul Euan Mackintosh—if the speculator-general had his eye on California, Macnamara was at least with the prevailing wind. He and Mackintosh may have given each other ideas and even shared the same roof, but speculator and enthusiast schemed independently, each aware of the opportunity afforded by empty California. There had been enough publicity about it in the previous decade. The British "glitterati" of Mexico City were also "literati," the only national group in the city to have its own book club which ordered from London every month. It was supported by Ambassador Bankhead.[7] Alexander Forbes' pioneering book on California would have been well-thumbed before Macnamara read it.

The Alexander Forbes Proposal

Alexander Forbes was the junior partner in the successful Barron and Forbes operation based at Tepic. It had, in effect, a monopoly of trade on the Mexican Pacific coast where Eustace Barron, the senior partner, was British consul. Nothing happened without his company knowing it from their vantage point a few miles inland from the major ports of San Blas and Mazatlán. Forbes gleaned every detail about California from captains, merchants and botanists. He never actually visited it until 1848, after the Mexican War, when he was involved with a mercury mine which he had obtained through the mediation of Eugene Macnamara.

A History of Upper and Lower California appeared in print four years after its author completed it in 1835. The date was significant: a large group of Mexican colonists had halted at Tepic on their way to California in 1834. A publisher's delay in London gave Forbes time to formulate more on colonization. It was the first promotion directed at Europeans for settlement in California, and Forbes made no bones about improving the trading prospects of Barron and Forbes. Little was known of the Californias save that Lower was arid and Upper was vastly more attractive, both being lately Spanish mission territory; the land was thought by many to be an island and on British charts it was still "New Albion." It had never been surveyed, nor had the missioners penetrated the interior. Forbes advocated a west coast steamer line between Panama and the Columbia River, citing Royal Navy opinions of harbors. As well as trade, a shipping line would bring settlers to a land "so devoid of inhabitants." He also urged a greater navy presence on the coast.

> In Great Britain and Ireland there are millions of human beings of superior intellects and varied acquirements who find it utterly impossible to get employment or food. No country can excel or vie with California in natural advantages, but while the population retain their present character of indolence and total want of enterprise, it must stand still. If on the contrary [under an enlightened government which knew how to promote colonisation] it could not fail to become known and selected as a refuge by the innumerable starving populations of the old world. I know of no place better calculated for receiving the surplus population of Great Britain [despite] antiquated prohibitions and absurd clauses such as the emigrant must profess the Catholic religion.[8]

The British press suggested government take note; some of the American press saw collusion already between British government and private business, the way Britain usually expanded its empire.[9] Forbes certainly never gave up his citizenship while living in Mexico and never became a Catholic, unlike so many fellow British residents in Mexico, who usually did so nominally, in order to marry or hold land. His book had the merits of clarity and timing, published just as the holders of Mexican Loan Bonds in England were given options on Mexican frontier department land in lieu of debt repayments: California was one of the departments named.

The Bondholders' Land Warrants

British merchant bankers loaned $33 million (£6.5 million) to the bankrupt young Mexican republic between 1823 and 1825. Political instability, the milking of Mexico by the same British merchants and the frittering of money on military spending, plus the lack of population to pay tax for the administration of vast territories, meant that the debt was not repaid. Even interest was withheld. By 1837, £11.5 million was owed by the Mexican government to private individuals, mainly in London. In a major renegotiating, bonds were issued and half the debt was converted into deferred bonds which carried no interest but gave their owners a ten-year option on northern Mexican Departmental land. After ten years, interest would be added to the bonds, but the land option would end. The warrants were open, not specific, and did not offer land free to the Bondholders, but at a favorable four acres per pound sterling ($1.25 per acre), the smallest allotment at 400 acres, the largest at 10,000 acres. As security, 100 million acres were set aside in the northern territories, obviously as a buffer against invasion from the United States or Russia. To this area was added a further 25 million acres in Texas and Coahuila, at least while hope remained of Mexico's regaining the Texas "Republic." Alexander Forbes, in a late chapter added after the 1837 debt restructuring, urged that California be settled by a company like the East India Company. Bondholders could take such a proposal seriously. For Mexico it would be the end of worrying about a vulnerable, eccentricity located frontier department *and* a paralyzing overseas debt all in one move. California would still go the Texas way, but towards Britain, not the United States.

John Diston Powles, the Topo speculator of 1828, was also a leading Mexican Bondholder as well as a director of Manning and Mackintosh in Mexico City. He urged that the Bondholders create a colonizing company, but they ignored him.[10] The Bondholders preferred cash and had waited a long time for it. If they even thought of land it would be Texas or part of Mexico near to the Gulf and, after 1841, in the West Indies Steamship Company network. In 1837 the silence deafened when Powles and Forbes suggested taking land in lieu of cash. The land arrangement had ten years to run and cash might easily materialize in that period: speculators are gamblers, addicts on hope. By 1845 the option had only two years left and little money had been seen. If war took place between America and Mexico, as seemed increasingly likely, the Bondholders could lose their money from Mexico, bankrupt after a war, *and* lose the land if Mexico lost the frontier departments; it had already lost Texas and the Yucatan Peninsula; California was in periodic revolt and too far away to control. Unrealistically, the Bondholders still hoped for cash.

Barron and Forbes pressed the advantages of a British naval presence off the west coast and the advantages to Britain of settling on shore. They won the support of Richard Pakenham, British ambassador in Mexico City, who forwarded his own version of the Forbes plan to London in 1841. Mexican control of the frontier departments, he felt, would soon cease, but any colonization would have to take place soon because the Americans had open designs on California. In London, just as Pakenham wrote, the expansionist Lord Palmerston was replaced as foreign secretary by the cautious and more sensitive Lord Aberdeen. Aberdeen took the stance he was to maintain for the next five years, that Britain wanted no more "new and far flung" territories with all the liabilities and expense which came with them. The halo effect of the presence of a single, small British warship still persisted, whatever disclaimers politicians uttered in private dispatches. Mexicans, Americans and British merchants themselves exaggerated the power of Britain to take over whatever she set her mind upon, however distant and exposed the lines of communication and reinforcement from home.

In London, the Bondholders' agents, the Mexican firm of Lizardi, floated its own bonds to raise money for the new consolidated debt as well as for their own expenses. In doing so they put the Mexican debt at $10 million higher than the Mexican government would acknowledge. Lizardi lost its agency and Euan Mackintosh in Mexico City moved into its place. Power over South America, once concentrated on single streets in London, was being challenged and displaced. Austin Friars Street, for instance, in the commercial heart of London, numbered Barclay Brothers at 12, the Powles brothers and the Columbian Mining Company at 13, William Taggart and the Pacific Steam Navigation Company at 14, the Peruvian Consulate at 15 and Frederick de Lizardi, Mexican Consul at 26.[11]

Sir George Simpson, governor of the Hudson's Bay Company also visited California in 1841, a few months after his company had set up a new base in San Francisco Bay. He too suggested that the Department of California be taken in lieu of debt repayments, but that it might be a waste of money to cash bonds when the local population could be induced to declare independence and hand themselves over to Britain without expense, war or liability. Simpson aroused grave misgivings in Washington and Mexico City, especially since his own expansionist trading company was setting up house in California. A tactless local company agent did not help by voicing fierce anti–American sentiments. The company abandoned California within four years and Simpson's book on the "destiny" of California to be British was not published until 1847, but his dispatches did make even Lord Aberdeen think again. Aberdeen vacillated right up to the eve of the Mexican war. At the same time proposals were being discussed among Britain, America and

Mexico that America gain Upper California by payment, which Mexico could use to defray the British debt, while Britain would cede to America the Oregon Territory as far south as the Columbia River. Mexico in turn would recognize Texan independence. It was a crowded stage already, but no drama in the Pacific was complete without the fastidious, meticulous and verbose Scots busybody, Dr. Robert Crichton Wyllie.

Wyllie

Dr. Wyllie, more than any other, inspired the Macnamara Contract. A leading Bondholder himself, with London offices on Fenchurch Street, not two blocks from the South American hub of Austin Friars Street, Wyllie published in Mexico in December 1843 and later in London a *Report on Mexico for Merchants, Emigrants and Mexican Bondholders* which he addressed to George Robinson, Chair of the Committee of Spanish American Bondholders. He had advocated taking land in California for some years, had written a preliminary *Report* in 1840 and had pressed Robinson since 1840 to get the Bondholders to form a colonizing company, but without success. He begged Robinson to get the 1843 Annual General Meeting "to overrule the Bondholders" and *make* them go for land. He corresponded that year at length (Wyllie did everything at length) with Alexander Forbes in Tepic, with his own cousin in Monterey, William Hartnell, with Robinson, and finally with Lizardi in London. Significantly, Wyllie also stayed with Forbes at Tepic in the summer of 1843, just before composing the *Report*. He was a partner in the Barron and Forbes Company and stood to gain from an anglophile California. From Tepic he plied Hartnell in California with 24 questions to which Hartnell provided the local information for the *Report*. Well into 1844, Hartnell was advising Wyllie of the recent gold finds near Los Angeles, of the need for thirty Jesuits in the department and of the 22 leagues of land he could get for the two of them. The rhetorical flow, the fine gilt tooling and the chromatic leather did not convince Joseph Tasker of Middleton Hall, Brentford, near London, who annotated his copy of the *Report*, "Notwithstanding vast resources, the Foreign and Domestic Debt is quite out of all proportion to Mexico's boasted wealth and means."[12] He spoke for the majority of Bondholders.

Wyllie would have been well remembered in Mexico City. His book, if not quite the stuff of the English Book Club, was certainly known in merchant and diplomatic circles. He inspired strong, often negative, feelings wherever he went. In January 1844 he stayed again with Forbes at Tepic on his way to make his home in the Sandwich Islands as British proconsul and then as Foreign Secretary to the King of the Islands. Throughout 1844 he waited for the Bondholders to call him to California, begging cousin

Hartnell meanwhile to take whatever land grants he could obtain for the two of them, before California was taken from Mexico completely. "Nothing could justify Britain's interference so much as previous grants of land under the Mexican Government to British subjects. Be ready to grab all you can for us if a crisis should threaten."[13]

Wyllie's report was realistic. He was frank about Mexico's excessive taxes against a backdrop of corruption, black market and smuggling. *Mañana* also dogged him: it had been impossible to get the open land warrants from agents Lizardi in 1840 in London because they had still received no instructions from Mexico, despite its being agreed three years before. He urged the Mexican government to develop tobacco, cotton, cocoa, and sugar, instead of mining. Agriculture, he argued, underpinned a country; mining was financially, morally and physically unhealthy as well as a dreamer's gamble. The coastal lands of California were as productive as the United States or India, "fit for the cultivation of the richest tropical products of those countries with labour cheaper than the slave labour of the USA." The climate was better than Texas for Europeans. He swore to the Mexicans that his proposed Colonisation Company was not a British government conspiracy. Lord Aberdeen and the London government "would not accept sovereignty even if it be offered by this government and petitioned by the Bondholders." It was sad, he felt, that Mexico could see no distinction between British private ventures and government policy.[14]

Wyllie warned that others were getting there first. A Belgian contractor (*empresario*) had already approval for 1,000 Swiss, German and Belgian families to take up Texan land in Tamaulipas, between the Bravo and Nueces. Each family could have 11 leagues of land, but they had to be at least 20 leagues from the frontier. Tax concessions for ten years would help defray expenses; they would all become Mexicans and form a militia under Mexican officers to preserve order and keep out Indians. If the offer were not taken up in ten years it would be null and void. Wyllie felt that such a powerful *empresario* was open to corruption. Worse, it was eating into the 25 million acres of land near the Gulf which was mortgaged on behalf of the London Bondholders. Farmers also like to cooperate—there was too much isolation built into these huge "ranges."[15] Thanks to William Hartnell, Wyllie knew his subject even though he never visited it. He reminded readers of an old British proposal from 1840 that Canada be settled with loyal veterans. He was also a keen Anglican churchman: in California and other departments, "the support of the clergy's respectability as gentlemen is of the highest consequence to the existence of religion here." The Catholic clergy supported the poor, and he stressed that he was saying that "as a Protestant."

He reminded that he had warned the Mexican government that the United States had strong frontiers and good tax revenues because the Federal government alone sold frontier lands, not the departments or states.

Mexico should survey its possessions, then advertise in Europe. Texas was an example of loss of control over settlers. Future colonists should be subjects of European monarchies—they were best at being loyal, as one-third of a million British had proved in the American Republic. He cited the Irish, Scots and English separately. "California and Mexico are the countries whose speedy colonisation is most important, to protect them from foreign aggression." They need "industrious inhabitants" and they need to help increase Mexican exports over imports, with cotton, silk, sugar, cocoa, coffee, rice, indigo and vanilla. Such a list would register immediately with anyone from the depressed plantations of Guiana.[16]

Wyllie reproduced Alexander Forbes' advice on California in full, although neither had ever seen the place. Colonists should settle on the coast, particularly on San Francisco Bay, in small agricultural communities. The "old lazy drones of the ancient hive" in California should be made to pay a shilling (25¢) an acre in tax to cover the cost of settling newcomers; it should not be defrayed from customs dues. Instead there should be free trade and no customs houses. The Colonising Company of Mexico City should hold all mineral rights. River gold, he confirmed, had in fact been found near Los Angeles. (There had been a find and minor gold rush in 1842 in Placerita and San Feliciano canyons which were producing about 2,000 ounces per year. Eustace Barron had just sent some of the placer gold from San Feliciano, near San Fernando Mission, to the Foreign Office. The British were well aware, early, of the promise of gold in California.) Forbes, however, ended his advice on a pessimistic note: Mexico would not accept the idea because of bad faith, corruption and restrictive legislation on trade and on colonists. California would be lost to America or France—witness Catesby Jones' attempt in 1842 to take Monterey. It would not be worth anything to Mexico and it would be really worth England's trying to secure the best of terms quickly. The Bondholders' agreement placed them halfway there already and "if the goods can be obtained for nothing, it is better than paying in bonds." From Liverpool, where much Bondholder business was based, the American Consul wrote to President Polk in August 1845, warning that "England has a mortgage on California," and advising, "Make Oregon the bone of contention to prevent [the loss of California]."[17] The intentions and political influence of the Bondholders were important, but hugely overstated.

Wyllie left Mexico City in December 1843, stayed at Tepic, presented Forbes with a copy of the *Report*, and was in Honolulu by January. Twelve months later, an Irish priest from an agricultural background, a monarchy and a Catholic country to boot, entered Mexico City. Within a short time he was proposing to lead several small immigrant agricultural settlements to the California coastal lands, starting on the Bay of San Francisco. It was as if Wyllie and Forbes had written his script, although it was not till later that he met either of them. He acted as Forbes' agent in 1846 and probably met Wyllie on the Sandwich Islands that same year. With the inspiration, the Irishman also shouldered some of the awkward baggage which went with it—the suspicion that he fronted for the British government and London speculators.

Macnamara's First Petition

Macnamara had basic Spanish but took help in composing his request. He signed *Eugenio Macnamara, Misionero Apostolico,* using his Guiana title at the end of the nine-page Spanish petition to the Mexican President, Joaquín Herrera.[18] The original was not dated, but to judge from Bankhead's comments, was presented either in May or in June, just before or just after Bankhead made his first report to Lord Aberdeen.

> I, Eugene Macnamara, Catholic priest and Apostolic Missionary, submit reflections on Upper California which is attracting much public attention. It does not require the gift of prophecy to foresee that within a little time this fertile country will cease to be an integral part of this republic unless prompt and efficacious measures restrain foreign rapacity. The unanimous voice of the country responds *colonisation* [Macnamara's emphasis] as the speediest and most secure means. Europe abounds with an excess of population and the Irish are the best adapted to the religion, character and temperament of the inhabitants of Mexico—devout Catholics, moral, industrious, sober and brave.
>
> I propose, with the aid and approval of your Excellency, to place in Upper California a colony of Irish Catholics. I have a triple purpose in making this proposition. I wish firstly to advance the cause of Catholicism. Secondly to contribute to the happiness of my countrymen. Thirdly, I desire to put an obstacle in the way of further usurpations on the part of an irreligious and anti-Catholic nation. I therefore propose that there be conceded to me an extent of territory on the coast of Upper California for the purpose I have indicated. I would prefer to place the first colonists on the Bay of San Francisco. This would be a proper step when it is remembered that the Americans have possession of Bodega, abandoned by the Russians a little north of San Francisco. I should bring for a start one thousand families. Afterwards I would establish a second colony near Monterey and a third at Santa Barbara. By this means the entire coast by which most danger is to be expected would be secured completely against invasions and pillages of foreigners. For each family I bring I will require a square league (*sitio*) free of all cost; likewise that the children of all colonists when they marry shall receive half a *sitio* as a national gift. I should likewise require exemption from payment of all taxes for a certain number of years; that the colonists on taking possession of their lands shall be protected by the Government and shall enjoy all rights. Other issues of less importance can be discussed later. These propositions have received the fullest approbation of the Archbishop. [If my ideas are carried generously into effect] they may dispense happiness to many and in the end tend to the consolidation and integrity of this great republic.

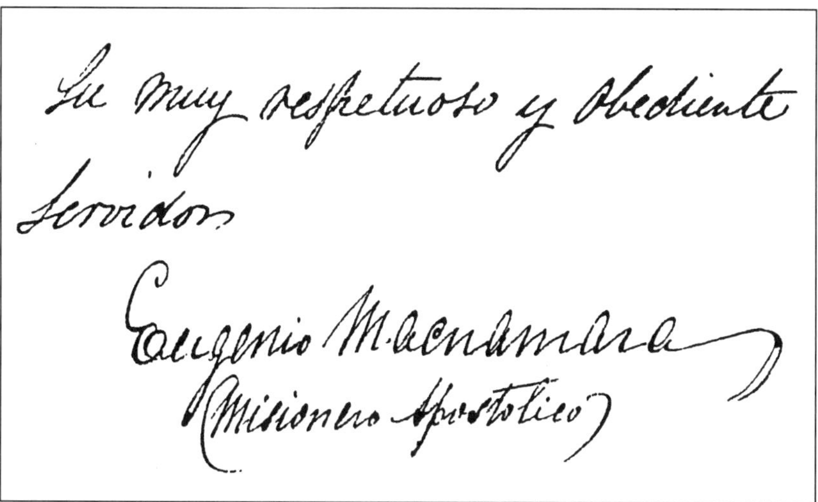

Macnamara's signature on the Colony Petition, May–June 1845 (*Archivo General de la Nación, Mexico City*).

It was clearly thought out, but an echo of Clancy's religious hostility to the Americans came through. Given the poor communications and disturbed allegiance between California and Mexico City, Macnamara could not have known that most of the coastal lands had already been granted away by departmental governors to existing settlers even while Forbes and Wyllie were promoting their schemes. It would have been impossible to find 7,500 suitable square leagues on the strategic coastal strip, but Wyllie was too far away to realize that. Nor could Macnamara have quite foreseen that the invasion danger lay not where Wyllie and Forbes tried to persuade the Bondholders, where American Commodore Jones had tried to capture Monterey in 1842, but from the newly scouted routes across the Sierra Nevada along which the present trickle of settlers would quickly widen to a river. The crossings led down into the great valley of the Sacramento and San Joaquin rivers.

Foreign Minister Luis Cuevas turned to ambassador Bankhead and asked his opinion of the Irish priest. Bankhead responded favorably, as he had on other occasions, and informed London he had done so. London remained silent. So too, frustratingly, did the government in Mexico City. Bankhead would have assured Macnamara that Cuevas had asked about him, to show that the matter had not been forgotten. Mexican ways, however, were slow. If California was still intact, then why hurry to preserve it? There were only twenty-four hours in the day, with enough and more to fill those hours. The following day might bring time for California: in Mexico the following day was *mañana*. One republican newspaper, *La Voz del Pueblo*, accused the government of relegating California to *mañana*. What was needed, said the editor, was "good colonisation law to protect the immigration of industrious populations, like the Swiss and the Germans."[19]

The Mackintosh Scheme[20]

Two months after he had first reported Macnamara's existence and scheme to London, Charles Bankhead wrote again to Lord Aberdeen on July 30, 1845, hoping, hinting and fishing for at least some response from that quarter, be it support or veto. The Oregon question was then in negotiation and war was likely between Britain and the United States. Bankhead warned that in any such war "The United States would without delay take possession of California. The Mexicans look to England as the power most likely to help them and notwithstanding their pride and prejudices they have not scrupled of late to discuss the expediency of disposing of the Californias to Great Britain in case she was willing to purchase them. These discussions are carried on by Persons outside the government. The government themselves dare not publicly entertain such a proposal. I shall be a properly silent listener." Bankhead then brought up Macnamara for the second time.

> Mr Macnamara's scheme, which I had the honour to mention to your Lordship in Despatch No 52, is still in embryo, although the Government see the advantages to be derived from a colony of Irish in the Bay of San Francisco, still they cannot be brought to give Mr Macnamara any positive assistance [for fear of public anti-foreigner reaction]. I do not feel myself authorised to offer him any official support, but indirectly I have endeavoured to aid his plans.

Bankhead included in his letter the colonizing proposal from Euan Mackintosh, speculator supreme, its financing ruthlessly and carefully thought through, unlike Macnamara's. "Mr Consul Mackintosh has placed in my hands for confidential communication to your Lordship a plan of colonisation upon a very large scale. I transmit a copy of his letter and enclose the proposition."

The Consul suggested colonizers needed inducements. "The proposal of the receipt of so large a sum as $10 million will eventually induce them to look more favourably on the scheme." He wanted to found the California Commercial and Colonising Company of Mexico (firmly on his patch and not in London beyond his control). It would import duty-free and have "the right to any mines that may be discovered during the twenty years in the lands rented to them"—mineral prospects in California were increasingly a major consideration. After twenty years there would be complete reversion of ownership to the colonists and ultimately to British protection, along with the duty "to maintain under arms a force of 2,000 men to repel any foreign invasion," and the pledge "to introduce into the Californias half a million European colonists" with a guarantee that all laws would be administered by a "mixed tribunal, half Mexican, half European."

Mackintosh submitted his case to London. Macnamara went directly to the Mexicans. Mackintosh had a partner in his firm go with John Diston Powles to negotiate personally with Lord Aberdeen. Macnamara had no apparent government contacts in London. Doubtless Mackintosh sounded out his high-level contacts in Mexico City too. His was the more hard-nosed business proposition, with the highest projection of colonists. Mackintosh was more used than Macnamara to thinking grandly, to diversifying: he had financial clout. At its most developed, the Macnamara Project, proposed by an unknown without money, never contracted for more than 15,000 settlers. There was total silence from London (save for a little private musing over Bankhead's letter by Aberdeen and the Mexican ambassador in September). The seceding of Texas to the United States that month, plus the gathering clouds of a Mexican–U.S. war eclipsed the Mackintosh plan. Aberdeen was cautious. He wanted the fruit from the tree, but not to be the dishonorable one caught shaking the tree in the first place. If, however, the fruit fell naturally, he would enjoy it with honor and peace intact. As long as California remained Mexican (or American by capture in a war with Mexico) England's neutrality was all-important. British admirals and diplomats were not to shake but to *watch* the tree and *see that* no one else got there. Such a brief was loosely defined, to say the least.

Urgency

Macnamara, alone of all the grand speculators in "paper empires," stood at the bar of the Mexican government. Forbes was more interested in immediate business than the grand scheme; Pakenham was posted to Washington where his views on California had to change; Simpson's company pulled out of California; Wyllie retreated into his new career as a foreign minister to a native king; the Bondholders waited for events to unfold and whistled into the wind for cash to come home; Mackintosh had so many irons in the fire that he flitted without regret from one scheme to another and the Mexican War proved to be a busy time for an opportunist, although he would be bankrupt by 1851. Macnamara was the only one whose scheme was translated into anything approaching reality. He still had no formal answer to his submission of May when word came back on the grapevine that finance was the problem. A bankrupt government in constant turmoil was unlikely to agree to an unfinanced scheme, whatever long-term benefit might accrue from it to Mexico. Macnamara had failed to propose finance. He had even demanded the land "free of all cost." Had he and Mackintosh combined their respective enthusiasm and expertise they might have made a successful team.

Macnamara acted on the hearsay and wrote a further submission, partly upbraiding the Mexican president for his slowness to act, partly trying to plug the gap in his petition. *Eugenio Macnamara, Misionero Apostolico* wrote and signed the whole three-page text in Spanish and submitted it to President Herrera on a date unknown, but which was probably late July.

> By the hesitation of the Supreme Government to enter immediately on the question of establishing an Irish colony in California, it appears the principal and only objection is the difficulty of obtaining the expenses of transporting the colonists. It is very easy to overcome without the government expending a single dollar. There are in my country many fathers of families who after selling the little land they possess, their cattle, furniture etc would be able to command 200 to 300 dollars [*up to £60*] with which sum they would have nearly enough to cover the expenses of the voyage and of their families. But, as it will be necessary to convey many other [*families" crossed out*] persons, who lack the means for paying the expenses of their transportation such as priests, doctors, artesans, young women etc it will be necessary to obtain money for the purpose. If the supreme government should assign me sufficient land in California to mortgage, I would be able to obtain money in my own country upon the land.
>
> The supreme Government should agree to concede me for a certain period of time for the use of the colonists the duties on importations of the port of San Francisco. The government does not receive much benefit from duties at that port. I take the further liberty to demonstrate that no time ought to be lost in this important affair. We are surrounded by an artful and base enemy who loses no means however low to possess himself of the best territory of this country and who hates to the death its race and religion.
>
> Before another year the Californias will form part of the American nation [underlined by Macnamara]. Their Catholic institutions will become the prey of the Methodist wolves and the whole country will be inundated with the cruel invaders; whilst I propose the means of repelling them, my propositions ought to be the more admissible in as much as I have no personal interest in the affair, save the progress of the holy religion of God and the happiness of my countrymen. As for the fidelity and affection of these [Irishmen] to the Mexican Government, I answer with my life; and according as may be brought over a sufficient number of colonists (at least ten thousand persons) I am of the opinion and may assure you that this number will be sufficient to repel at the same time the secret intrigues and the open attacks of the American usurpers.[21]

There was a creeping infallibility about Macnamara's pronouncements on everything in life. A frontier missioner, like the parish priest of Doonbeg-Kilkee, had to be versatile and often to have instant views. He was pronouncing on social dislocation, defensive measures, financial remedies and the future economics of a whole department he did not know, not to mention the duties of president of the Mexican Republic. Bishop Clancy too had claimed the Ecclesiastical right to direct the civil power. In fact, Macnamara's financial calculations were fairly accurate, but only for those with means and something to sell before they left Ireland. In 1846, for instance, the poor on

Macnamara's signature on the codicil to the Petition, July 1845 (*Archivo General de la Nación, Mexico City*).

the Crown estates of Ballykilcline in County Roscommon had an average capital wealth of $15 (£3) a head. The Crown gave them that sum for their smallholdings, cabins and the $3 (12 shillings) journey to Dublin. Livestock, which was real wealth on a small farm would fetch perhaps $110 and on a moderate farm $250. The fare to the east coast of the United States was about $15 and to Canada $12. The farmers Macnamara had in mind were a far cry from this and from the smallholders of Doonbeg, nearer perhaps to the prosperous smallholders of Borrisokane.[22] His defense calculations were also vague: 6,000 of his 10,000 were children.

Lobos Metodistas: "Methodist Wolves"

An American judge called Macnamara the most anti–American visitor ever to enter California. A California Franciscan in 1896 thought his anti–Americanism was so exaggerated that it proved the Macnamara papers were yet another anti–Catholic smear forgery. "Macnamara must have been very ignorant not to know that in the United States many Catholic institutions were thriving unmolested. 'Methodist wolves' confirms our suspicions that Frémont had more to do with the wording of the petition as it exists than Macnamara. It would not have influenced the Mexican government as Macnamara must have known."[23] By 1896 it had been forgotten that religious toleration in Mexico was neither law nor even in the wind in 1846, nor would it be for another fifteen years.

The Methodists, so-called for their founders' "methodical" approach to spirituality, started as a revival within the slumbering 18th century Church of England. John Wesley, their leader, preached throughout England, Ireland and in America, traveling a quarter of a million miles, but never formally broke with the English state church. Protestants outside of that body were "nonconformists," but tolerated. Methodists made inroads among the industrial poor of England, in rural Ireland, among colonial slaves and wherever there were people without a church ministry, either through inertia (in the Church of England) or legal disability (in the Irish Catholic Church). The Methodists had their good times and their bad. When the Mormons recruited throughout England in the early 1840s they took from what had been Methodist ranks; by 1846, nearly 5,000 British Mormons had left for the States.[24] They made their pitch at California, the first shipload under Samuel Brannan heading for the captured Mexican Department from Hawaii, literally passing Eugene Macnamara as he left on a British battleship for Honolulu in July 1846. That same year, the Mormons petitioned Queen Victoria for permission to colonize Vancouver Island, after the Oregon boundary was settled: suddenly they changed tack and settled Salt Lake, Utah, as New Zion. More recruiters went to Britain, until by 1860, 29,000 British Mormons had come over to Utah, away from the "Babylon" which was the rest of the United States.

The Tablet, staple reading of the British Guiana clergy, had followed the news of the Oregon Trail and the rival missioners who pioneered it. The first Methodists had arrived on the Columbia River in 1834 to evangelize the Indians and were joined by Presbyterians in the Willamette Valley. *The Tablet* of March 11, 1843, which would have arrived at Georgetown at the end of April when Macnamara was considering going to the Pope, reported the "impudence or hypocrisy" of a Methodist missionary in Oregon who called "Papists destructive of all godliness." The editor took consolation in the fact that the Presbyterians there were losing out to the Jesuits and hopefully, "the example of [the 18th century Jesuit missions of] Paraguay will be renewed in the Rocky Mountains." A year before, on May 21, 1842, the paper had reported how French Roman Catholic missionaries had the Methodists systematically following them, to cash in on their success: it called them bluntly, "wolves in sheep's clothing," a common Biblical condemnation of false prophets, used of each other by the feuding churches.[25] A Methodist Oregon Provincial Emigration Society to found a Pacific agricultural empire was set up in 1838, in Massachusetts, but dissolved by 1840. In the middle of 1845 its former leader, the Reverend Troy, offered to set up an "independent nation" in the West. The Foreign Office referred him to Mr. Pakenham, the British minister in Washington, but both turned him down on grounds of caution.

Bishop Clancy in Guiana had never needed *The Tablet* to excite his anti–Protestant sentiment. He described the Protestant missioners there as "ravening wolves in sheep's clothing," with the success of the Methodists in mind. There were three Wesleyan chapels in Georgetown by 1832, and the Methodists were held in high regard by Governor Light.[26] Any Irish priest brought up during what came to be called "The Second Reformation" of the decade after 1820, would know the impact at least short-term of the Protestant revival and Methodism in particular on parts of the Irish countryside. Clare was one target for the revival and Macnamara's Ennis had new

Methodist buildings. Their preachers even spoke Gaelic, which was more than the younger Catholic priests were able to do.

In 1839 Daniel O'Connell, Member of Parliament for Clare, addressed open angry letters to the Methodists of Manchester about their long record of bigotry in Ireland; they had opposed Catholic Emancipation while campaigning to emancipate slaves. In America in particular, the riots in Philadelphia in May and July 1844 were reported in the world press, what *The Tablet* called "Nativist anti–Irish riots."[27] A convent was burnt down then just as convents had been destroyed in similar riots in Charleston in 1839 and in Boston in 1834. A riot against Irish immigrants was increasingly a riot against Catholics. In 1836, Samuel Morse stated that the 1776 Declaration of Independence was a continuation of the Protestant Reformation, which was republican, not monarchist. He spied a monarchist plot by the Austrian Leopoldine Society to convert the United States (Clancy was a member and recipient of Leopoldine funds), coupled with their Jesuit "almoners and emissaries from the Pope's bodyguard, who can assume any character, either as angels of light or as ministers of darkness." These "priest police" to the immigrants "account Protestants as being worse than Pagans."[28]

Macnamara was not to know it, but Jedediah "Bible Toter" Smith, the California trail finder, who was warmly welcomed by the friars at San Gabriel Mission in 1827, was a Methodist. He admired the broad-minded tolerance of the Franciscans. In 1847 the first Methodist services were conducted in Santa Clara and San Jose, possibly in deliberate provocation of Padre Real, the eccentric remaining missioner.[29] The Methodists quickly became California's second largest religious denomination. Père de Smet, the Belgian Jesuit, traveled the Oregon Trail in 1841 in the company of a Methodist "preacher" and both men parted as friends after learning great respect for each other.

Macnamara's polemical use of the biblical "wolves [in sheeps clothing]" was still harsh, even though O'Connell, Clancy and many of his day would have endorsed his sentiments. He had also been accused personally of being such a "wolf," preying on the Georgetown nuns: perhaps the knife had gone deep. Before the end of 1845, even Bishop Clancy, in dementia, was urging what was left of his flock to join the Methodists rather than submit to Bishop Hynes. Ironically, despite the invective, California became the most tolerant of the States, "in religion, the great exception," where anti–Semitism, anti-Catholicism—and anti–Methodism—were little in evidence.[30]

Mexican Colonization:
The Híjar-Padrés Expedition[31]

While Macnamara and other outsiders dreamed up plans to populate Mexican California, some in Mexico City remembered an earlier attempt to colonize it. Two hundred settlers in California itself also remembered the trek. Macnamara might have learned from their experience and advice. It had been an all–Mexican project which started with such idealism and hopes that it was all the harder to have seen it collapse on Californian soil. At least Mexicans had themselves tried to people the land before asking the world to help.

Some mystery—Antonio Osio called it a "labyrinth"—has always surrounded this attempt to fill the wastelands. In August 1833 the Mexican government agreed to secularize all California missions as Spanish feudal relics—the rest of Mexico's missions were nationalized in April 1834. Administrators were to take over the temporal affairs of the Franciscan stations which lined the coastal belt of Alta California from San Diego to north of San Francisco Bay. The Indian mission subjects were to be given lands for themselves; obviously with such a dispersal of land the California settlers would benefit; the Franciscan padres were to continue church work purely as parish priests, supported by a state investment program, the Pious Fund, the confiscated former mission chest. To make it easier, more Mexican Franciscans would be brought in as the older mission priests with their Spanish background and memories faded away. It was not surprising that colonization should be taken seriously: an overall new order was being implemented for California.

Juan Bandini, Upper California representative to the Mexican congress in 1833, supported both secularization and colonization. His opponents scathingly called the expedition "Bandini's Colony." José María Padrés, a soldier of the independence war and former military *Comandante* in California, represented Lower California in the Mexican Congress. He wanted to fill both empty departments with people. In Upper California, the highly respected Governor Figueroa was in overall political charge. In Mexico City, vice-president Gómez-Farías acted as president on the retirement of General Santa Anna. Farías was keen for secularization of the missions and for colonization of what he believed to be a department with great potential. As a liberal, Farías wanted less clerical influence in the Mexican state. He and the well-heeled José María Híjar were personal friends of Padrés.

In mid–1833 Governor Figueroa fell ill and talked of resigning. On hearing this, Farías gave Padrés the role of military commander (*comandante*) in California and Híjar, that of overall civil governor (*jefe politico*). Híjar was also appointed colony director with Padrés as his deputy. The Pious Fund, confiscated from the secularized missions of California, was now earmarked for the expenses of colonizing as well for maintaining churches. Posters went up round the capital and 250 prospective colonists, including families, were recruited. Utopia was nigh: Lancasterian schools were to be set up; each family was to have $10 starting out cash, money for rations on the road, free passage from San Blas to Monterey, farms out of public lands, livestock, tools and starting-up rations for a year. A great send-off ball was held in Mexico

City in April 1834, appropriately in a derelict convent. Meanwhile, Bandini issued a 59-page prospectus for the Cosmopolitan Company of California, inspired by attempts to recruit colonists for Texas. The prospectus declared an intent to buy a trading vessel, transport the emigrants and conduct trade for the colony's benefit. It described the climate and soil of California and dismissed the popular belief that it was inhabited by fierce savages and castaway criminals.

The wagon train made its way to Tepic, above San Blas. Juan Bandini stayed with the column while Padrés and Híjar went down to negotiate a boat. San Blas with its mosquitoes and mangrove swamps was no place to linger. Alexander Forbes, Scots partner of Eustace Barron in Tepic, met the waiting colonists. It may have prompted Forbes to write his book on European colonization in California; he was fearful of a successful Mexican trading company competing with his own Pacific monopoly. "Ill considered and foolish," he called the expedition in his book, "not a farmer among them, just artisans and idlers." He had reasons for being dismissive and he wrote with hindsight, after its failure, which was not for want of farmers or useful people. While there were only ten farmers and many skilled artisans from carpenters to smiths, saddlers and shoemakers, Forbes did find easy jibes in the candymaker, teachers and goldsmiths: the party lacked laborers and healthy open-air types. Two ships were obtained, one a Mexican naval vessel to help out, the other the company's first trading vessel. They sailed north, but sickness decimated one ship before it put in to San Diego; the naval vessel made it to Monterey, landing about 120 colonists with Colonel Padrés. The remaining colonists recovered and made their way slowly from San Diego, mission by mission, up the Camino Real to catch up with the rest.

That same summer, Santa Anna came back from retirement to be hailed as "El Salvador" by conservative and church supporters, ousted "Judas" Farías and warned Governor Figueroa by special express dispatch from Mexico City, not to cede any authority to the colony leaders. He probably feared a breakaway department ruled by Farías' friends. The message reached Figueroa on September 11, 1834, the day he had designated a site in the Santa Rosa valley for the new town of "Santa Anna y Farías," the secular patrons of a new secular mission, just northwest of the northernmost mission, San Francisco di Solano. Padrés landed at Monterey with his colonists on September 25th from the corvette, expecting to be comandante immediately, but when he found Figueroa healthy and saw the orders from President Santa Anna, he asked if he could still be deputy-director of the colony, even if not department comandante. Figueroa agreed. When Híjar arrived three weeks later, he asked likewise to be director of the colony. That was also agreed, but Mexico City (and Híjar) had assumed that he would also be civil governor. Accordingly, as his orders allowed, Híjar ordered that the missions be handed over to him. Arguments continued into early November, exacerbated by the fact that among the colonists were 21 Mexican administrators already appointed for the missions. The Californios had expected that this task would be their perquisite. Figueroa referred to his Departmental Assembly which ruled that Padrés and Híjar should take charge of the colonists, but not the missions, for the sake of the Indians.

The colonists were in serious need of help. Most had assembled at the Solano mission for the winter. In March 1835, Híjar asked for help with the new town of Santa Anna y Farías, but Figueroa stated he lacked the money and the colonists lacked the skills and the brawn. Each family or individual should fend for themselves and find a place to settle as best they could. Clearly he was breaking up the group. After a brief insurrection by a number of Sonorans in Los Angeles who were not part of the Híjar group, Figuroa ordered the colonists to surrender all weapons in case they were tempted to rebel. Híjar and Padrés were dismissed their offices and despite protests, were placed on a boat with their families for Mexico. Two hundred colonists stayed on and settled, though not as a community. The California Department was never surveyed and mapped as Híjar's instructions ordered it should be, and the missions there were temporarily saved. There may have been local fear of commercial competition—as Barron and Forbes might have feared in their Tepic monopoly. Talk of not depriving the Indians did not sit squarely with the Indians reportedly welcoming the colonists as liberators and the prospect of a new start proclaimed for the Indian above all, but from which only the leading Californias, what Robert Wyllie later called the "drones," grew wealthy.

A decade later, and in different times, Híjar was sent back to California as government commissioner at a time of crisis, when American settlers threatened to swamp the department. Some suspected he was planning another Mexican project to control a reluctant California. The central government gave Eugene Macnamara a letter of introduction to Híjar, in view of their shared interest. The commissioner died in Los Angeles in December 1845, before Macnamara could get to California. In the same town lived Juan Bandini, ten years older and in ill health, advising on land grants and frontier security. He was to be crucial in the implementing of the Macnamara grant, interviewing and corresponding with the Irishman in some detail. The admission of foreigners to colonize the frontier departments meant the Mexicans had to swallow their pride; not easy for a nation which had only recently overthrown Spain to stand on its own feet. Foreigners usually had other motives and loyalties. Whenever Macnamara came up with his Irish proposal, it was always met with the counter-suggestion that the Irish should come to settle *along with* a balance of Mexicans, or even European Spaniards.

Through the first few months of 1846, when it was not discussing Ireland, *La Reforma*, the staunchly republican and anti-monarchist newspaper in Mexico City, published documents and descriptions of California, advertising its wealth and potential. The editor warned of the government's "selfish torpor and cruel indifference" to the department: "a year and it will be abandoned."[32] A request from Bishop García Diego of Santa Barbara for European missioners, with Commissioner Híjar's encouragement, was supported by the paper—save that they should be Mexican. Harking back to the Híjar-Padrés scheme, the paper admitted that "colonisation is vital and thereby its people would be its defenders," but proposed a Mexican military colony as the only answer. Soldiers on active service would defend it; reservists would cultivate it. As the editor composed his daily editions, troops were in fact being assembled (and disassembled) in an attempt to get a battalion of sorts from Acapulco to California. The Californians were understandably apprehensive, uncertain of the soldiers' role—defenders, depredators or colonists? Macnamara was asked to accompany the battalion. He was the first since Híjar and Padrés to actually set out for California from Mexico City with any sort of brief for colonization. The newspaper admitted that with a Mexican population of only six million and that in decline, it would be impossible to colonize without help from Europe, but even there, only the Spanish should be considered. For all Mexico's need of colonizers, its politicians had to tread carefully when considering what nationality of colonist to admit. Even the Catholic Irish could bring problems.

Five

Mañana.
Mexico 1845–1846

I will render The Californias before five years the most
flourishing portion of this Republic. I can bring to California, 10,000 Irishmen, a race who were never known
to be ungrateful to their benefactors.—(Eugene Macnamara to the Mexican Foreign Minister, 29th January 1846)

The *mañana* syndrome was hard for British or American Anglo-Saxons
to fathom. A Mexican foreign minister even described his people in a bizarre
mixed metaphor as "sheep who need the lash." At the end of 1845, in exas-
peration, the British foreign secretary, Lord Aberdeen, warned the Mexican
ambassador that his country was *rushing* into war with America. He put it
with sarcasm. "As it is always your custom to go slow, you might now do so
from policy."[1] By that same December, Eugene Macnamara had endured a
long *mañana*. Six of his twelve months in Mexico had gone on preparing his
proposal and its hurried financial codicil. Six months after presenting the
Proyecto to the government, he had heard nothing. A year had been lost.

Meanwhile Joaquín Herrera's world was collapsing. In mid–December,
1845, the troops of the Mexican reserve commander, Mariano Paredes, prepared to march on the capital. Paredes had refused to go to reinforce the
Texan frontier. While it was wise not to waste troops, he was saving them
for his own ends: Herrera was his doorway to power. Too liberal, they called
the president, too tolerant of Yankee offers to buy California and of Yankee
squatters already lording it there: he could not even get the California expeditionary force to its embarcation port. The loss of Texas overshadowed everything. "The Texas game" threatened the Californias, however remote from
the United States they might appear. Settler squatters were coming overland
from the States and the U.S. Army was out surveying the routes. A crescendo

of press and conservative politicians railed at Herrera, including many who had supported him earlier in the year when he showed determination over Texas. By the end of the year the conservative Mexican military felt bound to step in: national honor was at stake, although politics did take the army away from defending it. Outside observers detected more a thirst for power in these new patriots than a passion for honor. Herrera was also a sick man. Mrs. Bankhead, the British ambassador's wife, wrote scathingly to a friend in Oxford, "Herrera is ill. He is an old woman and the Secretary of State [Cuevas] ditto and something of the Jesuit. You cannot imagine a beautiful country more doomed and hopeless than this." No money, she concluded, and no energy.[2]

The Yniestra Battalion

President Herrera had ordered an expeditionary force to be raised in April 1845 for Alta California. At the same time he had sent a full division under General Arista to face the Americans across the disputed Texas border on the Rio Grande. The California force was to be commanded by Colonel Ignacio Yniestra, young, urbane and trained in a French *école militaire* during the 1830s. Herrera also sent two commissioners to California—something he was no longer able to do on Texan territory. The first, José María Híjar, the respected former colonizer of California, was to hear the complaints of the Californios. These were military and financial neglect by Central Government and the abuse of the national territory by U.S. squatters. Law and order had virtually broken down and California's tiny population had rebelled and exiled its governor, Micheltorena, early in 1845. The native Indians added to the miseries and insecurity of the legitimate settlers. The missions had also been destroyed. Herrera's second commissioner was Andrés Castillero, cavalry captain and expert mineralogist who had prospected in southern California in 1840. Castillero's task was to reconnoiter and to pave the way for the Yniestra force. He was also to negotiate with Johann Sutter the purchase of the fort at Nueva Helvetia on the Sacramento, in order to place a Mexican garrison at the overland entrance into California through the Sierra Nevada.

More battalion than division, the force was raised by May 1845. "Two thousand men for California, a splendid division of elite troops! Pay guaranteed for a year," sang *La Voz del Pueblo*. When the expedition faltered, the *Amigo del Pueblo* attacked it and its commander ceaselessly between September and December 1845, on grounds of corruption, inefficiency and frivolous spending. When the British ambassador in Mexico City wrote privately to Lord Aberdeen, "Mexico is about to send to the Californias an expedition to protect them. The Government greatly fear U.S. intentions," he also dropped a hint in the form of a report. "The sale of these provinces to England is talked of, if she would purchase them."[3] Aberdeen, reading the letter five weeks later on September 8th, showed no interest.

On the same day Bankhead also wrote his official dispatch to Aberdeen. The Yniestra expedition was "to aid the present very feeble force in California. It consists of 12–1,500 men, to embark from Acapulco where several vessels are waiting for it, to Monterey. It has been prevented from going by want of funds." He reminded Aberdeen of Eugene Macnamara's presence and intentions. "I should be glad if he would accompany this expedition with some ostensible authority from the [Mexican] Government, as he could then personally examine the facilities and prospects of a future Colony of his countrymen." Aberdeen, however, had already assured the Mexican ambassador, "We have closed our ears to those proposals and offers of that country [California] to England, as also proposals for establishing colonies there under our protection." Consistently, he closed his ears yet again to Bankhead's report, but inconsistently, read it aloud to the Mexican ambassador.[4]

Elements of the Yniestra force were already on the move the week Bankhead reported to Aberdeen. William Parrott, U.S. Confidential Agent in Mexico City, informed Washington, "Another portion of the force has left for Acapulco to embark. Colonel Yniestra, it is said, will soon follow. The military education of this gentleman was finished in France and it is said by well-informed persons that his command and political influence in California will be turned to French account, under the direction of the French Legation here. He certainly takes with him a large number of Frenchmen for some reason or other."[5] A week later, Eugene Macnamara was attached to Yniestra's command with a letter of introduction from Foreign Minister Cuevas to José Híjar, commissioner in California. The old and the new colonizers would meet. Pressure for the attachment may have come from Ambassador Bankhead, Archbishop Posada or Macnamara himself—he had the push. A multilingual chaplain to the expedition with French, Spanish and English, not to mention the energy and Irish "difference" from the Mexican clergy, would have been an asset. He also shared the commander's formative background in France.

> The Irish priest, Macnamara, goes to that department with the expedition in charge of Col. Don Ignacio Yniestra, and takes a project for colonisation with Irish families. Among the very honourable persons who have recommended this ecclesiastic to me, the most illustrious Archbishop has done so very earnestly, and desiring to gratify them in an affair that may be of advantage to the Republic, I make the same recommendation to you, charging you to examine well his project and inform the Government of what he may offer, in order that it may determine what is suitable, and likewise that you facilitate him as far in your power, and make his residence in the department agreeable. You will speak on the subject with his excellency the Governor in order that, in view of his advice and opinion, the Government may decide the more intelligently. To Don José María Híjar, Monterey.[6]

Macnamara's posting to the expeditionary force pitched him directly into the public eye. Less than a week later, word of his Proyecto was on its way to Washington. William Parrott wrote that the expedition was faltering due to lack of funds, but that "A young Irish priest by the name of McNamarrah" (*sic*) was preparing to go with it to organize there the immigration of Irish farmers.[7] All of Parrott's news arriving in September spurred President Polk to prepare a strong speech to the nation to be delivered in December, warning Europe against colonizing in California.

Macnamara held onto the Foreign Minister's letter of introduction for almost a year, and after news of Híjar's death in December came through from Los Angeles, still hoped to present it to someone of rank in California. When he did finally land there in June 1846, Governor Pico's scribes filed a copy with the Irishman's petition papers. In fact, Híjar had arrived on his mission in Pico's interim capital, Los Angeles, in June 1845 and, unknown to Cuevas, never left it. Governor Pico had little beyond paper influence further north towards Monterey, the traditional capital where his rival Castro held court and collected the customs dues. Híjar stayed quietly under Pico's wing until his untimely death, probably reminiscing with Juan Bandini who also lived in Los Angeles. "I do not recall what Híjar's mission was," wrote Pico years later, "but he did not interfere with government."[8] Pico spoke in eulogy at his funeral.

Híjar would have been a valuable ally to Macnamara, partly for his age and wisdom, but mainly for his colonizing experience. Director and lawmaker for the Cosmopolitan Company in 1833–5, along with Bandini, he knew the lessons to be learned from failing to colonize California. He would have offered two pieces of advice: enlist the support of the Californios themselves and do not try to make an agricultural colony without laborers. He might even have warned that it was too late. His own brief in 1845 was, according to Abel Stearns, American observer in Los Angeles and Bandini's son-in-law, "to enquire into affairs in California and recommend the reorganising of Government, Customs and Courts."[9]

Cuevas' letter of introduction to Híjar was a sign of the Government's good faith and interest in the Macnamara Project, even though the Council of Government had not yet debated it. Desperation may also have featured, that of a drowning government clutching a straw. The delay up to December 1845, however frustrating, was neither dissimulation nor lack of interest: *mañana* was simply Mexico, just as Macnamara's *bhlárna* was Ireland. Archbishop Posada's support was also a healthy sign. A kingmaker and conservative who sat on the Council of Government, he carried weight with the military rulers. He sent a letter of introduction with Macnamara to Bishop García Diego, the diocesan Bishop of the Two Californias. Posada and Diego were appointed at exactly the same time, hardly new brooms at 64 and 60 respectively, but fresh starts all the same. Diego approached Híjar on the latter's arrival in California in 1845 and suggested that one solution to the church's problem was "recourse to Europe where there are many zealous and well-educated missionaries." At the end of September, with Híjar's backing, he asked President Herrera directly for permission to "invite twenty, thirty or more missionaries from France, Italy or some other place in Europe."[10]

The expedition did not move north from Mexico City. On the contrary, by December 1845 it had managed to straggle 150 miles *south*, trapped in Acapulco and on the road there. The ships to transport it to Monterey had been withdrawn. Had Macnamara been with the expeditionary force, he too would have been stranded. He would have missed the final boost to his mission which came from confronting General Paredes after the January coup and from linking up with Admiral Seymour's British naval squadron in April 1846.

Rumor and Distortion

Although the Yniestra expedition came to nothing, it took time to do so and remained very real in the heads of the apprehensive Californios. As late as May 1846 Governor Pico lamented publicly the "non-arrival of the expedition announced in August of last year and which up to the present time we have not seen. There are some who doubt that it will ever arrive. The [Departmental Government] Committee would be most happy to hear of the entry of these troops into California, but at the same time, [it would be deplorable] should this force be sent without sufficient funds for their maintenance." He concluded gloomily that a sufficient force would run roughshod over the inhabitants, living off the land; an insufficient force would be ineffective against the Americans—and still live off the land.[11]

California was distant—it took three weeks for the faster letters and travelers to reach Monterey from Mexico City. In 1844 Bishop García Diego received letters from Mexican bishops one and even two *years* after they were sent. Paper was in chronic short supply and had been since Spain withdrew, ending the supply of European paper. A Mexican newspaper tax on all save the official government *Diario* meant little opposition press. "In all California there is not a subscriber to a Mexican newspaper. The Supreme Government sends the *Diario [del Gobierno]* and a few Mexicans receive papers from friends in Mexico City. No books for sale here."[12] There was no Californian local newspaper. A Sandwich Islands newspaper came in periodically with trade vessels. Rumor therefore flourished in California, shaping policy and fueling already deep-rooted suspicions. It was a society made paranoid by its minuscule size and isolation. Consuls, required to report back to Washington, London and Paris, had to sift through the chaff which constantly flew from the rumor mill.

Dr. John Marsh, a recent overland settler living in the hinterland east of Monte Diablo, wrote excitedly to Thomas Larkin, U.S. consul at Monterey, "It seems Mr Híjar of colonial memory has arrived, but with what object? and that one, two or three thousand soldiers are to follow, but for what purpose? Let them be stationed on the Eastern frontier where they can protect us from the [Indian] horse thieves." Abel Stearns, rancher, trader and U.S. agent, told Larkin the force was "some 15 or 18 *thousand* troops," with

Map of California

the financial backing of two British houses in Mexico. John Jones from Santa Barbara opined that Híjar was "a spy enquiring into the conduct of General Micheltorena."[13] A month later this "spy" was both "governing Pico entirely" and "keeping himself very quiet and visiting no one."

The expedition was the subject of rumor and counter rumor. Jones told Larkin a wealth of detail. "Mexico has bound herself to place 2,800 soldiers in this Department. A young man called Yniestra, educated in Europe, has been appointed Governor. Two English houses in Mexico City and Barron [and Forbes] in Tepic have become responsible for the payment of the troops. Two ships have been chartered and Barron offers to bring them. They are to found five Mexican *presidios* here and extend their settlements to the Columbia."[14] Naturally, they were "troops of the line, highly disciplined, not to oppress the Californians, but to maintain order and protect from foreign invasion."

Consul Larkin summed up what he knew in a letter to Juan Bandini. "The Government of Mexico are fitting out at Acapulco an expedition of troops for the purpose of putting out of office the Californio officers and reinstating the Government of Mexico. We have heard the number of troops variously stated. The new general is a Mexican, but educated in Europe with a perfect knowledge of the different languages spoken on this coast. The troops are now expected here in September, sent by the instigation of the English Government under the plea that the American settlers in California want to revolutionise the country. It is rumoured that two English houses in Mexico have been bound to the new General to accept his drafts for funds to pay his troops for 18 months."[15]

The troops did not move from Acapulco during the scheduled September: rumor embarked instead. "We look for the new troops in 20 days, bringing with them $500,000." In January word came from Los Angeles (picked up at San Pedro from Mazatlán, where it had been heard in San Blas, which had it on the best authority from Acapulco?). "The expedition for California is still at Acapulco and the vessels all ready to take the troops aboard." A day later, from the boundary between the Two Californias, Jones wrote to Larkin, "Mexico is in a worse revolution than ever. General Paredes with 12,000 troops has declared against the President and declared for a Dictator. Letters from the Government to Híjar state the expedition from Acapulco was to leave in December. 300 have died."[16]

In Mexico City on December 18, 1845, Theodor Hartweg, a German "botaniser" sent by the London Horticultural Society to collect plants and seeds from California, presented his letter of introduction from Lord Aberdeen to Charles Bankhead at the British embassy. (As a German citizen Hartweg could not hold a British passport.) As he headed out of the city afterwards towards the Pacific coast, Hartweg "met part of an expedition to be sent via Acapulco to California by General Paredes [Army commander-in-chief under Herrera] to bring that distant department to obedience; the general opinion is that the expedition will, for want of money, never reach California and that the troops have been sent away to keep them 'out of mischief' during the expected revolution." Hartweg, who confined much of his record to botanic detail, must have heard rumors from British expatriates as well as Mexicans. Much rumor concerned England and its intentions towards Mexico, California and the United States. Hartweg arrived with the most innocent intentions, but increasingly worried that few would believe "that a person would come all the way from London to look for weeds."[17]

The Mexican Ambassador in London

December was an eventful month all round. In San Luis Potosí garrison town General Paredes' troops declared for power and marched south on Mexico City. British Prime Minister Robert Peel's son, a Royal Navy Lieutenant serving under Seymour in the Pacific, stayed with the British Embassy on his way to England with dispatches from Captain Gordon, Lord Aberdeen's brother on HMS *America*. Eugene Macnamara, who must have met Peel, Jr., (and enjoyed the contact), sat out the frustrations of hearing nothing about his Proyecto from the Mexican government, seeing the military expedition to which he was attached run into the sand and hearing nothing more about California than its impending loss. He had never seen California, but was so involved in it already that it was central to his new identity, almost to the point of obsession. Theodor Hartweg also arrived from London that month, unwittingly putting himself (and his weeds) in the eye of a growing storm. Both Hartweg and Macnamara found the British embassy a refuge and a source of encouragement in the persons of its Irish ambassador, Charles Bankhead, and its Irish chargé d'affaires, Peregrine (Percy) Doyle. Macnamara seems to have lodged in the home of one of them. Doyle was impetuous, "casting care to the winds," and had once clashed seriously with former President Santa Anna. A small, home-made British ensign was displayed as a war trophy from Texas during a government reception. Doyle led a walk-out and London supported him. He was respected for his command of the language, knowledge of the country and his flamboyant "going native," down to a "Mexican suit fastened up the side with silver coins." Irish horsemanship matched Mexican dress. When Doyle went back to England on leave in 1846, Bankhead remarked that without him the British embassy "seems as quiet as an old Convent." The fastidious Dr. Robert Crichton Wyllie, however, found Doyle's manners "rough."[18]

Doyle wrote to his brother John, near Oxford, that Christmas, describing the California predicament as he must have related it to Macnamara and Hartweg. Even unseen, California was an attractive prospect. "These people, notwithstanding the good advice they have received for years, only wished to consent to the recognition of the independence of Texas when it was too late and, unless some other powers wanted to make an arrangement for their own with respect to California, that beautiful country will, as many fear, become U.S. property. The Oregon Treaty is worth much to settlers, almost all the Yanquee squatters have lately gone into the Californias and the accounts we receive of the fertility of the soil and the beauty of the climate are really marvellous. This country is going headlong to the Devil. There are now several people of about the same calibre trying to upset the Government merely to place themselves in power and rob as long as they can. Mexican patriotism simply means look after yourself."[19]

December was a busy month for others too. Lt. Archibald Gillespie kept his head down in Mexico City, disguised as a Spanish-speaking U.S. merchant. He carried instructions from Washington for Larkin and Frémont urging them not to stir revolt but to enlist by every proper persuasion the people of California to ask for inclusion in the United States. Gillespie memorized the instructions and destroyed the evidence.[20] Washington had been shaken by reports that the British were set to take California as well as hold onto Oregon further north, even at the risk of war. President Polk had been told of Macnamara's plan and of Seymour's large squadron. In December 1845 he warned Europe in his Senate speech to the nation that they were not to interfere with the Americas. That month Polk also formally confirmed Texas as a new state of the American Union.

In London, Mexican ambassador Tomaso Murphy had struggled for six months to persuade Lord Aberdeen to ally with Mexico against the United States. He dangled California, whether purchased, gifted or colonized, asking Aberdeen to "cooperate to prevent its loss." Publicly, Aberdeen was all things to all men, but no gunboat politician, unlike the bullish Lord Palmerston who both preceded and followed him in office. Aberdeen had already told the U.S. ambassador in March 1845 that Britain had not the slightest objection to Mexico ceding San Francisco port to the Americans. Murphy's attempt at persuasion continued until December, when Aberdeen and the British Cabinet declared for complete non-intervention over California, lest it damage the Oregon negotiation. Up to that point, Aberdeen had appeared open to suggestion, although he never ran out of reasons for turning down whatever Murphy suggested. He wanted the spoils of war without the risks of war. He did say, however, that if the Oregon talks collapsed, he would accept California and expect Mexico to keep U.S troops distracted. France, he reasoned, would not back Britain against the United States and might even go to war against Britain; Mexico was too inflexible, refusing to recognize Texas until too late; strategically the United States was in the superior position; British naval protection, which Murphy asked for California, would breach neutrality. At one stage in the months of discussion Aberdeen seemed to take the bait. Late in September 1845, Murphy suggested that a British colony in California would give Britain all the reason it needed to intervene should the Americans invade. It happened that Bankhead's dispatch from Mexico of July 30th had just arrived. Aberdeen sent for it and read it out loud to Murphy. It was the letter in which Bankhead explained the Euan Mackintosh project and mentioned Eugene Macnamara for the second (and final) time. Aberdeen, predictably, balked again, saying a new colony at this point in the Oregon negotiations would be rightly construed by America as an act of hostility. He then clutched at one last possibility.

Leaders of the Mexican Committee of the Spanish American Bondholders Association in London had been to see him that month, including Vice-Chairman John Diston Powles of Topo notoriety and partner to Euan Mackintosh in the firm, Manning and Mackintosh, together with another member of the firm. The Committee and Association monitored Bond speculators' interests. They explained to Aberdeen the 1837 Bondholder option on Mexican land and showed their open land warrants. The option had only two years to go and could still prove profitable all round. They proposed forming a company to take up 50 million acres of California land at a cost of £6.25 million, four-fifths of which would be covered by the land warrants, the rest in cash installments underwritten by the British Government. Aberdeen spotted the flaw. Even if the United States took over California, he pointed out, were she to respect the rights of British settlers there already, Britain would have no cause to intervene on their behalf. In the end the Cabinet ruled and by December 1845 discussion was at an end.[21] While Powles and other Bondholders continued to urge the government to annex California, they never set up a London joint stock company to raise money and settlers, as they had proposed to Aberdeen. Powles ruefully admitted it years later. While Macnamara and Mackintosh may have had the Bondholders' land option in mind and probably conferred in Mexico, both projects appeared at the same time and place by sheer coincidence and by dint of much publicized, empty land open to offers. Possibly they stole a march on others they knew to be negotiating from a distance, but they were independent of each other. Mackintosh was a man seeking power and money. Macnamara, like Bishop Clancy, may have had similar interests mixed with altruism: his successful contract in the end was for 13 million acres, not quite the Bondholders 50 million, but his was tangible, while theirs was notional.

General Paredes' Coup

Macnamara's passport expired on January 2, 1846, the day troops took over the capital. He failed to appear at Euan Mackintosh's British consulate, which technically incurred a twenty-*real* penalty.[22] It may have been the New

Year *fiesta* which, like a military coup also stopped everything in Mexico City; it may have been that he had needed no *Carta*, still notionally on attachment to Yniestra's army and to a forlorn hope that it might actually sail. There was confusion all round that New Year as the city was put under martial law.

On December 15, 1845, Comandante General Mariano Paredes in San Luis Potosí had proclaimed against Joaquín Herrera and announced a dictatorship "for the defence of the nation." The army was the symbol of the nation. Herrera resigned at the end of December when the army reached the gates of the capital. Paredes entered a silent sullen city on January 2nd without bloodshed, and proclaimed additional dictatorial powers, published in the *Diario del Gobierno*. Macnamara read the detail and three weeks later appealed successfully to Paredes' new powers to speed his Proyecto. His close ally, Archbishop Posada, chaired the *Junta* which conceded total constitutional authority to Paredes. That same first week of January, the general refused to receive William Slidell, the U.S. presidential envoy sent with money and power to pay Mexico in gold for both peace and land, the former dependent on the latter. At the same time, President Polk in Washington ordered General Taylor to the Texan border on the Rio Grande. Taylor did not arrive there until the spring, but the Rio Grande was not the border which Mexico recognized: that was the Nueces River, 150 miles further north. In February 1846 President Polk warned of war if Slidell were snubbed again in Mexico City. Paredes stood his ground and refused any audience. Slidell, his gold unspent, returned to Washington in May and urged war, just as news of an attack by Mexican troops on American troops north of the Rio Grande came through. War was declared on May 13th, on the grounds of Mexico's "incursion."[23]

On January 19, 1846, a note was delivered to Macnamara from Castillo Lanzas, the new foreign minister under Paredes. The Council of Government deliberations were now completed and the proposal was to go before the Chambers of Deputies and Senators. Lanzas omitted to say that the report had been completed on September 18, 1845, but had only been presented to the president on January 13, 1846. He even deleted from his letter to Macnamara the key Council exhortation that great haste should be made with the project.

> Having heard the opinion of the Council on the project of colonisation in California, presented by you to the Supreme Government, the Government, in accordance with the opinion of that body, has determined that "in view of the necessity which exists for some effective measures on that subject and on other concessions, proper for the action of the legislature, the matter will be referred" together with your memorial, "to the Chambers," ["*recommending the importance of very prompt discussion and approval*"]. I state this to you for your information, remarking that the subject will be thus attended to at a convenient time.[24]

Macnamara was indignant at so casual a response. He must have heard from the archbishop that the Council had recommended more strongly than Lanzas would admit. Lanzas, on the other hand, had had to cover for the failure of Cuevas to act: Cuevas was a conservative and centralist, the type who called liberal federalists "streetwalkers." General Paredes, though a monarchist, was not keen on the English-speaking world, feeling that they were all allied against the Latin race. He was a reputable drinker, which may have helped color his view of a world beyond Mexico which he had never seen. Macnamara, presumably still a Temperance pioneer, saw the world differently and exploded. On January 24th he wrote angrily to Lanzas, obviously intending it to be seen by the president. It was a release after months of waiting. His pompous hectoring smacked of Bishop Clancy, but behind the shower of rhetoric he argued no more than had been agreed three months before by Herrera's Council of State. He also decried *mañana*, "procrastination," as a national policy.

> I deeply regret that the President should come to this determination, as the exigency of the case requires in my opinion, prompt, strong and immediate measures. I trust I will be able to show you in a few words why the plan which I have had the honour of submitting to the Government should be taken at once into consideration. A statesman in viewing a question of this importance should have no other object in view than the immediate and future benefits to be derived from it to his country. Secondly he should reflect whether those benefits are to be more easily attained by immediate action or by procrastination; in my opinion it requires not much wisdom to perceive which course should be pursued in the present instance. If you procrastinate, if you yield to that infatuated premiss of the mind of man, to depend on the future in temporal matters, all will be lost.
>
> It is a well-known and undoubted fact that the combined attention of the Americans is now directed to the possession of the Californias, their squatters and colonists are passing in thousands over the Rocky Mountains, they reach the Oregon territory which they find barren and unproductive, and they naturally descend into the rich and fertile plains of California, and believe me that no force which you can oppose to them will be capable of checking them. Again it is highly probable that 'ere long the Oregon will be the scene of war between the British and the Americans. You cannot for a moment suppose that the victorious party will respect your territorial rights. Most assuredly they will not. Both parties are looking with wistful eyes to the beautiful bay of San Francisco and know that in modern times the axiom of "might is right" universally prevails. I am aware of the value of your time. I wish to be as brief as possible, yet let me give a candid and free opinion, that before two years the Californias will cease to be an integral part of this republic, if the plan which I propose be not speedily adopted.

Macnamara was warning against *both* Britain and America, although he changed his position later and claimed to be acting for the British Crown.

After venting his frustration, he turned from the role of moral scold to that of persuader. In his mind he had a whole nation (Ireland) behind him and a whole prospective new nation in front of him—or perhaps an Apostolic Vicariate. He lacked neither vision nor confidence, and shared them.

> Allow me to say a few words on the advantages of my proposal; if the President exercises that privilege which he undoubtably possesses and which I find bestowed on him in the additions to his Plan of San Luis Potosi as published in the *Diario* of the 3rd Inst [*exceptional dictatorial powers for the defence of the national territory cited verbatim in Spanish and underlined for emphasis*]. From this it is clear and evident that the President possesses the power of assigning to me the grant of land which I solicit. It will certainly be preparing for the defence of the country and let me add that when hereafter he will pass in mind and view the principal actions of his life, none will bring greater consolation to his bosom than this: I can bring to California ten thousand Irishmen, a race brave and hardy, loyal and devoted, who were never yet known to prove ungrateful to their benefactors, in confirmation of which I might refer you to the historical records of Spain, France and Austria. If my suggestions be carried out, I will render the Californias, before five years, the most flourishing portion of this republic.
>
> With regard to the opinion of the Council, of sending the question to the Chambers, I would respectfully suggest that that passage of their *dictamen* [*opinion, or judgment*] be referred to them by the President for reconsideration. As this is a highly national and patriotic question, I sincerely trust that the present energetic government will despatch it speedily and promptly.[25]

However much *Eugene Macnamara, Missionary Apostolic*, had "the honour to remain your very obedient servant," he was still an ambitious, frustrated man seeking a role for himself, chafing at the bit, half a year behind schedule and with California visibly slipping from his host republic's grasp, and thereby from his own. His outspokenness won him a hearing.

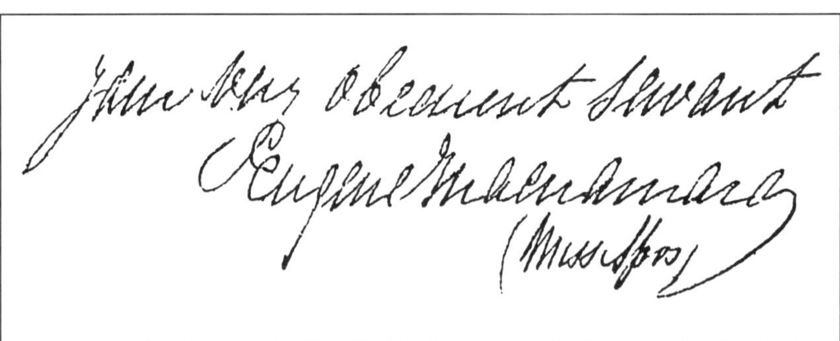

Macnamara's signature on his letter of remonstrance, January 1846 (*Archivo General de la Nación, Mexico City*).

On January 29th, presumably after consultation with General Paredes, Castillo Lanzas referred the whole file back to the Council of Government, together with Macnamara's latest letter. The Council met on February 3rd and backed Macnamara. Desperation in the wake of the failure of Yniestra's expedition may have gained him the politicians' support. Ironically, he had more prompt and effective support from Paredes, opposed to an English-speaking colony, than from Herrera, professedly for it. The archbishop, a key Paredes supporter, would have intervened for it; it was also rumored that Paredes had taken financial aid from at least one English trading house. Five months later, when he landed in California, Macnamara explained the delay to a resident of Monterey, possibly Padre Real, the Franciscan priest of Monterey and Santa Clara. Real was friendly with Thomas Larkin, the U.S. consul in Monterey and had a house a few yards from Larkin's fine home. Through Real or from Macnamara directly, Larkin learned what had happened between Macnamara and Paredes in February and duly told his agent in Los Angeles, Abel Stearns. "When Mr Macnamara called on President Paredes to converse on the subject, the latter objected at once saying the Irish would join the Americans immediately; that he wanted no immigrants whose national language was English."[26] By August when Larkin gave Buchanan in Washington his résumé of the summer's historic events, Macnamara's "call on Paredes" had become "several conferences with Presidents Herrera and Paredes."[27]

The Council's Response to the Macnamara Project

It is doubtful that Macnamara ever saw the report which the Council of Government sent to the Mexican Foreign Minister, Luis Cuevas, on September 18, 1845.[28] General Paredes would have been briefed on it, even had it in front of him, if he and Macnamara did confer in February 1846. The fourteen-page verdict on the Irish Proyecto was not only favorable, but judged the settlement vital to the Republic and its departments. The 17-man council was a conservative body, nearer to Paredes than to Herrera; its arguments were well constructed. "The richest country in the world, without inhabitants or a few colonists is just the same as the driest desert of Africa. The prosperity of the United States lies in its increase in population." The level of discussion during that summer's meetings was high and the experience round the table considerable. Macnamara's proposal was accepted in principle, as were the locations of his colonies around San Francisco, Monterey and Santa Barbara, but his financing was vetoed. The report was the work of wiser men than the initiating Irishman and it showed a thoughtful resolve. No mention was made of British Bondholders and their options, or of finance from or protection by the British government. The Irish colony was a purely Mexican affair and its *empresario* a private individual.

The Councillors of State accepted his motive in colonizing, "partly to prevent the usurpations planned by the neighbouring States of the American Confederation, and partly to procure for these families all the advantages of a more comfortable life under obedience to our laws and authority." They accepted his land requirements, "a square league in full ownership for each family he introduces and half a league for each couple before marriage to help found a family." Some tax relief and full Mexican citizenship were also agreed.

Fixed reference points were established "concerning the value of colonisation itself and to improve the means of attaining this end for a nation so endowed with natural riches." *Pobladores* in the "exuberant fertility of our mountains and valleys" would bring "work, the building of roads and canals by which exports can be made. Our wildest lands occupied by a large population would multiply the strength of our country, bringing respect and security, hope for every class, re-establishment of morals and respect for the ways of law." Mexico was in disarray, "destructive political passions have meant no protection for property or peace of mind for the individual, no confidence in the courts, a lack of confidence, material preoccupation, greed, extravagance and smuggling."

> California's massive elements attract the attention of daring adventurers in its position on the borders of the U.S. and Canada, by the Pacific Sea, an inappreciable position of power in which they have wished for many years to occupy even a single point, like the port of San Francisco which has been seen as an article to be bought by bargaining with our Government. The impulse to increase the U.S. population there, an enormous American wave, is irresistible.
>
> The forming of an army big enough to stop the incursions is extremely difficult, but colonising inhabitants would make good military auxiliaries, having their own property to defend. Colonisation would promote the principles of justice and enlightenment, as with the missions and *presidios* in 1823 when there was three times the population and four times the reclaimed lands. Since then it has all collapsed. Barbarian Indians wander everywhere and this state of wilderness encourages them to invade our Department bringing death and destruction with them.
>
> The Committee has no hesitation in approving the request of Priest Macnamara on grounds of the usefulness and urgency of colonising California, of enlightened politics and for the Republic's continuing to hold this Department.

The Council gave legal opinion that the approval conformed to the laws on colonization, that of August 18, 1824, whereby the population should be increased, and of April 6, 1830, whereby California should have immigrant families in equal proportion to any other department. Warily they accepted Macnamara's description of the Irish as "Catholic, loyal, moral, hardworking, sober and brave," and the *empresario* himself as someone who knows the traits and qualities of the different colonists of Europe and which would be most appropriate to our circumstances. He has no doubt that the Irish are the best endowed with these qualities, [but] nevertheless, the Commission while intending that the colonisation should be the fullest and freest possible, advise that it must be with certain unalterable restrictions—the ban on of slavery and the public profession of a uniform religion. The respect and compliance of the colonists for these, our State laws, is a requirement. This would be no trouble for the Irish who integrate both sentiments into their very education as the most profound of convictions.[29]

The commission approves without reserve, without taking away our declared preference for Mexicans, whatever is agreed in this instance, but feel that some part of these families should be Spanish from provinces throughout the Peninsula who find themselves in similar circumstances to the Irish and who are offered advantageous terms. An invitation should be sent out through our Legation in Madrid [as] proof of strengthening bonds of brotherhood between our nations.

The Council reviewed the old surveys of California, such as they were, starting with Humboldt forty years before. Ranching and population had declined since then. Much public sector land was available, quite apart from 7,420 square leagues of ex-mission land. The law of 1824 gave any colonist a square league of arable, four of pasture and six of uncleared rough, calculating each family at five persons. Macnamara evidently sought an allocation of 25,000 square leagues (*varas quadradas*), enough for 11 square leagues (74 square miles) for each of 2,250 colonists, and some land in bonus for the contractor himself, or for fewer colonists with land in reserve for marriage endowments; more would be allocated afterwards to attract more colonists.

Ignoring Macnamara's glib solution that the Irish farmers should sell their possessions for $2–300 before the voyage, the Council also advised against financing voyage and settlement from tax concessions in California. Evidently they had heard nothing of his conversational claim to official or private support from London; neither he nor they made mention of outside finance, save some extra land to raise capital in Great Britain. "Tax concessions would be unjust to existing inhabitants and would destroy the farmers of that Department, as well as national unity, colonisation itself and it would dismember the State. Their being Mexican citizens would not make sense." The Commission proposed a dramatic solution.

The Supreme Government should allocate financial resources for bringing in these families, bearing in mind the conditions of poverty from which they will be coming, and that they are labourers and smallholders of scant means, and that they will relieve the Government of the need to send and maintain troops in California. We propose that fifty men from our army be despatched, more than enough to conduct the first 300 families [1,500 people] from Europe and, if possible, that one of our Steamers should carry these passengers, ensure their peaceful disembarkation and impose respect for them in those remote and unprotected places.

Having conjured up the vision of Mexican troops taking shore leave at Cobh or Dublin, from one of Mexico's two steamer warships, *Montezuma* and *Guadeloupe*, only recently delivered from Liverpool amid a diplomatic row, the Council then acknowledged that the Chambers of Deputies and Senators would have the last word. Perhaps an alert Chamber Deputy might have observed that 1,500 men, woman and children would not fit on a naval steamer or any other steamer of the day, let alone cross the Atlantic with packed decks. The latest Royal Mail steamers on the West Indies run took only a maximum 100 passengers. On the other hand a naval vessel had assisted the Híjar-Padrés colony. Two resolutions were finally put to the Foreign Minister—that the "project of the Irish priest Don Eugenio Macnamara be acceded to on the terms laid down," and secondly that the whole affair, in view of its importance, be given "the Chambers' most immediate attention and decision." Perhaps genuine embarrassment made Castillo Lanzas omit the last line from his note to Macnamara—five months later.

More Rumor and Distortion

Mexico City was a maelstrom of rumor through winter and spring 1845-6, no less than California. Macnamara disentangled himself from the failed expedition to make his own way, unhindered, to that coast. He was now part of Mexican defense strategy, such as it was, by virtue of Dictator Paredes' emergency powers. Paredes, for all his mistrust of English-speakers, courted the British for their monarchist tradition. Charles Bankhead wrote a "*Secret*" private letter to Lord Aberdeen on March 10, 1846 (received May 6th), reporting that "The President intended to commission a person about to visit England to communicate his wishes on Mexico to Lord Aberdeen, which were to carry through the monarchy question and put Mexico into the arms of England, rejecting entirely the Spanish alliance." Bankhead later admitted that Paredes could not find anyone trustworthy enough in Mexico to take the message and the policy was not at all popular. Two months later, Paredes was begging Great Britain to accept California in hypothecation or collateral as long as she would protect it.[30]

On February 19th, John Black, U.S. consul in Mexico City, informed Washington excitedly, "It is reported here and I have no doubt there may be some truth in the report that Mr Bankhead has [today] passed a note to this Government asking the priviledge [*sic*] to land and pass through Mexican territory *twenty thousand* [Black's emphasis] English troops under the pretext of passing them to the Oregon territory. The English have some fixed and determined project in relation to this country and the non-consent of this government will not prevent their landing their troops, which will be done at all hazard and our country will be unprepared for such an event and we will find that the Oregon dispute will be tied up in Mexican affairs. The people here say they would a thousand times prefer annexation by the United States than submit to a foreign prince imposed on them by a foreign power."

Six days later Black ate his words. "You will see by *The [American] Monitor* that the number of English troops to pass through this territory has risen from twenty to thirty to forty thousand. Many think that no such application has been made." On March 14th, Black, now consul under John Slidell, special ambassador whom General Paredes snubbed, was again excited by news of the visits of the president himself to the British Embassy. He duly reported these to Slidell. "Paredes made no less than five distinct visits to Mr Bankhead at his house in the course of the day, an affair so extraordinary could not help but be noticed by the neighbours who, with reason, concluded that some very important business was about to be transacted between the Mexican President and HBM Minister." Slidell passed word to Washington, adding that even one visit "deviated from established etiquette," making Bankhead "a confidential advisor of the Mexican Government." Macnamara had taken out his passport for California the day before—John Black knew since he gave Macnamara a letter of introduction to American Consul Thomas Larkin in California—and the British conspiracy seemed to be confirmed. Bankhead's house was a known centre of intrigue. "Everything coming from California excites great interest here in the English circles. The British Legation is all alive on such occasions."[31] It was little wonder that Commodore Stockton, in 1847, advocated exiling General Paredes to St. Helena.

On the Pacific coast rumor and speculation were also rife. Thomas Larkin wrote to Jacob Leese at Sonoma north of San Francisco Bay that "England is all powerful, almost able to fight the world. Jonathan [America] will, in the case of a war with John Bull, receive some hard and ugly knocks for a year or so. He may take them patiently knowing John is growing old while he is just coming up the years and strength of manhood." The British seemed capable of anything. Much further north, word went back along the Oregon Trail in May that British soldiers in disguise were on the route as *agents provocateurs*, stirring up the Pawnee and Sioux to attack immigrant trains. In fact, two British travelers did set out in 1846 from Independence, Missouri, just ahead of the Donner party, in company with Francis Parkman, the pioneer diarist. One was an ex–Redcoat captain, the other was a London High Court lawyer, William Romaine. Parkman regarded the Englishmen as comic figures, Romaine an imperious fool and the captain an old woman. Their attempt at the Oregon Trail was an adventure holiday, a sporting sabbatical from England to see the mountains, and it was Romaine's second Trail journey.[32]

Sporadic rumor continued to bolster hopes and fears in California about the arrival of the Mexican expeditionary force, but only the French reported home in detail so late in the day. Perhaps the rumored French interest in the Yniestra battalion had been real. The French ambassador in Mexico City reported to Paris as late as April 29th that the expedition had "started to proceed slowly towards Acapulco where it should embark. Colonel Yniestra was to have embarked but he died in Mexico. General Juan Alvarez has risen in revolt [taking] possession of all the funds which the Government collected in Acapulco for the California expedition." From Mazatlán, a fortnight later, the French consul reported that "the Mexican Government despatched to Mazatlán a part of the troops composing the proposed expedition to California. A review was passed the other day. Little more than 700 men. Comandante General Gutiérrez flattered himself that the English Admiral would lend him his ships to transport this force to California. The idea was quite illusory. As for going by land, before the expedition would have made 100 leagues, desertions would have decimated the force. The officers and men are not particularly anxious to go to California. They have revolted and given Gutiérrez 24 hours to leave Mazatlán."[33]

Macnamara's Departure

On March 12th Eugene Macnamara visited Euan Mackintosh's Consulate and received his new *Carta* on the watermarked cartridge paper. There was no queue as only two others sought passports that day. *Carta di Seguridad* No. 455 in the Consular Register was issued, *gratis,* to *Eugine* (*sic*) *Macnamara, Religioso, Irlanda, resid. Mexico City.* No more detail was recorded. Unlike Theodor Hartweg, already out on the Mexican west coast with his London-bought rifle, Macnamara was unarmed and did not register for a gun permit. A day or two later he visited the British Embassy and received from Charles Bankhead dispatches for Alexander Forbes, acting consul in Tepic. Given the time Macnamara had on his hands in Mexico City, like a patient in a waiting room, it is likely that he had read Forbes' 1839 book on California more than once, as he had read Robert Crichton Wyllie's 1844 *Report.* Bankhead had already written a long dispatch to Admiral Seymour on March 11th which had just been sent to Tepic for Forbes to forward, but he wrote supportive letters of introduction for Macnamara to both Seymour and Forbes. Seymour later admitted privately to being struck by "so good a testimonial and strong recommendation."[34]

From the British Embassy it was a short journey to the archbishop's Palace between the Cathedral and the president's Palace at the center of town. Macnamara was a familiar visitor. Manuel de Posada y Garduno, archbishop of Mexico City, was a monarchist, a conservative and a nationalist. He succeeded as first Mexican-born archbishop in 1840 to a neglected diocese from which his Spanish predecessor, archbishop Fonte, had absented himself to Spain in protest for fifteen years. Macnamara had a good relationship with the archbishop and the understanding was extended to include Bishop García Diego of the Two Californias. Posada provided a letter of introduction for Macnamara and asked him to take mail for the bishop. Both bishops would see the Irish colony as a shot in the arm for California and for the church there, prostrated since the missions closed.

To a growing mail and document pouch Macnamara added the *Facultas* allowing him to preach and hear confession in French and English in the archdiocese. He also took the 1845 introductory letter from Cuevas to Don José Híjar at Monterey, although he knew Híjar was dead. It was still a valuable letter. Into the pouch went copies of the petitions he had placed before President Herrera in the early summer of 1845 as well as, presumably, some form of introduction from either Lanzas or Paredes. Finally, having arranged transport and guides, he rendezvoused with a companion for his journey, Frederick Beauchamp Seymour, Flag Lieutenant on HMS *Collingwood* and nephew to Sir George Seymour, British Commander Pacific. According to Admiral uncle Seymour later, the two became good traveling friends during the ten days on the road through Queretaro and Guadalajara to Tepic, where Consul Forbes offered them his famed roof and board. The public stagecoach, which went only as far as Guadalajara, allowed limited luggage and they traveled light, changing to horse and pack mule for the rest of the journey, rising each morning at 4:00 a.m. Theodor Hartweg had also been Forbes' guest from January to March, forced to wait for his considerable botanical safari baggage to arrive by mule train through winter in the mountains. Revolutionary armies, as well as travelers, needed mules. Hartweg left San Blas port for Mazatlán on March 15th. Macnamara and Lt. Seymour arrived at Tepic about a month later. San Blas was a long day, even two, away from Tepic and was no place to stay. "A vast swamp overflowing in the rainy season," one Royal Navy officer called it that month. Tangled forest tumbled down the slopes of San Juan behind the town to line the bay with a canopy of mangrove. The port was in decline by 1846, with only a ruined fort and an old Spanish dockyard to remind of its heyday.[35]

As Macnamara was negotiating a passage north, John Black in Mexico City reported belatedly to Washington on April 21st a visit he had received "some time since" from "an Irish priest who is a particular friend of the Archbishop and with whom I am on the best of terms." The priest had come from the archbishop and wanted Black to look into a delayed order of books for archbishop Posada from New York. Black thought the books a pretext. The priest had "turned the conversation to the question of Monarchy which had been agitated here, what course the U.S. would take if a Monarchy should be established in Mexico?" Black was an experienced diplomat and replied that the United States "would have nothing to say in the matter" if that were the Mexican people's will. The Irishman pressed: suppose a new Monarchy should "call in foreign aid and intervention to sustain such a government and that the federalists or those opposed to such a government should in like manner call in the U.S. for its protection and assistance, would the U.S. give assistance against the established Government of the country?" Black shifted his ground and referred the priest to President Polk's warning to Europe of December 1845. "I have since understood," Black continued, "that the Archbishop was much disappointed that England had not gone as far into this affair of Monarchy as was expected and in revenge for this disappointment he has hinted as a threat that he would be in favour of establishing 'one grand federation from Canada to Panama inclusive.' He still goes heart and hand in favour of Monarchy. He pants for the splendour of a court, but he goes the whole for a Spanish Prince and thinks any other would be tinctured with heresy. It is time for him to turn his throughts to another world, yet he clings as with youthful alacrity to the good things of this, as if he expected no other reward."[36]

Circumstances suggest the Irish visitor was Macnamara. He was close to the archbishop. He was privy to (and part of) the activity and excitement in British expatriate circles occasioned by the Mexican crisis. Black knew him well enough to provide a letter of introduction. It was said that he lodged with either Mackintosh, Percy Doyle or Bankhead. British Guiana clergy ordered religious books through an agent with branches in Baltimore and New York. Few Irish priests worked in Mexico, one noted by an American visitor who "at the convent of St Francis, Mexico City heard a sermon preached in English by an Irish priest for the benefit of the foreigners who spoke English, attended by about 100 people."[37] The only other Irish cleric, besides Macnamara, to register at the Consulate was John Urquhart, the roving Galway Dominican, and that for only two years, 1843 and 1844.

Two or three days after Black wrote to Washington about the Irish priest, Macnamara and Lieutenant Seymour boarded *Alexander Grant*, a 700-ton Cape Horn trader from Liverpool, plying the northwest Pacific coast. Macnamara would have recognized, from Guiana days, the bow nameboard, a leading West India Committeeman; he would also have met the son (and Mexican Bondholder) of the same name in the British community of Mexico City. On leaving Tepic the two had picked up mail for Admiral Seymour which had been overlooked at Consul Forbes' house. Forbes would have been intrigued by Macnamara and his project: the colonization he himself had advocated for years was now actively under way with the authorized *empresario* at Tepic already. Forbes had an added new interest. Barron and Forbes were mercury monopolists and the mercury mine of Santa Clara, California, discovered in late 1845 only a few years after the major gold strike near Los Angeles, threatened their business. Title had been confirmed in law to five proprietors—Andrés Castillero, government commissioner preparing for the

Yniestra force, Padre Real, priest of Santa Clara and Monterey, Lt. Col. José Castro, military Comandante of California and the Robles brothers, local ranch owners.

On April 15th Alexander Forbes wrote a letter asking for "correct information" on the mines and asked Macnamara to pass it to James Forbes in California: another document for the pouch. He also asked Macnamara to negotiate for him. James Forbes was privy to everything at the Santa Clara mine and two years later he reminded Alexander Forbes, "On his arrival in California, Mr Macnamara commenced his negotiations to obtain an interest in this mine, as your agent."[38] Macnamara's mission was increasingly complicated. A European colonizer, approved by a conservative anti–American Central Government, was sufficient defiance of the Monroe-Polk doctrine to provoke war. He was now, in addition, a mineral speculator and agent for the leading British merchant-diplomats of the Mexican coast. He was also a Catholic cleric who attacked American Protestants, although some of that may have been rhetoric to impress. As *Alexander Grant* left the shallows of San Blas bay for deepwater Mazatlán, four days and 150 miles away, Macnamara probably had no idea how deeply he was immersing himself in Californian and international politics. His next encounter, with the Royal Navy, which was to last six months, would also confirm in the eyes of others his role as European government agent and London speculators' front man.

Alexander Grant rounded the Tres Marías islands to take up the Trade winds. Once they were pointed out to him, Macnamara recognized the three Marys of Calvary from his scripture study—the Mother, the Magdalene and the wife of Cleophas. Every name in Mexico was rooted in Catholic piety, the legacy of the Spanish mission orders. Friar Juniper Serra had sailed for California from San Blas in 1769 to found his chain of Franciscan missions. Serra was the first to style himself "Apostolic Missioner" in the region. European Spain had been anxious then to forestall British and Russian designs on the empty, temperate Pacific coast. Missions and fortresses were the spiritual and secular weapons of total conquest. Seventy-five years later, the California void was still unfilled. European nations, including Britain, were still contending with each other as well as with Mexico and the United States for a land still virtually empty. The friars had vanished, their impact on the native people and landscape limited. Eugene Macnamara was the last "Apostolic Missioner" and colonizer in the old European mold to enter California.

Six

The Dealer.
Mexican California 1846

Will John Bull and Uncle Jonathan have another box-
ing match, or will they, like relations that sometimes
differ about each other's pigs and fowls trespassing on
each other's premises, after calling each other hard
names, shake hands and again be friends?—(Ethan
Estabrook, USS *Constitution*, Mazatlan, 1846.)

The voyage to Mazatlán on *Alexander Grant* was the Irish priest's first
experience of the Pacific. Once out from San Blas, past the Piedras, the coastline to starboard gradually changed from green jungle to the bare bluffs and
foothills of the western Sierra Madre running down to the sea. The mosquitoes remained behind at San Blas and Mazatlán was burgeoning, "no longer
a rural village, but a commercial town, full of busy merchants and traders."[1]
Flag Lieutenant Frederick Beauchamp Seymour as a naval officer and aris-
tocrat would have been shown every courtesy by the merchant vessel's captain. This would have included sight of the wheel house and its chart table
with professional exchanges. Macnamara, while no professional mariner, was
no stranger to a ship's ways after three crossings of the Atlantic and many
crossings of Irish and English channels. The officer reported to his uncle that
they got on well.

Contrasting Voyages

As they sailed northwest, William Clancy was also at sea, heading back
to Ireland from British Guiana. After two years of bitter exchanges between
the rival bishops, Clancy had finally gone, stripped of all dignity. Rome, London, Governor Light, the colony courts, clerical colleagues, the press and an

increasing number of local Catholics had turned against him. The Pope took away his title. Mental suffering compounded the physical, creating a lonely, prematurely aged man. West Cork in 1846, a year into the Famine, was no place for a sick man to return. The final exit was in total contrast to his grand entrance into the colony a few years before.

Bishop Hynes informed James Goold, his nephew in Ireland, of events in Georgetown, sometimes in a tone *The Tablet* would never have adopted.[2] Clancy was almost the last of the old mission establishment to go: Eugene Macnamara had left by the end of 1844; John McDonnell, Macnamara's Kerry-born colleague, had sailed for Europe in May 1845, after hanging round Georgetown as an outcast, accused of drunken advances to a wealthy plantation lady. Hynes was relieved to see him go. McDonnell adopted the Christian name Charles on joining the Jesuits in France in July 1846. He spent a year in (French-speaking) Quebec as the coffin ships were bringing the Irish Famine immigrants to quarantine at Grosse Isle, then went south to Fordham, New York with the Canadian Jesuit mission, where he died in 1852, aged 38, under his original first name.[3]

Clancy's state of mind was masked and muted by his illness. The noisy congregation at his breakaway Presbytery-Convent-Conventicle dwindled, although its hymns still disturbed Hynes in the next-door church, "captured" from Clancy late in 1844. Clancy registered 400 baptisms between June 1844 and his last on April 11, 1846. Hynes noted Clancy's movements over eighteen months. The postmaster kept Hynes informed of incoming and outgoing mail. Spies reported with gusto and spiced the boredom of British Guiana. Clancy fired off anonymous letters to local clergy, leading Catholics, members of Parliament in London, "written with the most hellish intent," and to Hynes himself, "in devilish spirit. I am not safe in person or character so near this skulking assassin."[4] Clancy claimed that letters from Rome told him that Hynes was being recalled by Pope Gregory; Hynes, with copies in front of him, countered that Rome was ordering Clancy to leave by Christmas on pain of excommunication.

Hynes watched one Saturday as Clancy strode out in "full pontificals" to attend a funeral, the week he was said to have downed 22 tumblers of brandy and water at a party. Catholics washed their hands of church, including converts who had been Clancy's mission trophies. By October 1845 "Georgetown is full of reports about Clancy's scandalous behaviour during his late trip to the Masaruni [penal settlement]—constantly inebriated. He is more painstaking in his wickedness than he ever was in the discharge of his duties." Clancy was found drunk in the street and drunk on his hospital rounds. In the colony's humid hot season, many who could not escape the dehydration, the lassitude, the boredom, the constant discomfort, the frustrated ambitions, the career backwater, the mosquitoes and sleeplessness which were British Guiana, drank to blot it out. Clancy had much to forget. "Another year has passed without ridding us of the wretch," groaned Hynes to his Diary on January 1, 1846.[5]

Clancy appeared to be in serious need of money. This concern even eclipsed the excommunication of January 1st. He had lost several court cases, with costs awarded against him. He held a yard sale (*vendue*) but few attended. He advertised for tenants to rent the presbytery, but Hynes warned the press that the building was not Clancy's to let. In the privacy of his Diary, Hynes was scathing about Clancy's Sunday services as "musters" or "demonstrations," the Presbytery-Convent as a "conventicle" and the remaining Presentation nuns as "Clancy's women." The small congregation of relatively simple people were "unfortunate dupes." In fact, the Apostolic Visitor became more vituperative the longer the ex–Apostolic Vicar remained. Clancy's presence corrupted Hynes. When Clancy sent more scattershot anonymous letters to destroy reputations, Hynes cried out melodramatically (and inappropriately, echoing Henry II on Becket), "When shall the world be rid of this assassin?"

The number of "dupes" fell, the singing stopped and the money ran out. In desperation Clancy stripped and sold the European roof shingles from the presbytery (March was still the hot season), took out the window panes and sold off a water butt which had been a gift to the church. "Two cartloads of trumpery" were driven from the presbytery to clearance auction and the doctor came to attend Clancy. More of his adherents returned to the official church and made public apology at Mass in front of Bishop Hynes. Clancy, the former anti–Protestant crusader, prelate of the Papal court and Count of the Holy Roman Empire, advised his remaining followers to join the Methodists rather than submit to Hynes.

Finally, on April 11, 1846, about the time Macnamara arrived at the Forbes house in Tepic, Clancy emerged from his presbytery "in a hired covered gig to pay his farwell visits. He looked terribly pulled down." Five days later at dawn, Clancy drove to the wharves. "Not a single white man, not a single respectable black or coloured person wished him goodbye. The house is in the possession of his ruffians, the gate is chained and an additional dog has been introduced. It is laughable, if not a little melancholy to see the little negro boy going about with Clancy's cap which he wears with no small pride."[6]) By noon that day, Hynes and two others had forced the gate and "captured" the presbytery. Clancy's lawyers climbed the gate to rant in the yard. Hynes stayed indoors. The police came three times to restore order and disperse a small demonstration on Brickdam, but by mid-afternoon "all was quiet." The sheriff sent Hynes the church registers which Clancy had put into his keeping. Hynes wrote to William Ewart Gladstone, Guiana plantation owner, to tell him of the episode.

It was August before Captain Riesen of the steamer *Parker* returned to report on Clancy's Atlantic crossing. "In a long passage and if water were scarce, [Riesen] would not desire to have a more accommodating passenger than that drunken vagabond Clancy, for during the entire voyage home he never allowed water to come across his face or hands." The Liverpool vessel was barely seaworthy, but Riesen had made Clancy haggle. Clancy died in Ireland in June 1847 and was buried in the grounds of Cork Cathedral.[7] He left a large, perhaps surprising legacy of £1,500 to two of the Georgetown nuns, by then back in Ireland in sympathetic convents, "for their mutual support and the education of poor children."[8]

As *Alexander Grant* sighted Mazatlán on April 26th, another bishop was preparing for his last journey. Francisco García Diego y Moreno, to whom Macnamara was carrying mail and a letter of introduction from the Mexican archbishop, took to his sick bed, "gravely ill and no longer able to attend to the business and pastoral care [of] this diocese." On April 20th he signed over his Episcopal authority to the veteran Franciscan missioners who made up his diocesan staff, Narciso Durán and José María de Jésus González Rubio. Ten days later he died at Santa Barbara mission where he had remained virtually trapped for six years, in a vast diocese which he could not cover, consisting of ruined churches, a diminishing number of priests, no funds, nominal Catholics and thousands of square miles of sheer wasteland. Not surprisingly, he died of "tuberculosis aggravated by acute depression."[9] Archbishop Manuel de Posada y Garduno also died in Mexico City that same day, a week after John Black had told Washington he should be thinking of "another world." Exactly a month later Narciso Durán, regarded as a saint (and an irrepressible practical joker), died at Santa Barbara, leaving Rubio alone as vicar general, the last Mexican cleric with authority over Alta California. At the same time in distant Rome, the conservative evangelizing Pope Gregory XVI died, remembered by enemies for his fear of railways, gaslight and liberals, but by admirers for his missionary zeal, condemnation of slavery and strengthening of the Papacy after its humiliation by Napoleon. He had laid out the stage on which Clancy, Hynes, Posada, García Diego, Durán—and now Macnamara—played their parts.

Admiral Seymour at Mazatlán

HMS *Collingwood* rode her anchors that Sunday, much more inshore at Mazatlán than she had ever been able to moor in the shallows of San Blas Bay. HMS *Spy* reported that HMS *Juno* was in sight: a lookout took *Alexander Grant* for the frigate expected up from Valparaíso. His eyes might have been suffering from the eclipse of the sun the previous day, recorded in the Admiral's diary. Seymour left nothing out. "Fine weather. Church service. Huge ship off, apparently that mistaken by the *Spy* for the *Juno*, the *Alexander Grant* of London. Dined in the Ward Room—the Rev Mr Macnamara dined aboard."[10]

Rear Admiral Sir George Francis Seymour (*F. Lucas, 1852; courtesy of the Marquess of Hertford, Ragley Hall, Alcester*).

Rear Admiral Sir George Francis Seymour was a veteran of Nelson's navy, a deck sailor from the age of 10. Both he and his father, also an admiral, had served on Nelson's flagship, HMS *Victory;* another admiral of the same vintage was Collingwood, to whom Seymour's own flagship and painted figurehead was a fighting memorial. Seymour took a pension at 28 with face wounds from French grapeshot, going ashore as an aide to King William IV and as a Lord of the Admiralty Board. He had served during the Anglo-American war of 1812, like the senior American officers who faced him on the Pacific in 1846. The experience and wisdom of a respected man as relatively "young" as 57 meant his recall to sea in 1844 to take up the sensitive Pacific command. He read, reflected, watched people and was intellectually inquisitive about the world around him. Physical fitness allowed him to swim ashore from *Collingwood* off the Mexican coast and take a five-day trek inland to see a silvermine. His landed aristocratic family had included the 16th century Queen Jane Seymour, third and favorite wife of Henry VIII (Tudor) and mother of the boy King Edward VI, Henry's only male issue.

The British squadron, mainly *Collingwood* with satellite frigates, sloops and steamer, had rounded Cape Horn in 1845 and made passage northwest via Chile, Peru and the Sandwich Islands. From Peru, in March 1845, Seymour signaled to Whitehall that he should be reinforced for a probable war with the Americans over Oregon and California. "At least 2 additional line-of-battle ships should be sent to this sea to provide for the essential services [including] to oppose or hold in check the ships of the U.S. Navy." He added wryly that the only two major battleships of his command, HMS *Collingwood* and *America*, were 6,000 miles apart on a station which stretched from Chile to Oregon. To worsen matters, he could barely provision. Mexico refused outright to allow British stores to be warehoused at Mazatlán or at Monterey; Chile likewise refused storage at Valparaíso. Seymour requisitioned the copper-bottomed Liverpool brig *Palinurus*, then in Valparaíso port, as a transport and store ship, placing it under temporary naval command. Months later and too late, Lord Aberdeen refused anything but a small increase of force, warning the Admiral that "the acquisition of British territory and of ports in the Pacific is a subject for Government [not Naval] considera-tion."[11]

Seymour's eyesight was no better for increasing age, wide reading and meticulous report and letter writing at night by candlelight. War injuries accounted for constant diary reports of headaches, toothache, insomnia and "headaching weather." After dining with Macnamara in the wardroom on the evening of April 26th and seeing his guest onto the cutter for the shore, he adjourned to his cabin where he used the small hours to write to Consul Forbes at Tepic and to Charles Bankhead in Mexico City, acknowledging let-ters Macnamara and nephew Frederick had brought.

> Mr Macnamara arrived here today in the English merchant ship *Alexander Grant* from San Blas and I had much pleasure in making his acquaintance. I wish he had taken up the matter of filling California with Emeralders some years earlier as the present prospect appears to hold out greater chance of its being inhabited by people whose objectives and moral qualities are not of so meritorious a nature. Mr Macnamara brought me your interesting letter of March 11th on Mexico and the United States politics which was mislaid at Tepic and not forwarded to me while I was at San Blas. Thank you also for the New York newspapers.[12]

Seymour had a soft spot for "Emeralders"—a gentler and less stereotypical nickname than "Patlander," "Mick" or "Potato Head" which went with the ape–Irish cartoons then appearing in *Punch* magazine in London. The Admiral's family ran estates in Ireland, like most English aristocratic families. Many crewmen in his squadron, including some Catholic officers since Emancipation, were Irish. His Protestant chaplain in naval uniform, Nathaniel Proctor of the Established Church of Ireland, came from Tipperary and had been through Trinity College, Dublin. On May 5th Seymour entertained to dinner Lt. Smith from HMS *Juno*, just arrived, a neighbor to a Seymour family Irish estate at Lisburn. Four times during his two weeks in Mazatlán, Macnamara was invited on board to the Admiral's table. The "intelligent young Irishman educated as a priest" impressed his host. The American newspapers provided news of the state of Ireland after the first Famine winter and Seymour's table guests, particularly Proctor and Macnamara, knew the land and its people, despite its being some years since they had last seen their homes. Conversation turned, inevitably, to the California Irish project. "I wish Mr Macnamara had better prospects in that direction for it is impossible not to be pleased with his apparent straightforwardness and intelligence. If I can help on his behalf, I shall do so as he is still here."[13]

Macnamara was truly stuck in Mazatlán. Commodore Sloat's command frigate, USS *Savannah*, 54 guns, then at anchor off Mazatlán with two U.S. corvettes and the British warships *Juno*, *Collingwood*, *Spy* and *Talbot*, was a deterrent to Mexican vessels from going to the California Department. The threat of war and fear of being trapped behind American lines were enough to stop most traders going north. Theodor Hartweg, the German botanist from the London Horticultural Society, had been stuck in Mazatlán since March 20th after he arrived from Tepic "in a small coasting schooner. I find to my great mortification that at present there is not the slightest chance of ships sailing for Northern California [and] no opportunity had afforded for the last six months. I approached Commodore Sloat for a passage to Monterey but was told in very few words that he cannot serve me. He could not let his movements be known [despite] their being well known weeks before he sailed!"[14] Hartweg gave up and planned to return to San Blas for a schooner rumored to be headed for California.

Macnamara was evidently in touch with Hartweg ashore—they may have been under the same innkeeper's roof. On May 8th Admiral Seymour decided to offer Macnamara "passage on board *Juno* as soon as she has completed her water."[15] The following evening, Macnamara was invited to dine aboard *Collingwood* once again, this time in the company of William Talbot, partner of Mott and Talbot in Tepic, and Robert Walkinshaw, the Barron and Forbes Company agent. Both merchant houses had been trading in California gold recently found in the San Fernando canyons. At the table Macnamara learned the good news of his passage, which would have been supported by special pleading from Forbes, who stood to gain by the priest's voyage. Macnamara took word back ashore and on the very next day, May 10th, Hartweg approached the Admiral. His cover letter from Lord Aberdeen would cut more ice with a British admiral than with a U.S. captain, now that a Royal Navy vessel was actually being sent north. "More successful was an application I made," Hartweg recorded in his Journal, "to Rear Admiral Sir George Seymour of HMS *Collingwood*, who kindly allowed me a passage in HMS *Juno* then proceeding to Monterey. Towards evening on the 11th of May I went aboard *Juno* and arrived at the quiet little town of Monterey after a passage of 26 days."

HMS Juno *to Monterey*

The evening they embarked for California, the two civilian passengers first dined on board *Collingwood* with Seymour and Patrick Blake, captain of the 26-gun *Juno*. The Admiral had already made a half-hour farewell inspection of the frigate in the afternoon. Dinner conversation would have touched on the fire and flares ordered in port the previous night to greet yet another revolution, this time against Paredes. "They were threatened with a fine if they did *not* illuminate!" Seymour noted wryly. General Gutiérrez, Comandante of Mazatlán, would have been a table topic too: he had boarded *Collingwood* to a 15-gun salute on April 18th to ask Seymour to carry the Yniestra battalion to California. "He was seasick. And he has not the manners of a gentleman" but it was for other reasons that Seymour refused the request. To justify the illuminations, Gutiérrez was run out of town by Yniestra's soldiers.

During the meal Blake made first acquaintance with his passengers, who outlined their purposes in visiting California. There was no operational secrecy about his own reconnaissance. "As it was known that Mr Macnamara and Mr Hartweg were to be embarked," Seymour earlier that day "advised Commodore Sloat the *Juno* was going to California to see what is going on." Diplomatically, Seymour did *not* mention that he had also ordered Blake "to examine the landing places near San Francisco [for] operations which may hereafter become necessary" and to find out more about the mercury mine

Forbes and Macnamara had discussed with him. "It will make the Americans more hungry than ever for California," he told Forbes on May 6th.[16] Two weeks later, Seymour confided in a letter to Captain Gordon of HMS *America,* brother of Lord Aberdeen, "I sent *Juno* to see whether the Californios had had the good sense to declare themselves clear of Mexico before it got them into a scrap! But I doubt they or any people with Spanish American blood in their veins having good sense about anything."

Sloat and Seymour dined, exchanged regular visits and played whist. Sloat had visited *Juno* on its arrival at Mazatlán after a salute of 13 guns and later sent over a chart of the Gulf of California for Seymour and Blake to copy. In Honolulu the previous October 1845, the two commanders had talked the political situation through at *Collingwood*'s wardroom table into the early hours. The rapport was good between the two old salts and former enemies—Sloat was nearly 70 and Seymour nearly 60—in charge of rival Pacific squadrons in a sensitive area.

Aboard *Juno* that night, after being rowed back from dinner on *Collingwood,* Theodor Hartweg dashed off a note to the London Horticultural Society to inform of his location.

> I have barely time to address you these few lines to let you know that I have at last obtained a passage to Monterey through Admiral Sir George Seymour on board H.M. Ship Juno. I applied to the Admiral yesterday and received orders to embark this afternoon.[17]

Blake ordered anchor weighed the following morning and set course northwest with southerly winds behind him. He had been at sea since 1813, and came from a minor blue-blooded family of aristocrats and admirals. His maternal grandfather was General Gage, formerly military commander in British colonial America. Blake's record keeping was brusque and may have matched his general manner. Passengers were entered on the Open Muster List as "Supernumeraries on Two Thirds Victual Allowance per order of C in C," which meant Blake was reimbursed for the expense and that Hartweg and Macnamara had to parade for muster roll each Sunday.[18] The entry was duly made in the logbook.

> 12th May Received the Rev Eugene Macnamara and Mr Theodor Hartweg Naturalist for a passage to California per Admiral's orders.

Seymour flagged them out of the Bay on the morning of May 12th and settled back to weeks of stand-by with a ship of 800 men—expeditions ashore, shell collecting, alligator hunting, cricket on the beach, letter writing, ship hull painting and reflecting on events. He did not want to go north before receiving further orders from London, so had to lie close to Mexico. It would be September at Honolulu before he would hear of the Oregon agreement in

June to the 49th Parallel between Britain and America. It would be mid–July before he, the Americans and the Californios heard of Washington's and Mexico City's final declarations of war in May. The battle on April 25th between American and Mexican troops north of the River Grande and Polk's final declaration of war against Mexico on May 13th spanned exactly Macnamara's brief time in Mazatlán, but news traveled slowly to the isolated Department.

A month later, about to leave the Mexican coast for California himself, Seymour wrote privately to a friend on the Admiralty Board, Lord Ellenborough. He harked back to the Macnamara project, which, despite its hopelessness, still excited him.

> It is evident that nothing but a large influx of British subjects into California could have had any lasting influence—Mr Bankhead sent me with a strong recommendation an active and intelligent gentleman, Mr Macnamara, educated as a priest, who had a scheme of taking 5,000 Irish to that Country and has gained some influence in Mexico—I ordered him a passage in *Juno* to California, arriving with so good a testimonial from Mr Bankhead and having travelled with my nephew from Mexico [City] who thought well of him, but I am afraid he is two years too late to be of any use in California.[19]

Patrick Blake ran a tight, perhaps demoralized ship: he had little time for "uneducated lower orders" and flogged some of them accordingly. *Juno* left Mazatlán after only a week's leave and replenishment, after being at sea 40 days from Callao. In that week one crewman drowned in Mazatlán Bay. It would now take the best part of a month, on the wrong side of the trade winds, to get from Mexico to Alta California and that without a single landfall. The frigate, half the length of the giant flagship, carried 250 men and boasted 26 guns, one-third the crew and armament of *Collingwood*. Macnamara would have had a tiny cabin, a junior officer's accommodation, and a hammock which would have been familiar from Guiana.

Two days out from Mazatlán, approaching Cape San Lucas on the Lower (*Baia*) California peninsula, the crew were assembled to witness Marine Taylor receive 24 lashes for insolence. On the first Sunday of the voyage, after muster call attended by supernumeraries Macnamara and Hartweg, Blake led Divine Service according to the rites of the national church. Macnamara may have absented himself, although many in the files of crewmen parading on the quarter deck were Irish of Catholic background. At 5:00 p.m. that evening they held a sea burial for Lieutenant Smith, the Lisburne man who had dined with Seymour on *Collingwood* only the week before.

When coastal fog and the distance from land allowed, they watched the desolate coast of Lower California pass by for what must have seemed an interminable 800 miles. An observer on another Royal Naval vessel was moved to note, "Lower California, although sterile, is from its formation, highly interesting. When the shades of evening have closed around, or before the daylight breaks, nothing can exceed the beauty or the magnificence of the barren peaks and cactus-covered rocks. The castles of feudal ages come before the mind in contemplating these extraordinary shores."[20]

For three more Sundays, the passengers attended muster roll call and Blake followed with Divine Service. Each day passengers and crew were issued their Navy ration of grog—rum, water and limejuice—though a Fr. Mathew medal holder passed on the rum. On Saturday, June 6th, as they prepared to come round Point Lobos into Monterey Bay, Blake paraded the crew for another flogging: a sailor was given 36 lashes for "continued dirtiness and taking another person's clothes." Since the serious naval mutinies of the end of the 18th century, a captain's power to punish had been limited to 12 lashes, but enforcement was difficult. HMS *Juno* dropped a single anchor in front of Monterey on June 7th. "June 9th Discharged Mr Theodor Hartweg, Naturalist," Blake logged tersely. Hartweg, normally a collector of detail as well as plants, recorded nothing of the four-week journey, not even the name of his sole fellow passenger. Life for him began again once ashore. "June 8th I delivered my letters of introduction and the following morning I settled down in the quiet little town of Monterey. The verdant fields and the pine-covered range of mountains at the back of the town form a pleasing contrast to the dried-up vegetation about Mazatlan." Macnamara also made his way into town, but the ship remained his lodging. Monterey boasted no hotels. Blake's orders had been to find out what was going on and to link up with Vice-Consul James Forbes. Forbes did not live in Monterey, but his ranch was near San José town, forty miles away. Word came back to Blake that Forbes had already gone south "some days previous," apparently to attend a convention (*Junta*) at Santa Barbara which Governor Pico had announced in mid–May.[21] *Juno* would have to go south to catch him up. Meanwhile, Macnamara had business in town.

The Speculators

Macnamara carried a letter of introduction from, among others, John Black in Mexico City. He made his way up the *Calle Principal*, intending to present this to Thomas Larkin, U.S. consul in Monterey who lived in the most imposing house in town. Captain Blake may have accompanied him to present credentials to Comandante José Castro, military commander in Alta California. Both Larkin and Castro, however, were away in Santa Clara, but the Franciscan Padre Real, former parish priest for the whole area from Carmel to San José, was in town and anxious to meet Macnamara, who in turn had been asked by Alexander Forbes to make sure he contacted the managing friar of the new mercury mine.

Alexander Forbes and Eustace Barron, his wealthy partner, then on a spending holiday in Europe, wanted the Santa Clara mine. Since its discovery late in 1845, an old cave had been enlarged into a mine by Padre Real and four Indian laborers. Indians had long used the vermilion-colored mercury ore (cinnabar) for face-daub, and even paint for the walls of Santa Clara church. The ore had a high yield, variously stated (sometimes deliberately *under*stated) at between 26 percent and nearly 40 percent, making the European ore from Almaden in Spain seem poor at 16 percent. The Santa Clara mine was later renamed New Almaden. Padre Real knew he was onto a valuable find, as did the other co-owners of the mine. With a minor gold rush near Los Angeles in 1842 and further gold prospecting going on, the mine was a stroke of luck. Its main shareholder was Captain Andrés Castillero, President Herrera's commissioner in California, preparing for the Yniestra battalion since mid–1845. No battalion materialized, but Castillero had another string to his bow as a renowned mineralogist. Alerted to the Santa Clara cave, he laid claim to it and was handsomely rewarded in Mexico with $5,000 cash and two leagues of land for colonizing. By law he could only own half of the 24 shares; Comandante Castro, Padre Real and two rancher brothers named Robles took up the other 50 percent.

War loomed with the United States and threatened the mine company's prospects; John Frémont made a point of coming down from San Francisco Bay to spend two days at the mine in January 1846; Consul Larkin sent mercury ore samples to Washington, just as he and Abel Stearns of Los Angeles had earlier sent California gold. Even if war never came, the overland immigrants still threatened the security of the find. Simplistically, the owners thought it would be safe if a British company such as Barron and Forbes agreed to rent and work it for a share of the proceeds. The arrival of Macnamara from Tepic by British naval vessel with an expression of interest by Barron and Forbes encouraged the Californios. Macnamara knew enough about the mine to impress—he had been briefed by Alexander Forbes; Forbes' agent Robert Walkinshaw, a miner and later administrator of the mine, had dined with Macnamara on board *Collingwood*. During a court case over claims to the mine in 1854, former Comandante Castro admitted, "Real and I considered Macnamara to be an influential person."[22]

José Maria Suárez de Real was a lively, forty-year-old who had come to California in 1833. He had seen the collapse of the missions under secularization, but his unorthodox lifestyle helped temper the isolation. He informed the bishop in 1846 that he was no longer accepting pastoral responsibility for the huge area between Monterey and San José, a move which may have been connected with the new mine, where he was, literally, deeply involved in excavating. British Vice-Consul Forbes regarded him as a friend in 1846, but years later spoke of his "reeking with concupiscence," having "several concubines at Monterey and a woman across the street from the Santa Clara mission."

In addition to a partner of his own, Suárez de Real had taken on the support of the children and two partners of his deceased predecessor at Santa Clara, Padre Mercado. The uncanonical but customary marriage of a priest was not uncommon in parts of Mexico. Rumor, which shaped California and constantly hovered over it like the raptors on the hot air currents, attributed to Real the disposal of mission furniture stored in his charge and, more seriously, the poisoning of his successor at Santa Clara in March 1846, before the latter even celebrated his first Mass. California thrived on gossip and considerable prejudice was shown by non–Californio settlers towards some of the last mission padres. Suárez de Real, who was also described as "a man of great shrewdness and learning," was so engrossed in the management of the mine and supporting his family, that he probably had neither time nor energy left to play the role of a Borgia. Bishop García Diego thought the Padre was tidying up his affairs while awaiting a Mexican ship at Monterey.[23]

Suárez de Real was waiting for Macnamara. The priests were strangers to each other and they both needed money. Macnamara had a secondary role as agent for the British merchants of Tepic. Real had mothers and children to support as well as himself, which could not be done on the trifling customary offerings which the Bishop reluctantly admitted were the only available income for his clergy. While the "ecclesiastical beggary" of these offerings made on the administration of the sacraments did not help a man's self-respect, whether in Mexico, Guiana or in Ireland, Macnamara did not even have that income on the road. Suárez de Real, on the other hand, could not leave California because of the danger of being disciplined in Mexico, thereby losing both his extended family and their means of upkeep. Comandante Castro, before establishing his headquarters at Santa Clara to raise a force against the rebellious trappers and Frémont in the north, left three pre-signed blank sheets of official paper with Suarez de Real, two of which the Franciscan used in transactions with Macnamara. With the third, the friar later bought an orchard.

Two days after Macnamara went ashore, he accepted an outright, unconditional gift from the Franciscan.

> In the port of Monterey, June 10, 1846, the undersigned co-owner of the mine of Azogue de Santa Clara, consigns through this instrument willingly and in perpetuity to Don Eugene Macnamara one share (*barra*) from the four which I hold the right to in this property. Witnessed by Juan Malarín and Antonio Pico. Signed by José María Suárez de Real.[24]

Two days later, Comandante Castro, *in absentia*, but through his signature on the official paper in Padre Real's keeping, gave Macnamara power of attorney to represent the mine owners' consortium.

> I give special, ample and sufficient power to Presbyter Don Eugene Macnamara that, representing my person and that of my associates, he may

contract with an English company to the exclusion of every other nation [to] work three properties of the mine for nine years, the products being one half for the owners and one half for the English company [or] two thirds to the English company, one third to the owners without charge. Witnessed by Jose Malarín, David Spence, Manuel Diaz, Antonio Osio [and over the signature of] José Castro.[25]

The transactions made Macnamara an even more "influential person," put a saleable asset into his hands and left him extremely well informed on mineral prospects in California. Real may even have taken him to see the mine. Macnamara's agreeing to take power of attorney, common business practice in Mexico where transport and communications were poor, saved Padre Real's skin and allowed the owners to feel that the mine was going into safekeeping— somehow under Crown protection—that old dangerous confusion which had long dogged Mexicans' dealings with the British. It was felt to be so important that they empowered Macnamara to agree even on the lowest possible terms.

Monterey was too small for secrecy and none was attempted. The arrival of a British warship was a newsworthy public event and the business of its passengers was followed with natural open interest. Larkin and Castro returned to Monterey and met the visitors before *Juno* sailed, but Larkin was disappointed that Blake had refused to bring mail from Mazatlán which might have clarified the state of hostilities between Mexico and the United States. On June 14th he wrote to his confidential agent, Abel Stearns, in Los Angeles, trading from San Pedro. Stearns was Larkin's—and Washington's—new eyes and ears in the south, a fellow Massachusetts man, Mexican citizen and owner of a vast acreage. Both men had also been exporting California gold to Washington for several years.

We have in Monterey the Rev. Mr Macnamara who arrived here from Mazatlan in HBM Ship *Juno*. The officers of the ship were by the captain prohibited from bringing letters. Mr Macnamara is a Catholic priest, an Irishman; has been in the City of Mexico all 1844 [*sic*] with Herrera; almost concluded a negotiation for the London Emigration Society to land ten thousand Irish in California. Paredes refused to allow any emigrant whose native language was English, adding that the Irish in California would join the Yankees at once.

Mr Macnamara dresses in Citizen clothes; has in my opinion full as much government and political information as theological. He and the captain of the *Juno* appear to be satisfied that no government course can prevent the destiny of California as it now appears to be going.

Mr Macnamara has correspondence for the Bishop; now goes south; will call on the Governor, I suppose. He brought to me letters of recommendation from our Consul [John Black] in Mexico City. He has a very good appearance; his actual business I presume to be of a private nature as Agent for his company to find available lands for the Irish. I should think his Government had cognizance of the business; perhaps affords assistance. Will you inform me of his motives and movements."[26]

The "London Emigration Society"

Like Bishop Clancy, Eugene Macnamara never hid his light (or lights he wished others to think he had) under a bucket. He had mixed enough with planters and financiers to know that even a hint of money and influence opened doors, especially mention of British investment money in Mexico. "The London Emigration Society," if it existed, left no record. Larkin, however, was partially deaf.[27] Macnamara had an Irish accent, however much leveled by residence abroad. A Clare man's saying "*Land and* Emigration Society" could have been heard by a Massachusetts ear losing its keenness as "*London Emigration Society.*" A Land and Emigration *Committee* did sit in London, offering advice on emigration to companies and groups, but only for those going to British territory. The full title of this Government body was the *Colonial* Land and Emigration Committee.

Perhaps Macnamara jumped the gun and thought California would be British territory by the time he and Seymour's naval squadron had finished. The Colonial Land and Emigration Committee would then be able to dispense help and advice, though not money. The Seymour Macnamara first met in Mazatlán was expecting "probable" war, with Oregon and California as the stake. A claim to "have almost concluded a negotiation for" impressive sounding London supporters could not be checked quickly in remote California. Macnamara seems to have made no such boast to Seymour, who would have known better. In January 1846 he had actually warned President General Paredes against Britain and her territorial designs. Twelve months before landing in Monterey, Macnamara had discussed the Land Committee with Ambassador Bankhead in Mexico, but at that stage he was simply floating ideas. He knew the Committee well from Guiana where it had been at the forefront of efforts to get immigrant labor. He may also have been prompted by *Tablet* reports in 1843 that O'Connell had founded a Catholic Emigration Society to press for state-assisted emigration which had stopped in 1828. Bankhead reported the conversation to Lord Aberdeen but evoked no response: "Macnamara can entertain no hope of an advance of money from Mexico, but he seems to think that if an additional grant of land was given in lieu thereof, he could raise money upon that portion in London, sufficient, with some aid from the *Emigration Committee*, to bring over his colonists to California."[28]

The Land and Emigration Committee dealt routinely but brusquely with cries for help from Ireland before and during the Famine. No request was recorded from Macnamara. "The large amount of spontaneous emigration out of Ireland means that HM Government has deemed it inexpedient to sanction any aid from public funds." One penciled endorsement noted that "Irish families are unacceptable on account of numbers of children." Subsidy was refused, but help was sometimes given in haggling over fares and in settling families "together in a body." Few land companies were willing to set up "villages" on the Wakefield model, therefore "we will only support emigration of tenantry if a Bond is put down by the landowners so that public money is not risked. Villages involve great risk in obtaining employment for 60 families in one spot." In February 1847 they rejected a plan to send an advance working party of convicts to Canada to clear ground and build log huts for Scots emigrants. A British consul in Texas warned the Committee to publicize the fact that a company calling itself the "British Mutual Emigration Association" had exaggerated the fertility of Texas and its directors were "men without character or influence."

Overall the Committee took the view that it was "no provision to throw great numbers of poor on large tracts of vacant lands," even through the respected Canada Company. Beyond the Empire there were simply "no prospects of appointing emigration agents to China," the Committee explained patiently to one inquiry, and warned another that "Ecuador is not a British settlement: beware of enlistment as soldiers for that settlement." Most revealingly, they told a Mr. Wright of County Monaghan on September 9, 1846, "the Government has not adopted any measure to promote emigration to the Oregon Territory and there are no opportunities by which emigrants can engage passage direct to that part of America."[29]

Larkin repeated Macnamara's claim, this time to the Secretary of State in Washington. "Mr Macnamara informed me that he was commissioned by a *private company* in London."[30] This definitely did not describe the Colonial Land and Emigration Committee and if it was not a reference to London-based Bond speculators, it was a sheer fabrication by Macnamara. Like Clancy, he used any available means to an end, especially re-creating himself to meet the need of the moment. A fortnight later in Santa Barbara he was further fabricating a tale of formal British Government support. Robert Crichton Wyllie, whose *Report for the Bondholders* Macnamara knew from Mexico, wrote to William Hartnell in Monterey in March 1844, "It is not improbable that the answer from the London [Mexican] Committee [of the Spanish American Bondholders Association] to my [*Report*] of December last from Mexico may lead me to visit California to determine how far English settlers there would enjoy greater advantages than in the Departments nearer to the Atlantic."[31] The Mexican Committee was, however, an informal private investor watchdog, not a joint stock company for raising money to colonize, let alone a subsidizing committee, although members did hold open land warrants from the re-shaping of the Mexican debt in 1837. John Diston Powles was vice-chairman of the Committee and chairman of the overall Association. His business partner, Euan Mackintosh, consul in Mexico City, with whom Macnamara had over a year's contact and whose colonizing plan for California was produced at the same time as Macnamara's, was their main agent. Powles wrote to Lord Aberdeen in May 1846 when Macnamara was in Monterey: his members begged the Government to intervene in the Mexican War, "to protect their commercial interests."[32] The dangerous confusion was being invoked once again. Two days later the Mexican Committee endorsed Powles' letter, although by then it was too late to save either their land option in California or their debt repayments. Unofficially Macnamara was invoking the same confusion to bolster his case, name-dropping, boasting, assuming a favorable change in Bondholder policy. Mackintosh must have told him in 1845 of Powles' and the firm's interview with Aberdeen, and Macnamara pinned too much hope on the success of their proposal. It may also explain his later bitterness towards "that asinine Aberdeen." Macnamara was overreaching, out of his depth in high politics and finance.

Powles alluded to Texas in his letter to Aberdeen. It could easily have been read as California and he may have meant it to be so; it showed that his and Macnamara's designs had nothing in common, and that they had never communicated. Powles turned failure to gain anything in Texas into lofty retrospective principle. He defended Mexico's part in the April incident on the Rio Grande and spoke glowingly of the "several hundreds of British subjects dispersed throughout Mexico carrying on their legitimate pursuits to the advantage of [Mexico and Britain]. If these persons were found to congregate themselves together in a remote and thinly populated province of Mexico and there to foment an insurrection against the parent state; then a declaration of separation and independence; and lastly an act of annexation to the British Crown, such a proceeding could hardly be viewed as otherwise than grievous towards the Republic of Mexico and not calculated perhaps to attract a moral sympathy in any quarter. It is now a matter of historical record that when the signatories to the act of annexation of Texas came to be examined, they were found to be nearly all those of strangers and not of native Texians [*sic*]."

Eighteen years later, Powles regretted that *no* colonization company was ever set up by the Bondholders. "California was one of the places specified in part satisfaction of Bondholders claims [in 1837]. Land warrants were issued. The Bondholders did not form any organisation to take up those lands. They trusted to the chapter of accidents to give—one day—a value to these lands. California subsequently fell into the hands of the United States. The British Bondholders lost by not taking possession when they might have done it without the least hindrance. They would by this time have had ample indemnity [gold discovery] for all the arrears of interest they gave up to the Mexican Government. Let not that lesson be lost."[33] Macnamara gambled on the launching of a private colonizing company in London to bring private money, just as he banked on Britain's eventual takeover of California to bring the public money.

HMS Juno *to Santa Barbara*

Captain Blake watered, provisioned and called muster on Sunday, 14th June, Macnamara answering as sole passenger. Three days later he gave orders to weigh anchor. Favorable following winds put *Juno* in front of Santa Barbara on June 19th, where "an American ship and a Sandwich Island brig at anchor" were observed. The following day, at single anchor inshore, *Juno* finally discharged Macnamara from the ration strength, but not before parade was held for another flogging, this time of six men who received 24 lashes each for insolence to the captain and disobedience of orders. Three days later, still at anchor, Blake ordered "four Marines flogged with 24 lashes for insolence and theft." Macnamara may have been glad to exchange the Navy's hospitality for more congenial company at the mission and a hammock for a bed. He already knew from Larkin at the last minute that the bishop was dead.[34] He was also, like Blake, under the impression that James Forbes was at the Santa Barbara Convention. In fact, the *Junta* had been canceled on June 13th by the Departmental Assembly in the same town and Forbes, under explicit orders from Lord Aberdeen in London to show no sign of British interest in intervention as long as Mexico still ruled, was more anxious to see Governor Pico at Los Angeles about a large grant of land in northern Alta California. He was one of many. Leading residents of Mexican California saw the writing on the wall and rushed for the land on offer in May and June.

Macnamara made contact with the Mission, still a Franciscan house thanks to a local Irish settler and doctor, Nicholas Den of Kilkenny. Den, the mayor or *alcalde* of Santa Barbara, leased the Mission and its eight league ranch for an annual rent of $100 in gold, adding to his small 3½-league ranch on the coast. This saved the Mission from being bought by a hostile buyer under the long, drawn-out secularization program begun in 1833. It also gave the diocese some revenue. In 1841, Den had also persuaded Bishop García Diego to live at Santa Barbara instead of at the designated seat of the diocese at San Diego and, although García Diego's dreams of palace, cathedral and theological seminary never got beyond piled stones, it was at Santa Barbara that he died in unpalatial but secure dignity. Padre Gonzáles Rubio, the remaining authority as vicar general in the diocese, informed Macnamara of the subsequent death of Padre Narciso Durán on June 1st. They would have paid their respects at the two fresh graves in the altar sanctuary. Turning then to practicalities, Rubio needed help and Macnamara in turn would have been glad of an official role to justify his title of "Apostolic Missioner" as well as any customary offerings forthcoming. On June 29th Macnamara's archdiocesan *Facultas* was accepted and extended to the Californias.

> Permit to hear confession and preach in English and French granted to the Priest Eugene Macnamara, native of Ireland and passing through this diocese, under the same terms as granted by the Archbishop of Mexico.[35]

They still talked of a previous Irish priest who had worked at Santa Barbara and had his letters on file. In 1837 Patrick Short of County Armagh,

former Irish College student in Paris, tutor in Mathematics at the Rue Picpus and exile from Honolulu, came to Santa Barbara after two years teaching at William Hartnell's ranch school near Monterey. Durán asked him to
take on Mission Purissima at Lompoc, just north of Santa Barbara, as a permanent charge, but Short declined the offer and left.[36] Hartnell and Larkin
in 1846 were still in touch with Short, by then teaching in Valparaíso.

The Santa Barbara Junta

On May 13, 1846, Governor Pico had called for a General *Junta*, or
Council of the United Towns of California, to be held at Santa Barbara on
June 15th. Fourteen members representing Sonoma, San Francisco, San Jose,
Monterey, Los Angeles and San Diego were to be elected on May 30th. To
these Pico added the seven members of the Legislature (the California
Assembly or *Deputación*), five soldiers and five clergy. In the absence of any
Mexican relief force, they were to address the California crisis. It was, in fact,
a Council of Despair, but the idea came from Juan Bandini, elder of the
Departmental Assembly and chairman of an emergency security committee.
Twelve of the total 32 would form a quorum: Pico knew that northern members might not appear if Comandante Castro objected. The north was less
enthusiastic to break from Mexico anyway and Castro had not been con-
sulted.[37]

Stearns alerted Larkin from Los Angeles the following day. "[At the
Junta] California will look for friends in another quarter. Overtures have been
made by British agents to the governor of California to declare its independence, at the same time requesting to declare itself under the protection of
that government and offering guarantees. This I am certain of." Again, rumor,
distortion and paranoia were shaping Californian reality. Stearns also noted
that Castro had asked to meet Pico at San Luis Obispo. Larkin replied that
he wanted Stearns elected to the *Junta* and would meet him there "at the
time." He hoped Juan Bandini, Stearns' father-in-law, would be there too.
Turning to the north, Larkin wrote asking Jacob Leese and General Vallejo
in Sonoma to come as members: otherwise, to come privately. Turning to
Britain was not the only direction the *Junta* could take. On May 26th Larkin
told Stearns that Consul Forbes was at Monterey, en route from San Francisco to Santa Barbara. Forbes was after land from Pico in the final handout,
"to enrich his children." Forbes dismissed the rumors Stearns had heard as
"entirely false respecting any offer made by British agents [although] it was
a common idea. The Governor may obtain sufficient from Consul Forbes to
give up any idea of looking to England." Forbes told Larkin that London
would "view with much dissatisfaction any other nation that interferes with
Californian affairs." Larkin later observed dryly, "Britain is welcome to *view*,

but events must have their natural way." Forbes also made the same disclaimer to the French consul, Gasquet, in Monterey.

Comandante Castro was a Paredes supporter. For a time he had rejected the appointment by Herrera of Governor Pico in 1845. Now he reacted with apoplexy. Frémont and the overland immigrants were on his mind and on his territory. Pico's *Junta was* "treason." (That very week, however, he had agreed to a "treason" himself, the transfer of his mercury mine to the British, with Macnamara's help.) From Santa Clara on June 8th Castro muddled his metaphors through indignation and brandy. "The insane hydra of discord … aborted … this most abominable scrawl … assassinating … the bosom of the mother country … a dangerous club … this volcano whose lava consumed … our rights [and] converted liberty into an abyss of evils … illegal, subversive, anti-constitutional, illiberal." Martial law was the only "legal resort" for security. Larkin saw a copy and acknowledged the writer's spirit: "If strong is well, it is certainly well written."

On June 1st Larkin told Washington that Forbes had promised "he would neither publicly nor privately advise the Governor to look to England and that if he was a private man he would advise to look to the United States. He wishes to meet me in Santa Barbara." Larkin suggested the *Junta* ask President Paredes to sell California to the highest bidder. On June 12th it was accepted that the Santa Barbara *Junta* would not happen, due to Castro's boycott. That day Stearns wrote that the Assembly had "deferred" the *Junta*. Larkin had already notified Forbes at Santa Barbara and Bandini at Los Angeles that he would not be coming. He told Stearns on June 14th that he had to wait for USS *Congress* from Honolulu and that he was "well informed that the Junta will not convene."

The Macnamara Petition

The day he brought *Juno* into Santa Barbara, Captain Blake paid $25 for a courier to James Forbes, by then in Los Angeles, one hundred miles south. Forbes' reply came on June 23rd and Blake sailed immediately to meet him at San Pedro port, near Los Angeles. He delivered a letter from Seymour, but found Forbes ill and anxious to return with *Juno* to the north. Having Forbes on board for some days was, for Blake, an efficient way of gathering intelligence while on the move. "I have availed myself much of his information."[38] Juno sailed into headwinds, doubling the two-day journey back to Santa Barbara. Forbes testified years later that he had gone "to Santa Barbara from San Pedro on learning that Eugene Macnamara had arrived at Santa Barbara" and that he had met Macnamara "at the start of July in Santa Barbara."[39] No record was kept of any meeting ashore and Blake did not log Macnamara's having re-boarded *Juno*.

On July 2nd, "The Governor of all the Californias came on board at 12.30. At 4.30 the Governor left. Saluted him with 15 guns."[40] Blake later told Seymour he had "had some interviews" with Pico and considered him Governor in "little more than name," although "well meaning, honest and generally popular." The four hours of talks between Pico, Forbes and Blake, representing the admiral as senior British official on that coast, were not recorded. Pico had composed a letter to Forbes at 1:00 a.m. on June 29th, informing him that "a multitude of invaders from the United States of America have entered [northern California], taking possession of Sonoma and tearing the Mexican flag to pieces. I have not had confirmed news that there has been an open declaration of war with that power. [The American settlers] are trying to have this section of the Republic of Mexico present as sad a picture as the Department of Texas, practically consummating another great theft." He knew an American warship in San Francisco Bay was also secretly helping the invaders. Pico had a copy of the Bear Flag proclamation of June 18th: "a band of bandits."

Pico intended to fight, but wanted to inform the British Consul that "the shores are unprotected and exposed to be occupied and blockaded by the American war vessels. Great Britain will doubtless give her protection. I solicit help for the Mexican Departmental Government as there is on the coast a [British] war corvette, in the hope that this will be enough to stop the Americans." It was a childlike belief in the power of a British sloop. Had Pico been able to omit "Mexican Departmental," then Blake and Seymour would have been enabled, even required, by London instructions to act in defense of a free California nation. They would, however, have to prove afterwards they knew nothing of the formal declaration of war between the United States and Mexico, which made dependent California a legitimate target and prize of war for the Americans and automatically neutralized Britain. The situation was fraught and the 15-gun salute probably did little to soothe the disappointed guest on his leaving. They were the only British guns fired on his or California's behalf.

Pico exhibited confidence in approaching the British. Given Forbes' London instructions and his avowed opposition to British interference, this confidence was hardly inspired by Forbes. Californian rumor did Forbes some injustice over his role in the Santa Barbara *Junta*: feeling ran high and the British, the old enemy, were thought capable of anything. However, Eugene Macnamara did approach Pico in Santa Barbara on June 24th to present copies of the petitions he had made to the Supreme Government in 1845, as well as Cuevas's letter of recommendation to Híjar of August 1845. The letter asked not only that Híjar help, but also that Pico be closely involved. Pico listened, but his mind was elsewhere. Years later, under oath, he denied emphatically, but awkwardly, that he had had discussions with Macnamara about placing anything under British protection, either a mercury mine or California itself.

He certainly passed on Macnamara's petition to the Assembly in Los Angeles, which passed it to Bandini's emergency committee. Macnamara appears to have been making his way south to Los Angeles, on July 1st, to meet both Bandini and the governor when he met Pico returning to Santa Barbara from Los Angeles to meet Forbes on *Juno*. He now had an exact location of land for Pico to approve, subject to the findings of the Assembly. "I don't even remember to have conversed with him more than half an hour," Pico later testified, "and my only recollection is that it related exclusively to the land he sought. It was on that occasion that I made the grant to him. Macnamara continued and met Bandini in Los Angeles."[41]

Wednesday, June 24th, had seen Macnamara's first mention of the San Joaquin Valley location for his land grant. It departed radically from the strategic coastline areas previously suggested—San Francisco, Monterey and Santa Barbara. Either the idea had been planted by a Californio adviser in his first days at Santa Barbara, or it had developed from a suggestion made by someone in Monterey the previous week. The Prefects of both towns had jurisdiction over the parts of the Valley nearest them. It was also the first time that "internal peace" was listed, along with "enemies who might invade," as a purpose of the colony. César Lataillad, Spanish Vice-Consul at Santa Barbara, to some extent Macnamara's mentor there, spoke of "the robbery of the Indians" a week before Pico himself spoke of resisting the "invasion of the savages." The advice may also have come from Rubio: despite every intention, the Franciscans had never penetrated the Central Valley. Certainly departmental security was a consideration in the Macnamara grant—in fact, in Californio eyes it was almost its *main* purpose. Everyone feared the Indians on the San Joaquin, impeding settlement on the grants made before 1846 and using the Valley as base and retreat for attacking property nearer the coast. Coincidentally the American settlers also invaded directly across the eastern mountains behind the San Joaquin.

It could also have been that the wary Californios wanted foreigners well away from the coastline, as Mexican law expected, but which the powers of a dictator like Paredes, on which Macnamara was acting, could easily overrule. It could even have been the lure and the lore of gold in the mid–Central Valley, known to the clergy of Santa Clara among others and possibly confided in Macnamara: Suárez de Real was by now a well-informed amateur mineralogist; Alexander Forbes, William Talbot and Robert Walkinshaw helped educate Macnamara in California's mineral prospects. César Lataillad, also enthusiastic that the colony be part of a cordon around California's frontiers, was the bridge between Macnamara and Bandini, the great mineral prospector of southern California, who came to see Macnamara as a future mining developer.

The land in the flood plains of the San Joaquin, known also as the Tulares (Swamplands), with its tributaries La Porciuncula (Kerns River) and Tres

Reyes (Kings) River, was an attractive proposition for agriculturists, if only it could be made safe and irrigated. Of thirty San Joaquin land grants made between 1836 and 1846, some were still being abandoned in mid–1846 because of the lawless state of the Valley. As late as 1852, John Frémont on Las Mariposas grant in the foothills, claimed still to be in fear of the Miwok and Yokut tribesmen. Tarantula and mosquito, reinforced by cholera and malaria, also defended their territory.

Whether or not Macnamara was aware of the grave dangers facing settlers in the San Joaquin, particularly east of the river up to the Sierra Nevada foothills, he petitioned for that specific land. He was there, he said, "to select land adapted to my object of colonisation, already exhibited, to the Governor."

> I contract to introduce in the shortest time possible 2,000 Catholic Irish families, industrious and sober, the whole of whose number would be 10,000 souls, subject to the established laws and to lend their services in defence of California against all enemies who might invade her, maintain internal peace and dedicate their efforts to this country. I solicit in ownership, the land selected between the River San Joaquin, from its source to its mouth and the Sierra Nevada. The limits being the river Cosumnes on the north and on the south the extremity of the Tulares in the neighbourhood of San Gabriel. I beg your Excellency to look favourably on my proposition, to the happiness of California, to propagate the holy religion we profess and to be helpful to my countrymen.[42]

Pico gave verbal consent, provisional on the advice of Bandini's committee and the Assembly. He would have expected to meet Macnamara again in Los Angeles to complete formalities. Macnamara made no *written* mention of government support from London, but he boasted of it in discussions down south no less than he had done with Larkin in Monterey. It is likely he mentioned it and his rapport with Admiral Seymour to impress during the half-hour on the hoof with Governor Pico, thereby increasing Pico's dangerous delusion about how much London and the Royal Navy were prepared to be involved in his crisis. It was after first meeting Macnamara that Pico requested naval help from Seymour. In the space of a week in Santa Barbara Macnamara impressed leading Californios by invoking Crown support for his project. Being a guest of the Royal Navy may have gone to his head. Larkin, who had also considered going to the Santa Barbara *Junta* in an impressive U.S. warship, decided against doing so, as "too imposing."

Macnamara certainly bragged to César Lataillad at Santa Barbara. Lataillad wrote on July 2nd to Juan Bandini, the elder statesman in Los Angeles, advising him that the Assembly wanted him to convene and chair the special committee with an agenda on claims to public land, including the Macnamara contract. Pico had already invited Bandini on June 23rd to the Assembly, but Bandini's health made his active participation in public life doubtful. Lataillad was impressed by the Irish scheme after conferring with

Macnamara, possibly in French. His letter recommended Macnamara very strongly and shows some knowledge of his mind. He also had his own land claim up for consideration by Bandini's committee of two.

The "10,000 Irish agriculturalists" Lataillad cited were Macnamara's "2,000 Irish families" of the previous day, allowing each family five persons and including in the paternal occupation the whole family. Lataillad supported, possibly even inspired, the Central Valley location, as part of

> a cordon of lands between latitude 38N and 31S [the San Joaquin estuary to the Colorado estuary], a secure barrier of holdings in the interior to resist the robbery of the Indians and prevent the secret and scandalous entry of the Americans of which Sonoma [the Bear Flag uprising] was a recent example. The land would be the colonists' property, although they would not inhabit for two or three years and Great Britain would make sure that no one from anywhere else would squat on their possessions. It would be politic to respect titles already conceded in the Tulares [San Joaquin] area.[43]

Lataillad emphasized Macnamara's support from the British Crown. Under Britain's constitutional monarchy, the "Crown" was the government of the day. The claim could only have come from Macnamara, who understood and used the dangerous confusion Mexicans, other South Americans and, indeed, the British themselves made of British government with British private business. The Land and Emigration Committee was a government, and thereby a Crown body. Lataillad continued,

> Macnamara had his difficulties in Mexico because it appeared that the costs of the voyage would be incurred by the [Mexican] Government, but in the end the colony will be subsidized by Her Britannic Majesty as regards the expenses, with huge resources placed at the disposition of this colony whenever it shall be agreed by this Departmental Government.

The Irish *empresario* was continuing the line he had fed to Larkin and others in the north, strengthening his petition, boosting his image as an important person and feeding more grist than ever to the Californian rumor-mill. Even though the story had changed several times in two years, its various versions could not be checked for months, if at all. In his own mind, too, he was probably naively convinced that London would annex California. Talk of untapped gold, silver, copper and mercury must also have influenced his thinking.

In 1858 James Forbes noted in testimony that "Macnamara left Santa Barbara for Los Angeles the day I left Santa Barbara on *Juno* for the North [July 3rd]." The day was inaccurately recalled, but Macnamara did go to Los Angeles to confer with Juan Bandini. As he made his way, he must have known that the card he was pretending to play, that of both private and British Government support, was, "in the end," bound to be shown for the brag that it was. His own grandiloquent blarney, like that of Bishop Clancy, rebounded on him.

Seven

Contract.
U.S. California, Hawaii, Mexico, 1846

When we had harpooned the whale, the British left us to make the most of the blubber and the bones—(Walter Colton, USS *Congress,* California coast, 1846.)

A hundred miles of road led southeast from Santa Barbara to the *pueblo* of Los Angeles. With early rises and changes of horse at hospitable ranches, as was the local custom, Macnamara could complete the journey in two days, despite the baking heat. Behind him, Blake and Forbes headed north in HMS *Juno* for San Francisco. Captain Blake had agreed with Macnamara a provisional rendezvous at Monterey on July 20th. The clockwise trade winds of the eastern Pacific favored Blake no more than they did Admiral Seymour, well out to sea and at times becalmed on a 3,600-mile detour from the 1,200-mile direct course between San Blas and Monterey. Seymour remained philosophical, sorting papers, reading Henry Dana on California and generally making good use of "a circular journey of learned leisure, 32 days from San Blas, as continual contrary winds took us halfway across the Pacific."[1]

Seymour to California: "A Lottery of Blanks"

On June 13th when Blake and Macnamara were still at Monterey, Admiral Seymour decided to go north from San Blas to meet them at Monterey. He had left Mazatlán for San Blas at the end of May to be nearer Alexander Forbes and the diplomatic pouch at Tepic. An express letter arrived on June 13th from Consul James Forbes informing Seymour of the *Junta* called by Pico "to get a protectorate."[2] Forbes indicated that southern members of the *Junta* would be divided between France and Britain, the conservatives for France, the others for Britain, but not really believing that Britain would act. The northern delegates would want a U.S. protectorate. Seymour decided to go to Alta California "to see if *Juno* has taken part." Blake lacked authority as well as firepower to make crucial on-the-spot decisions. The previous week, Commodore Sloat had openly headed north from Mazatlán in USS *Savannah*. Despite later legends, there was no semblance of a "race" between the two commanders. Sloat had waited more than two weeks after hearing news of the aggression on the Rio Grande and then had only assumed a state of war with Mexico. Seymour, further south and in another harbor, waited one week more and then proceeded. Inertia simply seemed a worse alternative. "I go with full expectation of seeing a Yankee ensign flying there. I have little authority for making the bite I wished, so it will be of little use to open my mouth."

Two days out from San Blas, he wrote to a friend in the Westminster Parliament, "As our government have not made a footstep in the concern, I shall not do so for them, without a fair chance of doing so finely. Things have not laid straight this side of Cape Horn and I am left to guess my way through the difficulties." As San Blas and its mountain shrank out of sight he wrote to another friend, Lord Ellenborough, a former colleague on the Admiralty Board, "In going to California, I am drawing in a lottery in which nothing remains but blanks, but I take the only chance of retarding the unfavourable result. I shall visit that Province in no sanguine temper, but desirous of judging if its situation is irredeemable. If I find on my arrival at Monterey that no good is to be done, I shall not stay longer than is necessary to assure myself of the safety of British subjects." Ellenborough thought San Francisco Bay was as vital to Britain as Malta and Corfu in the Mediterranean; during the Oregon crisis he had urged Lord Aberdeen, "while we are about it, to take possession, while we can, of the key to the north west coast of America."[3]

American propaganda and messdeck yarns made of Seymour a petulant loser and a nautical buffoon. Legend ignored the facts and, more importantly, the rapport between the two veteran flag officers. That Seymour and Sloat had fought on opposite sides in the 1812 war was a bond which civilians could not fathom. It was the same bond of respect between former enemies which created the Americas Cup Challenge at the end of that decade. Precisely by not trying to "race," Seymour missed the favorable winds which took Sloat to Monterey by the beginning of July, only 22 days out from Mazatlán. On July 3rd, as Sloat was at anchor off Monterey and Macnamara was briefing Juan Bandini in Los Angeles, Seymour wrote of his interminable voyage as a "circle, the centre of which is Monterey. Winds hang to the northward enhancing the tedium which places us out of the world for many weeks at best. This voyage abounds in learned leisure." Scurvy affected the crew; chair baths were rigged for hygiene, but it remained mercifully cool and no awnings were needed. They spotted (and shot) huge brown birds which Seymour verified as albatrosses from Captain George Vancouver's 1798 account of voyaging in the eastern Pacific. A class-conscious Royal Navy "skylarked after Quarters [sunset], the men divided from the petty officers on opposite sides of the becalmed ship." "Skylarking" was rough horseplay, sometimes "sky-high" in the rigging or on the tops, as a safety valve at the end of the day. Sunday brought more rest and a variation on tedium with Chaplain Proctor's sermon: "Not sufficiently plain and too declamatory."[4]

A young midshipman on Sloat's *Savannah* was sure that "Admiral Seymour had been following us for several months." Thomas Lancey on USS *Dale* heard that *Savannah* had staged mock hangings out at sea to put Seymour off guard, until he assumed she was heading out for yet another hanging. Mushrooms kept in the dark, the crew below decks recreated the world above. A landsman in California passed on the tale that Sloat had kept news of the Rio Grande aggression from Seymour, had sailed south after leaving harbor and had changed tack for the north under cover of darkness. Seymour, the legend continued, gullibly followed, heading in pursuit for the Sandwich Islands. The story improved with age. Ten years later, John Frémont's father-in-law, Senator Benton, recorded Seymour's incompetence as drawing room fact, not messdeck yarn: Sloat left Mazatlán "as if going to the Sandwich Isles," and thereby tricked Seymour who "went entirely to the Sandwich Islands before he was undeceived."[5]

El Proyecto Macnamara

On Monday, July 6th the deputies of the California Departmental Assembly convened at Los Angeles in Ordinary Session under Assembly President, Francisco Figueroa. His brother José had been Governor in 1835 and had shielded the Irish Picpus missioner Patrick Short at Monterey from a xenophobic Central Government. Macnamara's verbal request to Pico in Santa Barbara on June 24th, together with accompanying documents, had been referred to the Assembly. It was followed by the Irishman's formal written approach of July 2nd, already shown in outline to Pico on the road on July 1st. Three supporting documents, namely the two petitions presented by Macnamara to President Herrera before the summer of 1845 and the note of recommendation to Híjar from Foreign Minister Cuevas of August that year, were appended. The request was for 2,000 Irish families totaling 10,000 members to be given land from the eastern bank of the San Joaquin to the Sierra Nevada mountains. The Assembly referred it to Juan Bandini's security committee of two, responsible for the public lands and new title grants; it consisted of Bandini, veteran of the Híjar-Padrés colony, and Santiago Argüello, former soldier and Prefect of Los Angeles. Bandini gave notice that due to ill-health this would be his *finale* in public life.

The following day, July 7th, the Assembly met in Extraordinary Session to accept Bandini's and Argüello's judgment. It was passed to Pico with a covering note from Figueroa and Narciso Botello, respectively president and senior deputy of the Assembly. "This body agrees with the sentiments expressed by your Excellency, in your official [note] of the 24th of June, expressing your opinion and great desire that the said enterprise be carried into effect."[6] "The colony is not only useful, but in fact essential to this department," added Bandini, and recommended seven conditions which reflected both his caution and his experience.

The first three conditions were straightforward. One square league of land should be granted to each of 2,000 Irish families making up the 10,000 colony; sovereign public departmental land should be left between allocated plots. The colony should

> without prejudice to any third party, be on [*sobre*] the Rio San Joaquin in the direction of the Tulares, beyond the southern extremity of the Laguna Tulares, then up to the Sierra Nevadas, and then [in extension southeast] on [*sobre*] the Rio de Las Animas [Mojave] to the mouth of the Cajon de Muscupiabe [Cajon Cañon] on the north, to near San Bernardino.[7]

These remained the most detailed "verbal landmarks" outlining the concession. Surveyors and lawyers complained in later years on other sites that non-technical landmarks were all they had to go by, like the 19th-century chart and sand-table partition of Africa in miniature. "Over there" almost passed for precision. Bandini at least acknowledged that "third parties" had been granted land in the San Joaquin Valley already and existing titles were to be respected. The southeastern extension was also near "The Bandini Donation" by Cajon [de Muscupiabe] Pass, where in 1845 he had given land to several emigrants from New Mexico to found the colony of San Salvador, among them the Workmans from Ireland. Two years before that, he had allowed land there to an Irishman, Michael White. Any grant in that area had to be part of a defense strategy against Mojave raiding parties.[8] Jedediah Smith entered California in 1826 and 1828 along the Mojave River and through Cajon to San Gabriel Mission. Macnamara's request for land beyond the southern end of the Laguna Tulares took him, somehow, to San Gabriel. (The former wetlands of the Tulares had their southernmost winter limit just north of modern Bakersfield. San Gabriel is over 100 miles south of this, across Tejon Pass, the southwestern tongue of the Mojave desert and the San Gabriel Mountains. San Bernardino lies beyond that further still. Macnamara's advisers' topographical knowledge of the hinterland was vague.)

The fourth of Bandini's stipulations reflected the security crisis in

California. It was the most telling and yet the most ambiguous clause. The land should not be alienated to any foreign government or other owner, "nor in hypothecation or on any other pretext, without the agreement of the Mexican nation and the Departmental Government." The committeemen were on a tightrope, balancing national patriotism with the hopeless cause of Californian territorial integrity. Only a month previously, John Wilson had written from San Diego to Bandini asking him to overthrow Pico and declare independence to save California from a "foreign yoke."[9]

As a fifth amendment, the land should not be made over to *empresario* Macnamara in a parcel, but issued piecemeal as the colonists arrived, the total corresponding only to the number arriving. Congress in Mexico City was to be asked for several years exemption on essential start-up imports coming through San Pedro and San Francisco, the two ports nearest to access for the San Joaquin Valley, by the Estuary from the north and through Tejon Pass from the south. Duty exemptions on merchandise through Monterey and San Francisco should also be sought to the tune of 100,000 *pesos* per thousand colonists. That was already more than the Monterey Custom House, California's only revenue post, took in a year. Mexican customs dues were notoriously high and California's only public revenue. This generous final stipulation marked the despair of the moment.

The Macnamara grant was the sole agenda item for July 7th, a sign of its importance. As the seven deputies convened and deliberated in Los Angeles, Commodore Sloat sent his sailors and marines ashore three hundred and forty miles away to take the Monterey Custom House, the key to the success of the Irish colony. California became a forfeit of war and no longer Mexican territory. It would be some days before Pico, Macnamara, Bandini or Seymour learned of it, or that a formal state of war had existed since mid–May. Sloat himself did not know on July 7th, but acted on a presumption of war, spurred by Frémont's activity ashore. It was even rumored that he wanted to act earlier, on the symbolic July 4th. July 7th was later agreed by treaty as the date on which the legislative authority of the California Mexican Department came to an end. Neither Pico, his assemblymen, Macnamara nor anyone else could envisage this at the time. The legislature did not even dissolve itself until mid–August.

Bandini's work continued after the Assembly dispersed at noon on July 7th. On behalf of the committee, he asked Macnamara for further clarifications. A *diseño* or rough sketch map would have helped—it was required by law for grants, if not for contracts. He was being helpful, as well as thorough, when he asked,

> Firstly, whether of the land requested from the Rio San Joaquin inclusive up to the extremity of the Tulares on the south, you hold a plan or outline sketch, which might show local advantages and disadvantages. Please consider sending copies.

Secondly, how many square leagues do you consider it indispensibly necessary to have, to fulfill the colonising contract which you propose? If initially you do not have such a document, there should be at least a manifest of some sort, indicating which are summer grazing lands, the extent of colony lands in square leagues, the rainfall, watering places, irrigated land, rivers, streams, wells."[10]

Juan Bandini bowed out of public life on July 8th, unaware that it was the first full day of American rule in California. He wound up his outstanding correspondence, replying to César Lataillad in Santa Barbara and to James Forbes, courtesy Macnamara, who was ready to go north. He also wrote a note to Macnamara himself and drafted a circular to inform the Californios about the pending Irish colony.[11] Macnamara forgot to give Forbes, Monterey, his letter from Los Angeles and later apologized from Hawaii. Forbes had been in Los Angeles only recently and had time to converse with Bandini about the latest mineral finds.

"I have done what I believe necessary," Bandini told Lataillad, "to the good despatch of Priest Eugene Macnamara," and thanked Lataillad for recommending the scheme so strongly. He was now retiring "to the bosom" of his family for his health's sake.[12] To Macnamara he wrote of the mineral wealth of Alta California, "an immense quantity of minerals of all classes and in all directions. Gold, silver, copper, iron and semi-metals [mercury]. It is an Indian tradition that white water was found which you could not keep in the hand, between 30 and 34N Latitude and not far distant from the coast." Macnamara shared his letter from Bandini with Admiral Seymour on route to Honolulu, and the Admiral made notes on it in the back of his personal diary. "Bandini is at work in a copper mine which promises much with indications of gold and silver, but scientific miners are unavailable and he hopes to follow up his present experiments."[13] California's mineral prospects featured ever larger in Macnamara's mind.

Abel Stearns, the enemy's eyes and ears in the Department capital, followed events in Los Angeles with interest and good contacts. His single-story adobe, *El Palacio,* was a stone's throw from the Departmental Assembly house and Bandini was his father-in-law. On July 8th Stearns also wrote letters, including one to Larkin in Monterey, that "Mr Macnamara the Irish clergyman is here and leaves for Monterey. He has presented to the government asking for 2,000 leagues of land in the interior and on the River San Joaquin commencing north at the Arroyo Cosumnes and south or south east as far as San Gabriel. The Assembly has recomended favourably his plan of colonisation. The Governor will probably decree in his favour. He obligates himself to bring in 2,000 families and total number of souls 10,000, which if carried into execution will be quite an addition to our population." It would in fact have nearly doubled the settler population of the department.[14] Already, Indian riders had brought word to Monterey on July 1st of the opening shots between Mexico and the United States on the Rio Grande and of Macnamara's negotiations in Santa Barbara.[15]

It remained for Governor Pico to accept the Assembly's approval and refer Macnamara back to the Supreme Government. Either Pico had, as he later claimed, already conveyed the agreement, perhaps on pre-signed blank paper, dated ahead to July 4th, or he backdated the conveyance sometime in mid–July. Macnamara was back in Monterey, 250 miles from Santa Barbara, with Pico's signature to the contract by the time Seymour arrived there in *Collingwood* on July 16th. Pico was on the road north with his soldiers after the first week in July and, when the Assembly discussed Macnamara's colony on July 7th, was at San Luis Obispo. He reached his own Santa Margarita ranch on July 12th and reconciled with Comandante Castro there the following day, after hearing of the American capture of Monterey. Most likely, he backdated the formal agreement with Macnamara on July 12th or 13th at his ranch, where the Irishman caught up with him after leaving Los Angeles on July 8th or 9th. It would have required hard riding. The lengthy, detailed document was drawn up by José Moreno, Pico's acting secretary. "July 4th," the irregular backdating of the confirmation of contract, was a Saturday, a day when the legislature did not meet. It may have been a random choice, a taunt at American Independence Day or a devout, even significant acknowledgment of another, more important July 4, 1776, when Friar Juniper Serra refounded his first mission at San Diego, after its early destruction.[16] It was the main patronal feast of the new diocese, founded canonically on San Diego, but centered for convenience on Santa Barbara. Pico did note that the colony was, in part, for "the propagation of the Faith."

If, in response to Bandini's prompting on July 7th, Macnamara increased the number of settlers and thereby of square leagues petitioned, this would explain why Pico increased the contracted number of colonists by 50 percent in the final conveyance: *three* thousand families, totaling *fifteen* thousand persons, were each allocated a square league.

Considering the advantage to the country which would result from the occupation of those regions hitherto desert, alike in the advancement of agriculture and in the increase of commerce, the arts and industry, and in the propagation of the faith and that it would at the same time secure the Department from the frequent incursions of the savages who have heretofore diminished the wealth of the country by their repeated robberies; and moreover that the increase of the number of settlements by respectable families would preserve the national integrity and independence, supposing they would be so many more Mexican citizens in which case they would add to the growth of the country.

Having made the diligent examination required and using the powers conferred on me in the name of the Mexican nation and in accordance with the advice of the Departmental Assembly, I hereby concede for the colonisation of Irish families the land solicited by the said Padre Macnamara with the reservation of the approval of the Supreme National Government and under the following conditions.[17]

Pico accepted some of Bandini's advice and rejected the rest. He stipulated lands east of the San Joaquin River, with freedom of use but without right of alienation "either separately or as a colony" to any foreign country or of hypothecation to any other dominion unless with the consent of Mexico. He outlined the land within which the Irish could take the unoccupied portions, but compressed Bandini's extension to Cajon Cañon and the Mojave River to the point of identifying San Gabriel, his own birthplace, with the end of the Tulare wetlands. San Bernardino was not mentioned.

> In the interior beyond the twenty boundary leagues on the Rio San Joaquin from its source to its mouth and the Sierra Nevada, the boundaries being the Rio Cosumne on the north, and on the south, the extremity of the Tulares, in the vicinity of San Gabriel, without prejudice to paths, roads and public use.

If there were too much land for the colony, they might have other settlers, "any citizens or families whatever resident in the Department or others who have the legal requisites." The number of settlers was raised to three thousand families, each with a square league of 4,428 acres. If there were too little land in the prescribed area, "they must be limited to what is found. Should fewer than three thousand families arrive, all the excess of land between those limits shall remain for the benefit of the nation and may be allotted to Mexican families." Pico and Macnamara did not seem to know anything of the Council of Government's advice about European Spanish families or the amount of land to be granted. The San Joaquin Valley, east of the river, was quite inadequate for such huge tracts of land and some of its best had been granted away already. It was unsurveyed. South of the San Joaquin River were the wetlands, the Tulares Lakes. Beyond Tejon Pass, before San Gabriel, lay desert and mountain. Perhaps Pico was being consistent: a decade previously, he had helped frustrate the Híjar-Padrés colony.

Pico ordered that the decree, "Given at Santa Barbara on common paper on account of there being none that is stamped, this 4th July 1846, be recorded in the proper book and delivered to the interested party for his security and use." Paper was chronically short in the department. Official paper with the seal and year printed at the top was non-existent. José Moreno, interim secretary (and half–British), signed the document, confirming it had been copied and given to Macnamara. On July 8th Narciso Botello, senior assemblyman, grocer, saloon bar owner and gold prospector, wrote to Secretary Moreno a personal letter apologizing for his being taken up by the "Sr Presbitero Don Eugenio Macnamara" business. He had spent time talking with Macnamara and recommended the project highly to Moreno for its "huge advantages and security."[18] Effectively, the maverick Irish missioner now had at his disposal from a desperate Central Government and Departmental administration 13,284,000 acres or 20,280 square miles. In his home country, which he had not seen since 1841, a farmer was rated as "strong" with 30 acres or more, as "middle" with between 10 and 30 and as "small" with less than 10. The average around Doonbeg was six limestone acres and the poorest had but a potato patch. The San Joaquin concession by most, let alone Irish, standards was vast, yet by Texan standards it was guardedly reserved. It was also unusual in being made at the request of Mexico City, not by the department. When asked in court in 1859 why Central Government had taken on the Macnamara affair, Pico did not know and remembered only one other similar minor case. The American prosecutor tried to establish that Pico had been a fraudster, hiding behind a bogus Mexican Central authorization for Macnamara's concession. Pico, however, spoke honestly: it *was* an exceptional case.[19]

HMS Collingwood *at Monterey*

The Americans expected *Juno* and *Collingwood* at Monterey any hour. *Juno*, a sloop in comparison to the flagship, bypassed Monterey around July 10th with James Forbes on board and anchored further north in San Francisco Bay. There Blake kept to himself for a week, to the point of discourtesy to local American officers. *Collingwood* at 80 guns carried enormous firepower and would, in Larkin's words, "look down on the *Savannah* [54 guns] unless the *Columbus* [74 guns] is here as a shew off."[20] Admiral Seymour's lookouts sighted Santa Cruz on July 15th as *Collingwood* came in from the northwest on her circular voyage from the south to Monterey. The Admiral felt the chill of the coastal fog on his war-wounds. "I have suffered much this week from tenderness in the teeth, from cold."[21] At 5:00 in the afternoon of July 16th, 32 days out from San Blas, the largest ship in the Royal Navy dropped anchors at one and a half fathoms in Monterey Bay, sliding into line like a hawk's shadow over what some thought might have been its prey. It dwarfed the American ships. Anthems were played, salutes fired, while below American decks powder was opened and men stood at stations. "Find USS *Savannah* alongside two frigates in possession of the port. Commodore Sloat visited me." Midshipman John Wilson watched from the deck of USS *Savannah*: "Admiral Seymour who had been following us for several months previous, arrived the 16th and anchored in his flagship. On his appearing, Commodore Sloat sent orders, as I understand, to be in readiness in case the Admiral should be entering with hostile intentions, leaving the impression that the Admiral must have intended to prevent our squadron from taking possession of California." All hands on USS *Congress* were also called from shore to man battle stations. As late as September, Captain Kellett of HMS

HMS *Collingwood* (*Illustrated London News, November 8, 1945*).

Herald reported that the USS *Portsmouth* at San Francisco treated *Herald* as a hostile vessel with calls to arms and beating to quarters.[22]

It went round the American decks that Seymour had told Sloat, "You have played on me a Yankee trick"—a British proverb for double-dealing. Third hand, it was rumored that Seymour, on seeing the U.S. flag over Monterey, slapped his thigh, stamped his foot and threw down his hat, according to British officers present. In fact, headache, toothache and insomnia were more likely to upset Seymour than anything the Americans did. He arrived with no delusions. Sloat certainly found his visit "very serviceable to our cause in California as the inhabitants fully believed he would take part with them." He described the admiral as "amiable and polite." Commodore Stockton had come into Monterey with USS *Congress* from Honolulu at the news of the

Texas hostilities, some of his crewmen learning Spanish for an expected Mexican war. On July 15th Stockton anchored outside of *Cyane* in line abreast with *Levant* and *Savannah,* which all "present a very warlike appearance controlling the anchorage. [On Thursday afternoon, July 16th] *Collingwood* came to anchor outside *Congress* and *Savannah.* Our band greeted her with *God Save the Queen* which she returned with *Hail Columbia.* She looks majestic on the wave."[23] British ships-of-the-line at 80–90 guns outgunned U.S. line ships like *Columbus* at 74 guns, but the American line ships could outrun the British giants, whilst U.S. frigates at 50 or more guns outgunned considerably the British frigates of 26–40 guns. The British had the advantage in full-facing battle lines; the Americans looked to avoid such set-piece warfare.

Friday, July 17th was busy. The admiral summoned James Forbes to Monterey, "desirous of seeing you with regard to the interests of HM subjects resident in California. Finding that the country has been taken possession of by the U.S. in consequence of their hostilities against Mexico, it is probable that my stay will be very short. I shall await the arrival of *Juno* which Mr Macnamara informs me will be 20th July. Captain Blake will convey you from San Francisco if you prefer a passage in his frigate to the land journey." Blake had brought Forbes to San Francisco from San Pedro, discharging him at 4.00 p.m. on July 11th. "I have availed myself much of his information." Blake was a narrower man than Seymour, from a generation which had not fought and he did not hide his disdain for Americans or Mexicans. "Aggressors now step forward as the aggrieved. A proclamation was published at Sonoma by an uneducated person called Hyde [William Ide], part of a lawless gang of invaders and adventurers. There are few British subjects as such, but many British-born individuals, the most part being from the lower walks of life." He paid no courtesy visits to any U.S. ships in San Francisco Bay. On July 18th Blake left the Bay for San Blas, deliberately bypassing Monterey, unaware that Seymour was there with the Americans. "The presence of this ship [*Juno*] is no longer desireable here." He also left Macnamara stranded.[24]

Cold fog in Monterey Bay caused Seymour headache, but his code placed courtesy to visitors before personal discomfort. "Mr Macnamara, David Spence and Hartweg aboard. Visited by Commodore Stockton and Captain Du Pont. The latter gave me the Honolulu papers." A 17-gun salute for Stockton startled the gulls and pelicans on the bay. Spence, a Scots-born beef trader and Mexican citizen of Monterey, brought a copy of Sloat's proclamation of American rule. Macnamara showed off Pico's signed land grant as his trophy and spoke of his need to get back to Mexico. Theodor Hartweg (whom Seymour still referred to as "Hardwick") had been stuck in Monterey after only a brief research trip to the mountains round Santa Cruz: all horses had been requisitioned by Comandante Castro. Hartweg further feared that the trappers or "country people could not be persuaded that a person could come all the way from London to look after weeds which in their opinion are not worth picking up." Monterey was parched. "The fields and woods which were covered in flowers [when *Juno* arrived in June] are now gradually drying up from total absence of rain during the summer months." Seymour then called to return his respects to Sloat at the end of a first full day.[25]

On the following day the Admiral was well enough to return the compliment to Captain Dupont and visit *Congress*, where he met Sloat again. He took time off ashore with Lieutenant Walpole and others to ride to David Spence's ranch and beef-packing station to see *vacqueros* rounding up cattle. They also showed him the stripped Carmel Mission and the River Carmela. He was the first official British visitor to land in American California. Sunday brought a lull in the social rounds and Seymour took the opportunity to write to his son Francis, an army officer in London. It was his private voice. "The presence of *Collingwood* and *Juno* here has been unnecessary, but that would not have been the case had the people the good sense to declare independence in time. I feel I was entitled to instructions on a subject which I called to [London's] attention at various points beginning March 1845 when I predicted what has since happened, but have not had a syllable in answer. I am writing, as you will see, in bad spirits. Things have gone wrong in both the quarters which have principally occupied me. I do not want to stay in these seas a day longer than the usual period. 'Jonathan' [the United States] has improved his position, but I hear of 23,000 Mormons coming to California disenchanted with the state."[26] As the Admiral wrote, HMS *Juno* passed south unnoticed.

Consul James Forbes arrived by the cutter after dark on Monday, 20th July, having taken the road from San Francisco via the looted remains of his home at Mission San José. He slept on *Collingwood* and then "spent all morning with me on California affairs. Called on Commodore Sloat and introduced Mr Forbes as Acting Consul. He had a salute from *Savannah*. Forbes, Macnamara, Spence and Hardwicke [Hartweg] dined with me." Thomas Larkin also visited *Collingwood* that day and exchanged courtesies, but the admiral stopped short of a consular salute: American territory warranted no consul. That evening, over the wardroom table, Macnamara detailed to Forbes his power-of-attorney and intentions over the Santa Clara mine. Forbes digested it with the meal. The priest also described his approach to Larkin for advice about his Mexican land concession now that it was on American territory. Larkin knew the outlines of Mexican law, but nothing of emergency powers or the distinction between an *empresario*'s contract and a settler's grant. In any event, the contract depended on Mexico City, not on Pico. Larkin told Washington of the conversation.

> Mr Macnamara informed me that the Governor and Legislature gave him a deed for 3,000 square leagues of land dated 4, July 1846, he engaging to introduce into California 10 thousand Irishmen, and he applied to me for

my opinion of his rights now our flag was over California. I replied that a Governor of California had no power to grant over eleven leagues in a single deed. This act shows a new feature in British policy to obtain a title to California, although Mr Macnamara informed me that he was commissioned by a private company in London.[27]

Macnamara was a stranded British subject, needing to pass the American blockade to Mexico. Seymour was due to go to the Sandwich Islands and then to Tahiti. He offered to take Macnamara to Honolulu from where the priest could find a Royal Navy ship for Mexico. Macnamara accepted, promising James Forbes he would write to keep him posted of matters of common interest—the land contract and, even more important, the mercury mine. Forbes had other ideas, but kept them to himself. Macnamara seems to have been quite fooled by the canny Scots trader. Seymour's enthusiasm for Macnamara was also on the wane, possibly through his own ill-health, possibly as a result of losing patience with anything linked with the Latin Americans. He may also have begun to see another side to the *empresario*.

The Guests at the Wardroom Table

On July 19th the livening town of Monterey, which had never known such international attention, saw a squadron of 120 trappers, Frémont at their head, ride through to encamp on the heights above, among the pines "where the July sun made the sea-breeze and the shade welcome." They were there at the request of Sloat and Larkin to protect settlers against marauding Indians from the San Joaquin Valley. "Many of my men had never seen the ocean or the English flag. They looked on HMS *Collingwood* with the feeling of the racer who has just passed the winning post. Three nations were represented in those quiet streets." Toward the end of the admiral's week in Monterey, when Macnamara was in the wardroom, Captain Frémont and Marine Lieutenant Gillespie in "blouse and leggings" came aboard. Frémont later denied that real trappers wore such impractical costumes, only those in paintings. Their conversation with the British officers and the Irish priest should have been awkward, if their role in California was to save Manifest Destiny from these same British agents. A decanter and glass combined with the courtesies of a gentrified Royal Navy might have lightened the meeting, which may have been the first time Frémont had actually heard of the Irish colonization project. He made no mention of it in a long detailed letter to Senator Benton of July 25th. It would soon provide a useful alibi for him, although later in life he showed sympathy and admiration for Macnamara. Their meeting on *Collingwood* cannot have been too negative an experience.

"Received visits from Messrs Frémont and Gillespie. The trappers had been ready to show their skills as marksmen on shore," noted the admiral.

Top: Wardroom table, HMS *Collingwood* (*Illustrated London News, November 8, 1845*). *Bottom:* Wardroom table, thought to be from *Collingwood*, Ragley Hall.

Frémont too remembered that "The English Admiral looked on, with his officers, with great interest." Other witnesses reported that the sharpshooters "delighted the officers of *Collingwood* and reduced their store of silver dollars." Walpole had seen them in books, "the class that produced the heroes of Fenimore Cooper's best works." For the rest of his life Frémont was to be nicknamed after a Fenimore Cooper bestseller, *Pathfinder*. To Seymour, trappers were in the same category as brown albatrosses and Governor Gutiérrez of Mazatlán, but he would have been courteous, while curious. Stockton's chaplain, Walter Colton, found Seymour "an officer of great amenity of deportment. He has been several times on board *Congress* and has been much impressed. He and most of his officers are connected with the English nobility, but assume no airs. He had no instruction from the British monarchy to raise the English flag in California, a mere assumption warranted by not a solitary fact. When we had harpooned the whale they left us to make the most of the blubber and the bones."[28]

One evening Frémont sat alone on the beach at Pine Point. Hindsight colored the memory, forty years later. "Looking out over the bay, the dark hulls of the war vessels and the slumbering cannon still looked ominous and threatening. But the Cross of St George hung idly down from the peak of the great ship, the breeze occasionally spreading out against the sky the small red patch which represented centuries of glory. There lay the pieces on the great chessboard before me with which the game for an empire had been played. At its close we had, to be sure, four pieces [ships] to one, but that one [ship] was a Queen [Victoria]. I was but a pawn and like a pawn I had been pushed forward to the front at the opening of the game." Strangely, he reported nothing of this in his correspondence of 1846.

The situation was unambiguous and Seymour's priority was now Honolulu. As the trappers entertained (and the ex–Royal Marines among them insulted) the crew onshore on *Collingwood*'s final day in harbor, "shooting at marks put up on pine trees," the admiral wrote his final letters of the visit. He advised James Forbes that Sloat's was "a provisional occupation only, pending future decisions on the outcome of the contest. I recommend to you the strictest neutrality between contending parties, and prudence and circumspection." He sent a copy to Sloat to emphasize the correctness of British behavior and to make the point. Sloat provided *Collingwood* with mast spares and provisions, given the Royal Navy's lack of store facilities along the Latin American coastline. American officers provided books for Seymour and his officers to read, and east coast newspapers which included news of the "great distress in Ireland." Post too was exchanged—whatever their politicians' stances, the two navies respected each other as former enemies with a shared language and traditions. They carried for each other private and state correspondence of the most sensitive nature.

Seymour also wrote to the dejected Governor Pío Pico of Alta California, a task made easier by the fact that they had never met. "I regret deeply [the American attack] but as the Province remained under the authority of Mexico at the time of the attack, I could not be justifed in interfering." It was a belated response to Pico's plea to James Forbes in Santa Barbara on June 29th for naval help. Forbes duly forwarded Seymour's reply with his own cover note which Pico acknowledged courteously, from Los Angeles on July 29th. The expectation of British help ran deep. As late as August 9th Comandante Castro placed on record with James Forbes his own correspondence with U.S. Commodore Stockton, "as authentic proof of my behaviour and to place it in the knowledge of the nation that you so worthily represent." Pico and Castro, no less than Seymour, deserved better than the evasions which London offered.

It was calm in the Bay on July 23rd when Seymour paid respects to Commodore Stockton on his assuming command of the American squadron that morning from Commodore Sloat. Macnamara was aboard *Collingwood*, not as a passenger on the ration strength, but with the Admiral's retinue. *Collingwood* put to sea at 1:00 p.m. and was promptly becalmed in the coastal fog. Frustration gave way to distraction as the crew crowded the rails to watch "mountainous black fin whales sporting round the ship." It inspired yet another American messdeck legend. Surgeon Rogers recorded that Seymour did not leave at all, but hovered just below the horizon, beyond the fog, "gathering a large force to attack U.S. shipping at anchor." In fact Seymour watched the whales and spent time alone in his cabin reading Henry Dana's *Two Years Before the Mast,* on California, which he had bought in New York on a private visit in 1840, and Frémont's 1842 narrative lent by Captain Dupont of USS *Congress.* There was even theological discussion, enough to note on July 28th, "Air comparatively warm at night. Mr Macnamara gave me the verses in the Testament *[I Corinthians 3, 13–15; Matthew 5, 26]* on which Catholics found their doctrine of Purgatory." It may have arisen from a friendly wardroom discussion between the two Irish clerics, Macnamara and Chaplain Proctor, in Seymour's hearing. It must have been good humored: Seymour had no time for sectarian bickering. The Catholic doctrine of Purgatory, a purging of sin prior to Heaven, was being reintroduced into Seymour's and Proctor's Anglican churches. The Anglo-Catholic movement created much division among Anglican Protestants and would have been a topic of conversation between clerics thrown together at close quarters. With Tipperary in common and the Famine an universal concern, the two were not short of conversation. Village life aboard *Collingwood* with its gentry, crew, goats, hens, geese and evening fiddle music, a cross between Noah's Ark and Windsor Castle, also afforded plenty of promenade space and distraction from the tobacco-and-port atmosphere of the wardroom.

Seymour appeared at table less frequently by the start of August. "The sudden change in weather has weakened me," he confided to his diary, between reading Sandwich Island papers. He also noted in the end blank pages of the diary the letter Macnamara had received from Juan Bandini about mineral prospects in California. It was the Admiral's last reference to Eugene Macnamara. When he wrote his formal report for the Admiralty on the California affair after conferring with Captain Blake at rendezvous in Honolulu in late August, he made no mention of the Irishman and even wrote as if warning about colonizers. "In addition to a considerable force, a large body of emigrants *on whom reliance could be placed* would be necessary to establish any British ascendancy and without these I think it preferable that no attempt should have been made to connect the honour or the interests of Great Britain with the possession of California."[29] Macnamara was a growing embarrassment.

One final Monterey eyewitness wrote just after *Collingwood* sailed into the fog. Louis Gasquet, the vain and highly excitable French acting consul, was under house arrest for refusing to recognize the American occupation force's authority. He had been on the streets of Monterey both in June and July when Macnamara was in town. Jesuits were a European political legend, particularly in France, and they had been allowed to re-enter Mexico in 1843. To most Europeans, a priest acting suspiciously had to be a "Jesuit," but a Jesuit agent acting for Protestant Britain was something altogether unique.

> [*Juno*] had brought an Irish priest, M. Eugene Macnamara, who it is said is a Jesuit and whose worldly manners, spirit of intrigue and dexterity in affairs show him to be of the same family with other members of the celebrated [Jesuit] company. He had come to ask of the Governor and he got from him the concession of an immense tract of land nearly eighty [*sic*] leagues, for the establishment of an Irish colony. This gentleman affected to say quite loudly that his action was uninfluenced by the English Cabinet although all his steps had been well planned in advance, and I am well convinced that he undertook nothing of his own motion. I am thoroughly convinced that England and her agents have not lost the hope of establishing themselves in California. They regard the American occupation as very precarious and they are putting themselves in a position to replace them. M. Macnamara has laid a stepping stone; the others will soon follow. This must be well understood in France if it is to be opposed and if advantage is to be taken of the good will that [the Californian] chiefs and population manifest for us.[30]

Despite the passing of forty years, Frémont claimed to remember in 1886 exactly what he was thinking in 1846. He camped in the ruins of Carmel mission just after *Collingwood* left and wrote a long letter to Senator Benton, his father-in-law, explaining events to date in California. He claimed in 1886 to have thought as he wrote the letter, "It ended my mission as well as that of Macnamara," but he made no mention of Macnamara in the letter home.

The London Bondholders Awake

Rumblings of war were heard some months previously on the London Stock Exchange. The Spanish American Bondholders had failed to raise a company in London to finance and arrange colonization. Up to 1844 at least, they had been overwhelmingly hostile to the idea of developing land on the Pacific, preferring to consider Texas, if anything at all. The real hope was for an economic miracle in Mexico and to have cash dividends instead of the long-term headache of land speculation. Like those of the rats of Hamelin, their cries suddenly rose from a squeak to a crescendo. Charles Graham, company partner to John Diston Powles, wrote to Lord Aberdeen in late April 1846, begging him to buy California outright for its harbors *and its gold*, just as the United States had barefacedly annexed Texas. If the United States took California and the Mexican mines, "she would repudiate the whole of the debt of this country. Ten years of my life has been passed in the Americas" and he offered to place his experience at Aberdeen's service.[31] Louis McLane, United States ambassador in London, reported to Washington that "the Mexican creditors, whatever their feeling towards the U.S. may be, will take no course calculated to sacrifice their interests."[32] He wrote just after a stormy meeting of the Bondholders which railed against the Americans. The prospect of the Americans going to war against a prostrate Mexico was highly unpopular in England. A Mexican agent was also in London looking for further advances from the Bondholders. In June 1846 the overall Bondholder committee under John Diston Powles begged Aberdeen to consider the losses they would sustain in a Mexican-U.S. war and to mediate "from desire to protect their communal interests."[33] Throughout the following twelve months the United States refused any offers of mediation from the London Government, although British diplomats in Mexico City did help secure cease-fires in the summer of 1847.

On June 4th the full Committee of Mexican Bondholders met in London, chaired by George Robinson, with Powles as vice-chairman. The meeting was advertised and reported in *The Times*. In contrast to the rowdy general meeting of the Bondholders in May, "the expediency of compromise" was the tone of the day. They voted to ask Aberdeen to intervene lest the war become "protracted and sanguinary" and asked further if the mail packets would still ply. In fact the United States continued to allow the Royal Mail packet ships to enter Vera Cruz harbor throughout the war blockade as they were such a vital line of communication. The Mexican creditors, however, banked too certainly on British mediation between the belligerents: in the same meeting, they voted to allow further loans to Mexico under a fresh *refacción* of the debt, "on the express ground that British interference on behalf of Mexico might be relied upon." In July, Henry Parish, an old South America hand, wrote from Caerphilly Castle in Wales to the foreign secretary, protesting at losing "New Albion, San Francisco, which belongs to Great Britain in virtue of its having been discovered by Sir Francis Drake and formally conceded by the native chiefs to Queen Elizabeth."[34] This *cri de cœur* came as much from the purse as from any sense of historical injustice. For months Mexican bonds stagnated "flat … heavy … depressed" on the Money Market as reported in *The Times*. On September 26th, London finally learned of the capture of California by Sloat.

Hawaiian Interlude

Fourteen days out of Monterey *Collingwood* anchored in Honolulu Roads on August 6th, two miles out from the town, beyond the reef which surrounds Oahu Island. Its deep draft did not allow it to moor nearer. It was the only warship of any nationality lying off Honolulu. "The ship was surrounded by two or three hundred wooden canoes full of noisy natives and fruit, vegetables, fowls, ducks, goats, geese, turkeys, pigs and fresh eatables. Our old tortoise on board even woke from his sleep, left his corner and wantoned on the fresh food. The excitement among the natives was tremendous, hundreds came merely to look at us. They had never seen so big a man of war."[35] Consul General Sir William Miller came on board to greet Seymour and brief him. Miller was introduced to Macnamara at some point and heard of his work in California. Macnamara's voyage was over and he climbed down into the ship's cutter for the journey into harbor with reassurance from the admiral of continued assistance from the Royal Navy and orders for him to be taken aboard the requisitioned storeship *Palinurus* when it arrived with 100,000 loaves from Valparaíso. HMS *Juno* was also expected before the end of the month. Louis Maigret, from the Franco-Irish Picpus missioners, ran the Catholic church in the Sandwich Islands. Macnamara probably stayed at the mission, but neither Maigret nor his colleague, Calixte Lecomte, noted him in their journals. Lieutenant Walpole, who had little time for missioners in general and Catholics in particular, made of Maigret an exception: "Of him, no eulogy would be too high."[36] Maigret's house and church were two blocks from Consul Miller's house.

Onshore, Macnamara would also have met Robert Crichton Wyllie, Scots foreign minister to the king of the Sandwich Islands, and author of the Bondholders *Report*. It is highly likely that Wyllie, who boarded *Collingwood* on August 11th to pay his respects to Seymour, recorded Macnamara's visit in Volume III of his diaries. The estimated forty volumes of personal records, 350 pages each, disappeared on his death in 1865.[37] Wyllie was still in touch with his cousin William Hartnell in Monterey and in even closer touch with James Forbes.

In December 1846, when Hartnell came to see Wyllie at Honolulu, Miller complained formally in a despatch, "It is strange that Mr Vice Consul Forbes does not write to me as I have more than once requested him to do so *and this* [Miller's emphasis] is the more remarkable since he seldom or ever fails to write to some other Person residing at Honolulu whenever an opportunity offers." In fact, Forbes was pressing Wyllie to send Sandwich Island laborers for the Santa Clara Mine, which could not be exploited without laborers or mineralogists. British naval officers also had little time for the pretentious Dr. Wyllie. Seymour had to treat with the King through Wyllie, and Wyllie's manner offended him. (The King, on the other hand, amused Seymour, whose deep voice His Majesty described as "speaking from his bottom.") To his son in London Seymour complained, just before leaving harbor in early September, of "all these scoundrels who have installed themselves as ministers of his Hawaiian Majesty—never was such a gang got together. Wyllie is the most out and out specimen of regular Scotch with the most extensive talent for writing immensely long letters on any and all subjects. The Sandwich Islands is a hornets nest but it will be a fine Yankee colony one of these days." Wyllie did help make peace after *Collingwood*'s men broke into a Grogshop and drank their fill, but only after appointing a banker who paid the owner all they took. "The men were perfectly sober (*sic*) and too numerous to be interfered with by the Police," who waited until three sailors were alone and "beat them almost to death."[38]

Seymour left for Tahiti at the beginning of September. Consul General Miller observed nearly two hundred Mormons go through Honolulu for California in July, led by one Samuel Brannan. They boasted they would set up a California independent of the United States. Such independence would help the British cause. Miller gave these "armed organised squatters" a letter of introduction to James Forbes, as one-third of them were Scots and English. The question of what would happen to California arose in every conversation and featured in the major newspaper of the islands. As late as the end of August Miller dispatched to London, asking "whether California will form part of the Union or an independent Nation" and added, "I have my house full of visitors and guests and have written the foregoing amid embarrassments." Macnamara may have been one of them. Late in September Consul General Miller wrote to Lord Aberdeen enclosing a letter from the captain of HMS *Modesto* in Vancouver. "Nothing of importance has occurred in the Oregon Territory up to the 27th of last August excepting the near approach of about 3,000 more immigrants from the United States, part of whom have been induced to vary their route for California, a system of squatting by irresistible numbers." The bearer of the letter, William Romaine, the London High Court lawyer vacationing along the Oregon Trail that year, told Miller after leaving his ship *Toulon* fourteen days out from the Columbia River, that "about 5,000 Mormons were on the road to California."

> Mr Romaine proposes leaving here in company with Mr Macnamara, a young Irish Priest, in the first vessel that sails for San Blas or Mazatlan. Mr Macnamara came here in *Collingwood* from San Francisco [*sic*] and, it seems, recently obtained from the Mexican Government the grant of a valuable and extensive tract of land in California which was conveyed to him two or three days only previous to Commodore Sloat taking possession of that country. Mr Macnamara tells me that it *was* [Miller's emphasis] his intention to have brought out a great number of Irish Emigrants to California.[39]

A ship was taking mail to California that week and Wyllie wrote to James Forbes at Monterey. By the same post, Macnamara also wrote to Forbes, venting the most negative feelings. Consul Miller had noticed that the land project was already in the past tense: the mercury mine was taking its place as Macnamara's priority.

> I send you a few hurried lines in accordance with a former promise. Here I am still, very much annoyed at being detained in this half savage place having nothing to do and my anxiety to reach Mexico amounting almost to madness. I am daily, nay hourly expecting the arrival of the *Palinurus*, transport ship, which is to carry me to San Blas. The only English man-of-war here is the *Juno* with our friend Captain Blake.[40]

He noted three ships of Seymour's command, including HMS *Collingwood*, which had gone on to Tahiti, and five more on the Columbia River, including HMS *Herald*, surveying under Captain Kellet. Commodore Biddle's ship, USS *Columbus*, had also passed through, "destined to cooperate with the squadron on the coast of California, but now that the storm has blown over, she goes to Valparaiso." Biddle and Seymour were old friends and had made warm exchanges, but part of Macnamara's loathing of Honolulu may have been the scores of sick American sailors put ashore to recover from scurvy during Biddle's time there. Macnamara also objected to the Oregon settlement on the Columbia River.

> England gives up all the good harbours of the northwest coast and gets nothing in return. Thus has the country been again sacrificed by the asinine stupidity of old Aberdeen. Every Englishman with whom I have spoken on the subject, seems utterly disgusted at the whole proceeding and none moreso than the officers of H.M.'s Navy who looked forward with pleasure to a brush with the Yankees, but who now must hide their diminished heads, while 'Jonathan' [the United States] may well boast, if not of his bravery, at least of his superior sagacity.

Macnamara was unaware that Forbes had already taken charge of the mine from Padre Real, had purchased shares from the Robles brothers and was signing receipts for the first consignments of ore. Forbes knew that Macnamara was out of his depth.

I fully expect to leave this before a week, and soon to enjoy a palaver with our mutual friend Mr [Alexander] Forbes. I am most anxious to set about forming a company to work the mines of Santa Clara. In the event of my succeeding, of which I have very little doubt, would you consent to take charge of the whole concern? Pray let me know in your next letter. I am very desirous of doing something about that grant of land. I will give the Yankees as much annoyance as I possibly can in the matter. May I beg of you to write to me by the very first opportunity to Mexico. Send your letter to me under cover directed to Mr Bankhead. I enclose a letter [from Bandini] which I got for you at Los Angeles but which I forgot to deliver when we last met [on *Collingwood* at Monterey]. I shall write to you again when I reach the City of Mexico.

I forgot to mention that by last accounts the Americans were rapidly advancing into the very centre of Mexico, and it was even feared they would overrun the country if England or France did not interpose. The illustre sangre Mexicana [*sic*] seemed to be below par. I remain, my dear Mr Forbes, Your very sincere friend, Eugene Macnamara.

Palinurus, an "English hired stores ship" of 500 tons, arrived, according to Consul General Miller, on August 6th "with provisions for HM Ships around here and is to proceed tomorrow for Mazatlan." Her Valparaíso bread was duly unloaded. According to Blake's logbook on *Juno*, HM Transport *Palinurus* No. 27 returned again on October 2nd. Her two officers seconded from *Collingwood* in Chile, Lieutenant Lucas in charge and the Honorable Arthur Cochrane as Mate, joined Blake on *Juno* for morning service on October 4th. Blake then "provisioned heavily" from the stores ship which sailed on October 11th. Macnamara, increasingly sharp and irritable as both his prizes slid around, in and out of his grasp like mercury, joined Romaine on board. It was a contrast to the great *Collingwood*—cramped quarters, a silent cargo and just 18 crew. Romaine would not have noticed. He told of life on the Oregon Trail in a crucial year; Macnamara told of being at the eye of the California storm. Neither was short on opinions or words.

May 1846 had found Romaine with a retired British officer at Fort Leavenworth. In Pawnee Indian country Romaine pursued buffalo on horseback as if at foxhounds in his native county of Surrey. An American thought him "noisy and obstinate, overboiling with conceit, assuming direction of affairs of which he knows nothing," and gladly left him four weeks later. Romaine, he felt, had a "glaring want of courtesy and good sense."[41] The Jesuit missioner, Père de Smet, described Romaine more kindly and perceptively five years earlier. Romaine was on his first adventure holiday on the same Oregon Trail, while de Smet and other pioneers were on a serious journey of life. "Fond of travel," de Smet wrote of him, "already seen four quarters of the globe, in many respects estimable, but he cherished so many prejudices against the Catholic religion. [Yet] I treasured one of his beautiful reflections: *'we must travel in the desert to witness the care of Providence over the wants of man.'*"

Perhaps Romaine, the Cambridge-educated son of an Anglican vicar, shared this "beautiful reflection" with a frustrated Macnamara on his second encounter with an "Apostolic Missioner." On a journey of a month and ten days they may have wearied of each other in the close quarters of a small vessel. Lieutenant Lucas finally brought *Palinurus* into Mazatlán Bay on November 9th and waited to provision HMS *Herald* coming down from California. *Herald* carried a German botanist aboard, Berthold Seeman, who recorded the entire survey voyage under Captain Kellet.

"On the 12th November we entered the port of Mazatlan and found that our letters were at San Blas and that *Palinurus* transport was in the bay with stores and provisions for us." On the 17th, 18th and 19th of November Kellet logged three days work "receiving provisions from Transports and stowing holds. From *Palinurus* store ship, bread, rum and vegetables, sugar, soap, etc." Kellet also took on board Macnamara and Romaine, sailing with his passengers at noon on July 21st. Seeman may have known of Theodor Hartweg, the other German botanist on British contract in those waters. German scientists were meticulous recorders. "On the 21st of November we sailed for San Blas having on board as passengers Mr Romaine and Mr Macnamara. The latter, a Roman Catholic priest, has the intention of founding in California a colony of Irishmen who would swear fealty to Mexico and resist the further encroachment of the Americans. This project nearly forestalled the occupation of San Francisco by the United States and should, in all probability, either have led to the establishment of an Irish colony or compelled the British Government to occupy the country." The tale had lost nothing in the telling, but was definitely moving into the past tense.[42]

Favorable following breezes made for a speedy voyage to San Blas. Romaine and Macnamara prepared for a prompt landing as San Juan mountain loomed closer above the decrepit port. Macnamara's pouch was full. He had letters from Captain Kellet to Acting Consul Alexander Forbes in Tepic, one from Kellet for Forbes to deliver to Seymour, and a letter to Forbes from James Forbes which the British vice-consul had managed to slip on board HMS *Herald* at San Francisco in late September, "where I least expected her, according to my last words from the Admiral. I am in charge of the quicksilver mine and am going to work it and am on the point of striking a bargain for four shares."[43] He later claimed in court to have received the mine and shares from Padre Real before the end of 1846. Macnamara delivered both letters to the grand house at Tepic, unaware of James Forbes' preempting of what he considered to be his own initiative on the Santa Clara mine. It incensed him when he did learn of it.

"You of course will be glad to learn all the news of Oregon and California," Kellet wrote to Alexander Forbes after his ear had been bent by Romaine and Macnamara. He felt that after six months "It would require a fleet to turn [the Americans] out if they wish to hold [San Francisco Bay]."

Mormons, "all mechanics," were swarming into the new territory, "well armed and with the intention, it is said, of settling on the San Joaquin River." The last could have been a Macnamara "Methodist wolf" gloss—many English and Scots Mormons were recruited from the Methodists. One of Kellet's crew deserted at San Blas—two had already fled at San Francisco. Impressed men still manned the lower decks of the Royal Navy in 1846. Kellett moored *Herald* briefly at San Blas, to refill the waterbutts and collect mail.

Mr Romaine and Mr Macnamara landed immediately and a courier went up with them to Tepic to bring back our letters. In thirty six hours he returned with the long expected communications from home. Tepic is only 22 miles in direct distance from San Blas; by the road however, which is tedious and fatiguing, it is 56.[44]

Eight

The Demon.
Mexico, Washington,
California 1847–1896

Go tell your Queen and Parliament,
  to Aberdeen make known
That Macnamara's little scheme
  by Frémont is o'erthrown.
—(Thomas Lancey, USS *Dale,* 1846, *San Jose Pioneer,*
  April 17, 1879)

Macnamara was still at the Forbes house in Tepic on November 28th, a week after his landing from HMS *Herald.*[1] On that day, "currently resident in this place," he exercised his power-of-attorney over the Santa Clara mine. After showing the town public notary his authorization, he negotiated a contract with the 72-year-old Alexander Forbes, representing the Barron and Forbes company. Forbes must have told Macnamara that James Forbes was already working the mine and had acquired four shares, after reading the letter which came up with Macnamara from HMS *Herald.* It may have surprised the priest that he had been deceived, but one local witness and fellow shareholder would have understood: Comandante Castro, a refugee from the American occupation of California, stayed at Tepic throughout that winter and for the rest of 1847. He had last met Macnamara at Pico's Santa Margarita Ranch on the Camino Real on July 12th. In a buyer's market Barron and Forbes did well from the deal on November 28th as Macnamara settled for the minimum terms authorized by the owners. The contract was later ratified in Mexico City by Castillero, the majority shareholder.

That same day, Alexander Forbes wrote a dispatch to Charles Bankhead which Macnamara was to carry to Mexico City. He informed the ambassador of shipping news on the coast, but regretted that James Forbes, vice-consul in California, had nothing new to report. He made no mention of the mine deal described in Forbes' letter. The venture was permissible under Foreign Office regulations for diplomats, but it was out of order in wartime when Seymour and Lord Aberdeen had clearly set their faces and even warned Forbes directly against any breach of neutrality. Perhaps Macnamara too was expected to be discreet in his conversations with Bankhead.

The company was war profiteering. Between December 1846 and April 1847, Comandante Castro financed his refuge in Tepic by the sale of his four mine shares to Barron and Forbes for between $800 and a final $1,300 per share. Guardedly, he still called it a "silver mine with alloy of gold and quick-silver." The Robles brothers of Monterey sold James Forbes two of their four shares in September 1847. In January 1848 Padre Real sold three of his four shares to Alexander Forbes for $1,500 each, but complained of being swindled, and in August 1849 sold (or re-sold) his (or Macnamara's) remaining, disputed share to Robert Walkinshaw, Barron and Forbes' agent at the mercury mine.[2] No one admitted to having bought out Macnamara's share, but Macnamara did complain of having been short-changed. Ironically Walkinshaw and Macnamara had been table companions in May 1846 on *Collingwood* at Mazatlán, just as Macnamara set out for California. An odd clause in Walkinshaw's share contract with Real gave the agent "power to reclaim the same *from any person living*," presumably from Macnamara. Obviously it was unclear in 1849 whether Macnamara was dead or alive, and even if alive, whether he was still in possession of his mine share.

The Go-Between

Macnamara may have sold his mine share to Alexander Forbes in November for the going price of around $1,000. The merchant world was deep water for him to tread, but his silence did have a modest price tag. James Forbes wrote to Tepic from California on July 14, 1847:

> I have seen a letter from Mr Macnamara to Padre Real in which he complains bitterly that he has not received enough for his services in negotiating the mining contract with you; that he ought to have had one share from each of the [shareholders]; that I wrote inaccurate statements to you; and sums up with a furious tirade telling Padre Real that he is a man of great influence with HM Minister [ambassador] at Mexico [City], of whom he is the most intimate friend; that I had better be cautious or I will lose my official situation! and other absurdities which manifest his principles and how little he is aware of my independence of spirit to be affected by such threats. I am sorry I cannot send you a copy as Padre Real is absent. The letter was written in the supposition that I should learn its contents. I am ignorant as to how my letter to you [of September 1846, via HMS *Herald*

in November] could have given the Reverend gentleman such umbrage and I beg you to send me a copy of that same letter and also to inform me whether Mr Macnamara is yet in Mexico.[3]

Macnamara at least achieved the permitted minimum terms, negotiating a distant mine in enemy-occupied territory with skilled hagglers. Barron and Forbes did not dare invest in the mine until immediately after the March 1848 peace treaty between the U.S. and Mexico. Months after that, James Forbes was still pursuing the Macnamara share. He reprimanded Alexander Forbes for having had any dealings at all with Macnamara

on the lowest terms, least favourable to the owners and most favourable to you. [It] raises doubts about the validity of the contract and Eugene Macnamara's right to the one share offered to him in consideration of the due discharge of his agency on behalf of the owners to obtain for them a beneficial contract. [You have done nothing] to conciliate the mine owners to this undue proceeding of Mr Macnamara. Rev. Real having appointed me to be his agent for the management of the one share promised to Mr Macnamara upon the condition stated. I trust you have not purchased the share of the last named person.[4]

Either Padre Real or James Forbes—or both—lied about Macnamara's share. Real had made it over unconditionally in 1846, without the "condition" which James Forbes claimed. In fact, Forbes had agreed to Castillero's retrospective confirmation of the Macnamara deal in May 1847, but by 1848 he felt "the vast magnitude of the undertaking and the interest of the owners" should have come first. If any "consideration" had been agreed, it was not written into the legal form: the share was firmly conveyed, not "offered" or "promised."[5] The power-of-attorney given Macnamara in Monterey also allowed him the discretion to go not only for lowest recommended terms, but to go *below* those terms if no other way of closing the contract was possible. The owners were desperate in the face of enemy invasion. In post-war days, when the mine was producing most profitably for Barron and Forbes, it was easy to regret wartime haste and losses, while forgetting the sheer lack of laborers, mineralogists and security in 1847.

At the end of November 1846, with Pico's contract still safe in his hands, probably share payment and possibly even a little "consideration money" (the Mexican "bite") in his pocket, Macnamara left the comforts of Forbes' house in Tepic for Guadalajara and Mexico City on a journey of nearly two weeks, through the mountains in winter, rising at 4:00 each morning. He would have had plenty of company since the pilgrim crowds were descending on the capital for the national festival of the Virgin of Gaudeloupe. His stagecoach arrived on December 12th, the feast day itself, in a capital very different from that which he had left the previous April.[6] Archbishop Posada, his patron, was six months dead. General Paredes had been ousted by those constantly recurring Mexican factors, Gómez-Farías and General Santa Anna. American forces under General Taylor had invaded as far as Monterrey, 600 miles north of Mexico City. Washington was planning a seaborne invasion in the spring of 1847, through Vera Cruz, to take the capital. President Polk even toyed with promoting Senator Thomas Benton, Frémont's father-in-law, from retired Colonel to Active List Lieutenant General, thereby keeping the war in the family and balancing the politics of the Army command. In California there had been fresh Californio resistance between San Diego and Los Angeles. Great Britain, far from intervening, as Macnamara had hoped, now distanced herself even further as a neutral from the plight of Mexico.

In Mexico City, Captain Andrés Castillero was keen to sell his shares in the Santa Clara mine to Alexander Forbes, but Forbes' agent, Francisco Negrete, merchant of Guadalajara, reported that Castillero would not make any move until he saw Macnamara. On December 15th in Mexico City, Negrete invited Macnamara to meet "in my house for a couple of hours when we talked about the mine and Señor Castillero." The following day "at 11 we met again with S. Castillero and a lawyer" hired by Negrete. Andrés Castillero agreed retrospectively with Macnamara and Negrete to Macnamara's "special but full" power-of-attorney from Real and Castro at Monterey in June, and to his "effecting the contract for which he was empowered" with Alexander Forbes "for himself and in the name of the English company [Barron and Forbes] he represented" at Tepic in November.[7] On December 17th they all signed before a public notary of the city. Castillero acknowledged the "want of formality" in the Monterey transaction and promised to get the "explicit consent" of his mining partners "to remove any doubts" about Macnamara's power-of-attorney. The two leagues of land for colonization given as a reward by Mexico for finding the mine, were conveyed by Castillero to Alexander Forbes, along with five of his shares sold for a total $4,000. Around them the Mexican states were in collapse. California had gone the way of Texas, Arizona and New Mexico and was out of the war. Gómez-Farías, the old liberal of 1833, became prime minister and a reborn conservative, while the one-legged General Santa Anna rode out of Mexico City at the head of a newly mustered army of 18,000 to meet the invader head-on. The entire international dispute was now playing out on Mexican home soil and Macnamara was sidelined.

He seems to have lived for at least some of 1847 in the house of one of the British diplomats in Mexico City—Mackintosh, Bankhead or Sir Edward Thornton. He threatened to use his influence with the ambassador against James Forbes when he wrote to Padre Real early in 1847. Dr. John Baldwin, a fluent Spanish speaker and former resident of Mexico City, returned there as a negotiator with General Scott's occupation forces when they entered the capital on September 14, 1847. Three months later, during John Frémont's appeal to Congress for compensation to the California settlers of 1846 for their part in the war, Baldwin was called as a witness to the threat from Macnamara.

> I made the acquaintance of the priest Macnamara [in Mexico City], and from sources entitled to credit, I was informed that he had, under the auspices of the British legation, projected a plan to colonise California with emigrants from Ireland. His project had met the approbation of the Mexican government, and he went to California. A fierce opposition was contemplated by the republican members of [Mexican] Congress when he should return with his matured plans from California. This resistance became unncessary in consequence of the conquest of California by the arms of the United States. Macnamara lived in the family of either the British Consul or Chargé d'Affaires in Mexico.[8]

Euan Mackintosh was still British consul; Charles Bankhead, though increasingly sick, was still ambassador; Sir Edward Thornton, Jr., was British chargé d'affaires. Percy Doyle, whose place Thornton had taken, returned from an 18-month leave in November 1847, just after Bankhead had been made invalid home; the ambassador traveled dramatically to Vera Cruz under Mexican military escort in October with a safe-conduct through American lines. Thornton and Mackintosh both worked as go-betweens for the warring sides on Mexican soil. Neither made mention of Macnamara in their known papers. He may have been an embarrassment, given the desire on the part of Britain to be a neutral intermediary. He was also, suddenly, quite unimportant. The Mexican War preoccupied everyone and in Britain other events took over completely from talk of California, Texas or Bondholders.

The Irish Famine

The U.S. ambassador in London, Louis McLane, described the change of climate in Britain: "The present Government will not attempt to give direction to Mexican affairs; although perhaps in the event of the cession of the Californias to the United States, some consideration may be asked for such rights as British subjects pretend to have acquired there. But as yet, this Government, as far as has come to my knowledge, has preserved in the whole matter the most profound silence. Another cause exists for the great disinclination of England to interfere with Foreign Nations, a disinclination which, in comparison with her past history, must be called extraordinary. That cause is Ireland."[9]

It is hard to imagine what rights "British subjects," other than Macnamara or the Bondholders, could even "pretend to have acquired there," apart from the Santa Clara mercury mine which had only just passed to Barron and Forbes. British investment in California was minimal. The land warrants held by the London Mexican Bondholders were open for any Mexican frontier departments, but were agreements in principle, not specific grants. McLane meant what all other observers meant by "Ireland" in 1847—the Irish Famine. The word "Famine" was widely used in the British Press in 1846. Irish churches invoked the Collect prayer, "In Time of Famine," as early as winter 1845-6. Admiral Seymour read of it disbelievingly in the newspapers forwarded to him in the Pacific, but put it down to the hostile American press, which "always contrives." *The Tablet* front-page leader of September 9, 1846, was headed simply "*FAMINE,*" describing it as "the most entire that for hundreds of years has been known in any considerable quarter of Europe." It dominated *The Times* throughout the autumn and winter of 1846-7, eclipsing reports about the Mexican war and the collapse of Mexican Bond values.

"Famine" described the first year, including winter 1845-6, of the airborne spores which were to blight the Irish potato crop for four out of five years. Potatoes blackened where they grew and where they were stored; the smell was rank. A greatly increased Irish population had come to depend on the efficient, nourishing tuber which could be grown on poor soil in the smallest of holdings. When it failed, life failed, so great was the dependence. There had been frequent local failure, including two in County Clare during Macnamara's youth. The failures between 1845 and 1849 were Ireland-wide. Doonbeg village was described in 1847 as "a wretched nest of filth, famine and disease," so bad that Michael Comyn gave up his house and lifestyle in protest.[10] The British government, paralyzed by the unprecedented scale of the disaster, followed an ideology of "self-help," "free market" and "survival of the fittest," to the point of apparent lack of pity. Many British citizens on the other hand were moved by the plight of the Irish. While government remained aloof, Queen Victoria herself donated a personal £2,000 ($10,000) to the famine fund; President Polk sent what he called his personal "mite" of $50, but vetoed the use of public money, despite a Senate Bill for half a million dollars in relief for Ireland. The Pope donated various amounts by diocese or organization, and appealed through an encyclical to the worldwide Catholic church. Choctaw Indians, Jews and Quakers also contributed generously from across the Atlantic. Private entrepreneurs hired U.S. Navy vessels to bring relief supplies to Ireland. The British residents of Mexico, in the middle of a serious war, also collected for the Irish in the winter of 1846-7 and Macnamara would have been among them. Lord Palmerston, British Foreign Secretary, thanked them for £523 "to the relief of their fellow subjects at home, the distressed Irish and Scots."[11] All told, after four failed years, the Famine wasted a million Irish lives through starvation, cholera and typhus. Poor records mask a much higher figure. It also accelerated the flight, much of it to America, of another million by 1850. The rest of the century saw four million Irish leave for America, Canada, Australia and England.

The anti–Irish saw flight and famine as Nature's sifting of the fit from the flawed. Some clergy, even bishops, spoke of "a judgment" for lax religious observance, or of God's plan to evangelize the world through the Irish emigrant. *Punch* magazine mocked the tragedy, saying Daniel O'Connell was Ireland's real blight. It took *The Times* until 1849 to accept that the Irish needed exceptional help on purely humanitarian grounds. Even the landed gentry suffered, losing their revenues (and in a few years their lands) as rent-payers died or left. Emigrants and their families came increasingly to see migration as forced exile: Gaelic had no word for "emigration" save "exile." An American "wake," as if for the dead, would be held well into the 20th century for departing relatives before embarkation. "West" was where souls went after death. The Irish migrant "dead" felt guilty, as if deserting their own in need. In fact, their own *needed* them to emigrate to take the pressure off the subdivided land.[12]

As Europe's biggest peacetime disaster, the Famine could not have been exaggerated. It did, however, suffer over-simplification and, like religion or the English, was made to explain too much in Irish history. Myth had the attraction of simplicity. *All* emigrants who left, even *before* the blight, became its "victims"; *all* landowners came to be seen as pitiless, rich Protestants starving Catholic poor. The truth behind the halving of the population of Ireland from the time of the Famine was much more complex. The emigration syphon had long been flowing by 1845, with over a million gone since 1820. Many Protestant clergy worked for, and dozens died among, the starving peasantry with no part in the "religion for soup" abuse practiced by extremists. Wealthier Catholic middlemen and landlords rack-rented, evicted and starved their tenants as cruelly as any proverbial Protestant estate owner. Some Protestant gentry gave aid to the point of bankruptcy. No religious denomination had a monopoly on humanity. The harsh public workhouse system, built for poor relief in normal times, could not cope with a disaster it was never intended to face, but became a symbol, as if the underplanning had been deliberate. Emigrants also re-invented themselves, like holiday romancers, presenting themselves as direct victims of atrocity or as political refugees, in faraway lands where stories could not be checked.

Eugene Macnamara's land scheme for California, proposed in the spring of 1845, was not responding to a Famine which had not yet occurred, but to a more general European (and Irish) population crisis. Throughout the winter of 1845-6 and afterwards, the Famine was widely reported in Mexico. On February 15, 1846, *La Reforma*, the staunchly republican broadsheet, used it as an example of what could happen under a backward European monarchy. That the British could argue about allowing maize into Irish ports while allowing wheat and barley out of the same ports astounded the Mexican press, whatever an editor's politics. It was happening at Limerick and at Kilrush, just south of Doonbeg and Kilkee. Macnamara's resolve was probably strengthened by the bad news from home, but he was not the only Irishman in Mexico with an eye to the land.

The Enticing of Irish Deserters

In August 1846, the Mexican caretaker president, José Salas, promised an office (*dirección*) for the encouragement of colonization, with an interim committee (*junta*) "to promote foreign immigration to people our immense territories" for the "security of the republic." By November the office was formally constituted in the building of the Office for Industrialization, to save costs.[13] Like the Macnamara scheme, it was too little too late, but there were enough Irishmen (nicknamed *colorados* for their notable red hair), resident in Mexico to take advantage of access to the *Junta de Colonización*. Nicholas Synnott, a "preceptor" of Mexico City, teamed up with Isaac Murray and his sons, manufacturers in Puebla since 1843. Possibly they came with the Irish linen trade to that city where three English houses imported huge amounts of wool, linen and cotton, choking off local industry.[14] Murray and Synnott approached the new *Junta* in September with florid expressions of loyalty to Mexico, "to offer our humble services to the Government in this honourable war." For a consideration.

They pointed out that one-third of the U.S. Army was Irish (it was in fact about a quarter). They claimed that Irish soldiers could easily be persuaded to desert on religious grounds, such as the anti–Irish and anti–Catholic riots in Philadelphia during 1844. They also noted that all General Taylor's deserters so far had been Irish. Taylor, in September 1846, was on the outskirts of Monterrey, conducting his war in the Mexican heartland. They asked that Synnott be commissioned as interpreter to the Mexican commander with a brief to entice the Irish: he had, they said, a gift for language. Once Irish deserters had been lured, they should be allowed their own battalions and regiments: the more deserters, the greater the Mexican army and the smaller the enemy. The Irish knew the meaning of "Victory or Death" in war. At the end, they should be allowed land in the Californias, retaining horses, arms and six months pay as bonus. This colonist militia would solve the age-old problem of what to do with foreign mercenaries after a war; it would also harness proven loyalty. The colonists would be committed to defending California, since the Americans would give no quarter to former deserters.

In addition, they proposed, families should be brought direct from Ireland, including a proportion of young women for the military colonists to marry. Young and footloose soldiers would be better motivated to work the land if they had families. Synnott and Murray, as *empresarios*, would be conceded lands for this colony and would themselves earn a bonus of 20 square leagues. Murray's commercial links would allow him to sell provisions and tools at good prices, putting his own capital up front as outlay. He would go immediately to any lands conceded and be there to apportion land and supplies when the soldiers returned from the war: at a moderate cost, *un precio modesto*. Until he had been fully reimbursed, Murray asked to be civil and military commander of the colony. The veteran militia would be under his command, with land allocated by rank and length of service. A captain, for instance (Synnott's eventual rank), would enter California after war service of one year and claim 2,000 acres, with 1,000 more should he serve a second year. The signatories were also realists:

> If through one of those fatal mischances, which do happen in war, the Government were forced to cede California to another power, the colonists would be entitled to make their homes in another frontier department, on the same conditions, giving to them and to the undersigned a similar amount of land.[15]

The San Patricio Battalion

John Riley of Galway deserted from the American forces before the hostilities of April 1846 were formalized into war in May. He formed a Foreign Legion of 48 Irishmen, half company strength, in the Mexican Army. By August 1846 it had increased to 200, still mostly Irish. He named this small battalion the *San Patricios*, after Ireland's patron saint and possibly to honor the first Irish colonists in Texas. Men had reason to desert from the American forces, where discipline was often brutal and where an Irishman could feel he was ruled by class and religious prejudice. President Polk himself feared a breakdown in the Army in Catholic Mexico and had discussed it with John Hughes, the Catholic Bishop of Baltimore, in May 1846. Bishop Hughes had contact with the Mexican bishops. Polk appointed two Jesuits as unofficial chaplains to provide to some extent for Catholic soldiers in the U.S. Army. It was, after all, only two years since the Philadelphia riots.

American commanders in Mexico did attempt to keep their troops from despoiling the Catholic and, to some of them, quite sinister religious culture of the land. Abhorrence was felt on both sides. *El Trueno*, on February 12, 1847, spoke of the "Protestant prejudice which animates our northern neighbours," a commonplace assumption in Mexico. The American officers promised the population on many occasions that the Catholic religion would be as respected as it was in the United States. While the Philadelphia riots could reasonably be cited as American Protestant bigotry, they were not the whole story: a Protestant pastor sheltered the Catholic bishop during those riots. Polk himself also gave the Presbyterian minister of Philadelphia short shrift—"A knave and a fanatic"—when the latter objected to his appointing the two Jesuits and demanded his own chaplaincy.[16]

In fact, few Irish soldiers pleaded religious reasons for deserting. Service conditions, the carrot of promotion and disagreement with the war played a greater part. There were also other deserters besides the Irish. However, the racial stereotype which underpinned belief in Manifest Destiny translated too easily into religious terms—thrifty Calvinist facing lazy Catholic;

republican virtue against monarchist autocracy; Latin and Irish alike "lazy, loud, undisciplined, ignorant, devious, unfit for self government or for leadership."[17] With its backdrop of Spanish mission churches, wayside shrines and every placename redolent of pre– and counter–Reformation piety, the very stage itself on which the Mexican war was fought was haunted by the Black Legend of wicked Catholic Spain. The Pilgrim Fathers themselves had brought Hispanophobia to America within living memory of the Armada crusade against England.

The Colonization *Junta* advised that Murray should not have a monopoly on trade with the settlers. On October 2nd, two weeks after the proposition was put to the *Junta*, Synnott wrote to Bernardo Angulo, its chairman, accepting the changes advised by the *Junta* and explaining that Murray had dropped out. Speed was of the essence for both sides; invasion had focused minds enormously; *mañana* was no longer the public policy it had been in 1845.

Synnott was commissioned as a captain to interpret for the commander and it may have been no coincidence that defections were being actively invited from November 1846. With California a U.S. prize of war, however, it was difficult to convince deserters that it was any longer in Mexico's power to grant Californian land. The option was given "of emigrating to whatever frontier Department they might select." Synnott was to receive, when the war ended, an *empresario*'s bonus of land equivalent to that granted to all the Irish military colonists much more than the proposed grant to a captain. Synnott would also be *Intendente* of the colony and the government would cover costs of tooling, seeding and anything else needed. They had vetoed Murray's monopoly on the ground that his greed could stifle a new colony. They may also have known Murray by repute: Mexico's need was greater than that of any foreign profiteer. There was no mention throughout of the Macnamara concession, itself already too big for the river valley from which it was to be apportioned. Much giving away of Californian land, by both Central and Departmental authorities, took place without survey knowledge of exactly how much suitable land was available to be offered. The department could have been promised away twice without anyone being aware of discrepancies: in fact, much of it *was* being promised for the second time.

The confused state of the Mexican administration added to the confusion about California. Within the cabinet it was said that Secretary of State Baranda was "getting secret aid from the English residents of the City and particularly from an Irish priest who for some time has been planning a colonisation project in California." The form of "aid" was not specified, but Santa Anna's foreign minister regarded the priest (who can only have been Macnamara) "as a secret agent of England." Plans to lure deserters from Scott's army were still being discussed in the Mexican Cabinet in the spring of 1847, "offering them 200 acres of land each after the war as inducements."

Congress turned against the idea, mistrusting "gringo" deserters on principle.[18]

Inevitably, Macnamara's name was linked with any scheme involving Californian land and the Irish. Indignant American observers demonized him. From November 1846 onwards, Mexican priests in Monterrey were reported to be enticing Catholic U.S. soldiers from Taylor's army. Priests-at-war were in an old Mexican tradition stretching back to the Aztecs: Miguel Hidalgo and Jose Morelos were still within living memory, heroes of the fight for independence from Spain. Ireland, too, had a similar tradition. At Puebla and Jalapa priests were accused of being guerrilla leaders and of enticing Americans with offers of land. They also killed them: Padre Cenobio Jarauta's name was a by-word by the autumn of 1847, "styling himself a priest, yet nothing but a student, the coldest, bloodiest, guerrilla chief in Mexico," and he fought on, months after the signing of the Peace Treaty in 1848. Clergy at San Luis Potosí called the Americans "vandals vomited from hell to savage the nations." (Santa Anna called them "clowns at a Carnival" and Foreign Minister Ramírez described their conduct as "restrained barbarism.") A priest was arrested in Guadeloupe on a charge of enticing U.S. soldiers to desert. In all, few priests were accused, but enough to arouse anger among the enemy in the heat of war. At the same time, General Scott ordered his men to salute all Mexican officials, including priests in cassocks.[19]

American diarists and correspondents were less than complimentary to Mexican priests. An older, deeper prejudice surfaced. Nicholas Trist, the U.S. commissioner to Mexico, set the tone by writing to Secretary of State Buchanan of "Lazy, ignorant and stupid monks ... the round of purely animal enjoyments which makes up their lives ... their greed for money and property mixed up with idol worship, fanaticism and burning of candles."[20] Ralph Kirkham, serving with General Scott in the early summer of 1847 at Puebla, a city largely ruled by the clergy, described how "the rascally priests live well enough, for they have the fat of the land and dress in broadcloth, but [even] in rags it would be easy enough to recognise them by their fat well-fed bodies. They are a good set of rogues." It was a recognized stereotype, and a stock part of campfire chatter. "If a Mexican buys an American horse," Kirkham said in another letter home, "he pays the priest a round sum to bless it." Macnamara was the most easily identifiable of those demons, Irish and Latin treachery and superstition personified from before the war even started. The legend was so strong that it became seriously accepted fact. "The Mexican Government's most promising plan was to buy up Scott's Irish soldiers through the priest Macnamara, recently conspiring in California, and facilitate their desertion by having Santa Anna attack Puebla."[21]

Certainly in the spring of 1847 Lt. Robert Anderson wrote to his wife of seeing the first "addresses in bad English calling on the Volunteers to desert, promising them rich lands." Synnott's gift for language was evidently not making itself felt. On the capture of Mexico City, Anderson reported Scott's order of 22nd September, "informing us that there is a company headed by some cowardly officers and false priests to assassinate our brave little army. The principal conspirator is said to be an Irish priest called Macnamara who has been tampering with our soldiers, offering them lands in California if they desert. I hope, if the evidence is conclusive against him, he will be hung."[22]

Anderson was a fair and tolerant man who respected Mexican religious practice, but the demonized, generic "Macnamara" was beyond even the most tolerant man's pale. Captain Kenly, another fair-minded American officer who would "make no reflection on the Church and its clergy—they have done wonders in reclaiming an idolatrous people," acted as defense lawyer for "the curate of Naolimo" who had "helped corrupt the rank and file of the U.S. Army by money and promises."[23] Macnamara was never named in Scott's Order of the Day, published in the army newspaper *American Star* on September 24th. It spoke only of "a conspiracy by several false priests to entice our gallant Irish Roman Catholic soldiers to desert under a promise of lands in California which our arms have already conquered." Mere assumption linked the Irish deserters with Macnamara because of the land offer. In fact, while Anderson was inveighing against Macnamara in his letter home of September 23rd, Dr. John Baldwin, with the American Command in Mexico City, was making himself known to Macnamara and hearing about him from friends in Mexican society. Macnamara was under the roof (and protection) of one or other of the British diplomats in Mexico City. Two of these, Thornton and Mackintosh, mediated between the Americans and the Mexican Provisional Government at Queretaro, 150 miles away. It is unlikely that Macnamara's playing a subversive role from under their roof would have been tolerated by the diplomats, since it was both British policy and commercial interest that the war be brought to a speedy conclusion. Unless Macnamara made his way to Vera Cruz and the Royal Mail Packet with Bankhead's entourage under safe conduct and diplomatic protection in October—no witness recorded that he did—he would have had difficulty in leaving a blockaded Mexico. The forlorn Irish deserters who did survive the war were paid off with $50 each upon registering at Euan Mackintosh's consulate in Mexico City. It was more than any other prospective Irish colonist would get.

The Macnamara Project Sealed[24]

Early in the new year, 1847, Macnamara submitted his grant from Governor Pico to the Office for Colonization for recommendation to the Mexican Congress. It took up 18 pages. By then, General Santa Anna, the crafty and vain hero of his own one-legged, one-man version of Mexican patriotism, was president as well as commander-in-chief. Bernardo Angulo's

Dirección of Colonization debated money owed by Macnamara for the land and the legality of Pico's concession. In fact, they fiddled while Mexico burned. The bureaucratic excursion into unreality reflected the understandable reluctance of embattled Mexicans to surrender any land to any foreigner, however Catholic and anti–American.

The *Dirección* calculated the price Macnamara should have been paying for the grant, on a sliding scale of five tariffs between ten *reals* and one-eighth of a *real* per acre. He had never offered and never been asked for payment, nor was he operating under the Bondholder's agreement of 1837, unless he had talked the Mexicans into thinking he worked for the Bondholders. The London creditors' warrants entitled them to an option on 125 million acres (27,900 square leagues) of Mexican frontier land at rock-bottom preferential prices ($1.25 an acre = £1 for four acres), but not *gratis* and not specific to California. Possibly Angulo's committee was considering Macnamara as a possible source of money. The Church was being asked to fill the empty war chest with forced loans and new taxation in 1847.

The *Dirección* then tested the legality of Macnamara's claim and found it flawed. The legal snake ate its own tail and lost track of the link between its two ends. It was inevitable in a scheme conceived, hatched and bred under three successive, diametrically opposed Mexican governments, including one which had assumed dictatorial powers. Angulo's committee denied Pico's authority to make such a grant, although Pico clearly made it at Central Government request and subject to Central Government approval. The proceeds of such sales, they said, should go, by law, towards paying the national debt, yet the Council of Government in 1845 had never discussed payment in its detailed report, save for how to meet the colonists' expenses. Chairman Angulo then claimed foreigners had been banned since 1842 from provincial lands—except by express permission of Central Government: only Central Government, he objected, could alienate Departmental land. The *Dirección* then approved the Project and recommended it to Congress and President Santa Anna. It was as if no one had read the file very closely—perhaps because it no longer mattered. The Irish families were to occupy their land by 1852. Each individual was to be limited to one square league of irrigatable land, four of arable and six of pasture, which turned Pico's contract for 3,000 square leagues into one for *eleven times* as much. One hundred thousand dollars worth of goods would be allowed duty-free through San Francisco. The enjoyment of any minerals on the properties would be subject to the laws of mining.

Sometime before November 1846 someone sent details of the Mexican church to *The Catholic Directory* in Dublin, in time for the 1847 edition. If they came from Mexico, they would have been sent at least two months before that, by packet, to make the deadline. The informant reported Archbishop Posada's death on April 30th (as well as the ages of remaining bishops between 70 and 96). Bishop García Diego, however, who had also died that day, was reported still alive, leading some 60 religious in California, which suggested that the informant knew little of California. Previous to 1847 *The Directory* had never mentioned the Mexican Church. Clancy had been adept at using this yearbook for self publicity; Macnamara would have made a more accurate submission. Besides, it still listed him in British Guiana. The pointed silence of three years was only finally broken in the 1848 edition.

Frémont's "Bugaboo"

John Frémont rose dramatically from lieutenant to lieutenant colonel in a space of months during 1846. As early as his first expedition to the Rockies in 1842, Frémont had been briefed by his father-in-law, the expansionist Senator Thomas Hart Benton, and knew it was more than a survey. His second expedition followed in 1843 to the Columbia River, southeast to Nevada Territory and west over the Sierra Nevada to Sutter's Fort in California. A third expedition took him again to Sutter's Fort in 1845. Sour relations between Sutter and Frémont reflected those between Mexico and the United States. Frémont sought supplies from the coast instead and, after seeing the Santa Clara mercury mine, arrived at Monterey where Comandante Castro permitted him to winter in the San Joaquin Valley. In defiance, Frémont took to Mt. Gavilan north of the Salinas Valley, where he ran up the U.S. flag to bait Castro. The bait was not taken and Frémont turned north for the Oregon border. At Klamath Lake, Marine Lieutenant Gillespie, who had crossed Mexico in disguise, caught up with Frémont and delivered messages from Washington. Whatever the messages—they seem to have been unremarkable—Frémont promptly returned south. He camped at the Sutter Buttes as rumor swept among the American settlers that Comandante Castro was expelling all foreigners from the department. In imitation of the Texans, the settlers raised the Bear-and-Lone-Star flag at Sonoma. Frémont, while not an instigator of the "Bear Flag Revolt," certainly trailed it and reinvented its causes and impact afterwards.

In July, Frémont and Gillespie led a band of settlers, later styled the California Battalion, to Monterey where he met Seymour and Macnamara briefly before embarking in August for Los Angeles to suppress the last of the Californio resistance. There they were still under the command of Commodore Stockton, senior naval officer in California. Unfortunately, Marine Lieutenant Gillespie's arrogance as commander in Los Angeles provoked a Californio backlash in mid–October. As a result, Frémont had to take a fresh battalion of mounted rifles south during the winter. At the same time, General Kearney and a column of volunteers were marching overland via New Mexico, Arizona and the Colorado River to cut off the California Department from Central Mexico. Kearney took over Stockton's authority in the south, but Frémont refused to accept this when Kearney suspended him from duty. The insubordination culminated in a Washington court martial at the end of 1847. Frémont was found guilty of mutiny, insubordination and conduct prejudicial to military discipline. He was also Senator Benton's son-in-law and had promoted Manifest Destiny. Polk had the "mistaken hero" pardoned and reinstated.

Once over this career hurdle, Frémont turned to compensation for himself and the California settlers who had helped in that theater of the Mexican war. He appealed to the Senate, claiming to have gained the independence of California under the Bear Flag even before learning of the Mexican War. Once war and occupation were declared, "the fruits of the revolutionary movement passed to the United States. The peaceful possession of California checked the designs of the Californians to put California under British protection and prevented the fulfillment of the great grant to Macnamara, the original papers of which I have here."[25] He sought over half a million dollars for the expenses of his Battalion and merchants who sold to them on credit, but he had to prove that there had been grave threats to American interests and that they had organized for defensive war accordingly. The reality was that Frémont, a U.S. Army officer, had entered a Mexican Department illegally, then aided and abetted a revolution on that Mexican soil without any mandate to do so. He needed to find a justification after the event and Macnamara was conveniently at hand.

Frémont stated that "the Californios designed to create as large as possible a British interest in the country, to convert, wherever it could be done, public or Mexican property in California into British property." He then adduced a new reason for the Bear Flag rising, but in remarkably vague and evasive terms. "The action of the authorities in the grant to Macnamara *was appreciated by* the revolution in the North." He called witnesses who sang the same refrain. Gillespie claimed the Santa Barbara *Junta* of mid–June, "planned and arranged through Mr Forbes the British vice Consul and an Irish Catholic priest by the name of Macnamara, had been prevented from assembling *in consequence of* the rising of the settlers. All this intrigue of British agents was broken up by Captain Frémont." The whole petition was economic with the truth: the assumption *"after this, therefore because of this"* was never challenged. Under cross-examination Gillespie too retreated behind unverifiable generalities. "The subject of the transfer to England and of Mr Forbes and Macnamara's using all their influence to accomplish that object was the topic of common conversation throughout the country *after* the rising of the settlers in the north." The rising was on June 14th. Gillespie admitted elsewhere to having learned of the *Junta* and of Macnamara only on June 30th. It may even be doubted that he knew of Macnamara before meeting him in *Collingwood*'s wardroom on July 22nd.

One by one they trouped to the witness table with more hearsay and opinion than fact. They all mentioned, in the same breath as Macnamara, the British settlers and prospectors Workman and Reid, who had procured land from Pico and Bandini in the final days of the Mexican Department. The more British interests in California that could be named, the stronger the conspiracy threat would seem to have been. Captain Sam Hensley, a settler in California since 1843, affirmed that he knew "the authorities were about to grant certain tracts of land in California to an Irish priest to establish a colony of British subjects, the said priest Macnamara having been brought to California in a British vessel of war. *My impression* is that the *timely* movements of the settlers in the north, Frémont and others prevented the conclusion of the transfer." Seven of Frémont's topographical engineers agreed that "the revolution put an entire stop to such grants." Another American who had been at Sutter's Fort when Frémont returned with Gillespie from the Klamath, confirmed "there was a good deal of talk about England taking possession of the country. They knew England had a mortgage on it. A British man-of-war was on the north west coast and would be down in the summer to take possession of California." It was easy to see how *Juno, Collingwood, America* and *Herald* all conflated into the threatening warship, but harder to see how a single ship could threaten a continent. Pressed about Macnamara, Midshipman Wilson of Sloat's USS *Savannah* "recollected seeing him at Monterey, engaged, *it was said,* in negotiations with the English Admiral, Seymour, in relation to a grant of land which had been made to him by the Mexican Government." A junior officer from *Savannah* also testified that he knew "*from sources entitled to confidence* in the latter part of 1846 that a majority of people of California desired the protection of England; the opinion he thus formed was strengthened by the fact the English frigate *Juno,* about the same time the *Junta* met, had landed an English subject named Macnamara at Santa Barbara, of whom *it was said* he had obtained a grant from the Mexican government of one third of the richest portion of California." Lieutenant Minor was on shore duty in Monterey and watched Frémont arrive. "The appearance of this body of men and the well known character of its commander not only made a strong impression upon the British admiral and officers, but an equally impressive *and more happy one* upon those of the American navy then in Monterey."

The Senate Committee asked the same question of each witness: "What effect did the revolutionary movement have in stopping sales and grants" being made in a hurry to Mexicans and foreigners to keep the missions and public lands out of the hands of the Americans. The witnesses all agreed that the mission and land grants were being made with "alarming haste" and at "inconsiderable, almost nominal prices." Macnamara and his grant were "a topic of free and very general conversation in all the intelligent circles of California." Col. William Russell "entertained the confident belief that the most valuable portion of the beautiful valley of San Joaquin and the wealthy

Missions of the country would have been ceded and granted away, but for *the opportune hoisting* of the Bear Flag." Only Frank Ward, merchant of San Francisco, disagreed bluntly:" "I do not think the revolutionary movements under the Bear Flag had any effect in stopping these grants, as I know of some that were made within three days of the hoisting of the U.S. Flag by Commodore Sloat." Macnamara's was one of them, but he probably never learned of his own fame in Washington. Despite Ward, the case was proved.

Frémont's actions did prompt John Sloat to take Monterey, even if under a misapprehension. Sloat was angry and puzzled when, at their meeting in Monterey on July 19th, Frémont disclaimed any Washington orders for his action. Macnamara, supposedly with the British Empire actively behind him, was a powerfully distracting Goliath which David could claim to have helped slay. Frémont took to Washington from the scatterings of Pico's departmental archive the dossiers of the five most important California land grants, including the Macnamara concession. Pico himself had abstracted the most important title deeds to take back to Mexico, but had to leave them behind at John Forster's ranch. The Macnamara papers were published in Washington as evidence of the huge threat to the Monroe doctrine which Frémont had thwarted. Frémont's biographer echoed that "by virtue of this grant of land to Macnamara the whole country would have passed under British protection," adding San Francisco Bay to the San Joaquin contract for good measure. "The American flag was floating over California, hoisted in consequence of Frémont's achievements. The whole scheme of Macnamara's grant, the Irish colony and a British protectorate was scattered to the winds. Frémont is therefore entitled to the glory of having secured California from falling into the hands of a foreign power and preventing a disastrous collision between this country and Great Britain."[26]

Senator Benton, Frémont's proud and protective father-in-law and Polk's adviser on Manifest Destiny, gilded the lily. His son-in-law, he said, "put himself at the head of the people to save the country, snatching it out of the hands of the British. For 200 years the eyes of the British have been on California [and he prevented] the transfer of the public domain to British subjects, the British Vice-Consul Forbes and the emissary priest Macnamara ruling and conducting everything: and all their plans so far advanced as to render the least delay fatal. It was then the begining of June." Myth was simpler than reality—and chronology.[27] Forty years later, Frémont himself remembered Macnamara more kindly: by then the demon had served his purpose.

Demon Macnamara

Macnamara was last sighted in Mexico City by John Baldwin, who left for Washington in November 1847. Rumor persisted that the Irish priest took passage for Europe, rounded the Cape and died at sea. William Rudall, a young English businessman on the Pacific coast of Mexico since 1842, wrote to the Mexican Sonoran, José Velasco, from Guyamas in October 1849. Velasco was compiling the story of his native Sonora from documents collected over sixty years, and Rudall's letter went into his archive. In Guyamas, Rudall had met one "Dr Delis, a practical miner" attached to a Mr. Whiting's Company in California, which in July 1849 was "ruined as a result of strong opposition from the Americans to Mexicans, Chileans etc." It is just possible that "Delis" was an Irish doctor, Daly, resident in Mexico 1844–52, who turned to mining at the Real D'Oro in 1845. Delis was certainly a friend of Macnamara. One Whiting managed a Barron and Forbes cotton mill in Tepic.[28]

Delis had returned to Guyamas and Rudall took notes of his conversation. Forecasting a doubled population of California by 1850, accompanied by a gold yield "larger than the income of Great Britain," Delis wanted to "add its riches in mercury to its gold. Mr Forbes' mine alone, worked without machinery and in the crudest way imagineable, he reckoned to produce a daily profit of $1,000." California "has only a very small area fit for farming and as it will not become a manufacturing country, it will become an importing country. Its wet, cold and changeable climate determines what its principle imports will be. England as usual will account for most of the trade." Rudall then remembered Macnamara.

> A tract seventy leagues [182 miles] long was granted to Father Macnamara to establish a foreign colony by the former governor of California, Pió Pico. I well remember that this tract runs from north to south between the latitudes of Monterey and San Diego and it is probable that this land will lead to litigation, as Dr Delis, a friend of Macnamara, told me; that the land in question was really granted for the purpose mentioned by the Governor of California before the Americans entered in 1846 and the grant was confirmed in Mexico City by President Santa Anna before last year's April armistice. According to what I have learned, Macnamara is in Europe pursuing his claim.[29]

James Forbes spent the next decade defending his rights in the Santa Clara Mine (under its new name of New Almaden). In 1858 he testified,

> Macnamara is dead, as I have been informed. He died, as I have been told, in 1847. It must have been later, because in 1847 he left the [west] coast of Mexico and went around Cape Horn. I had intelligence in 1848 or 1849 that he was dead.[30]

No vessel of the Royal Navy in Pacific waters logged the taking of Macnamara on board after 1846. From 1837 all deaths at sea in British vessels had to be registered in Great Britain. Macnamara's name was not so registered, nor was his name registered as dying in the British Isles in the 19th century.

He may have died on a ship of another nationality or died ashore elsewhere. The fact that he failed to "make mischief" as he had threatened over the land grant and the fact that he did not make a claim before the California Land Commission suggest that he was dead. It meant that his huge land contract was consigned to the wastebin, nullified after 1852 under both Mexican and American law, because it had neither been taken up (under Mexican conditions) nor verified (under U.S. requirements). The colony became a utopian memory, literally no-such-place, so much so that while a respectable lawyer could still pour scorn on Macnamara in 1852, a fellow Irish priest in 1878 denied the Project had ever existed and a California Franciscan in 1896 accused Frémont of forging it.

The Encirclement Conspiracy

Just before his disappearance into the stuff of Black Legend, Macnamara was again invoked in Washington, this time by the breakaway Mexican Department of Yucatán, the Maya jungle peninsula. It had declared independence in 1840 with the help of Texas. At the end of the Mexican war, the Yucatán commissioner to the United States, Juan Sierra O'Reilly, pleaded with the U.S. Secretary of State not to treat them as part of defeated Mexico, but to help against the British and Mexicans. The Royal Navy had attacked and blockaded the Yucatán: the nearby British commercial protectorate, the "Kingdom of Mosquito" (Belize, later British Honduras), was arming the Maya Indians against the Yucatán authorities. O'Reilly asked Washington to follow the Monroe Doctrine with proper consistency. In February 1848, between the Frémont court martial and the Frémont compensation appeal, O'Reilly rehearsed the grievances of Yucatán, particularly against Britain, "a power which employs its strength according to any other rules than those of morality." He accused the British of seizing Yucatán ships and of abusing the Royal Navy's power in threatening bombardment on behalf of the Mosquito King. He cited Macnamara in the same breath as the naval bombardment. The belief was certainly strong in 1841, claimed O'Reilly, that

> The two Californias and the Yucatan were hypothecated for the payment of the English debt [and it has been] corroborated by certain incidents, not the least important of them being the authorisation granted by the Mexican Government to a certain Irishman, individually, to colonise an immense quantity of square miles in the Californias, the extent of which, not now precisely in my recollection, embraced nearly the whole of those provinces."[31]

The interests of O'Reilly's lobby coincided with those of the expansionists and Frémont supporters in Washington. Frémont's compensation claims were debated by Congress in March 1848. Senator John Dix carefully allowed that Frémont had kept California "out of the hands of British subjects and *perhaps* out of the hands of the British Government." He cited an active, undermining British presence on the Mosquito Coast, where the isthmus was most suitable for a canal. "We seem to have restricted Monroe to *North* America now." He and O'Reilly had certainly talked. The Macnamara scheme was, he said, an example of the typical British progression from private home, through ditch, fort and colony, to perpetual occupation. India and Canada were ready-made illustrations. He attacked the Irishman's bigoted "stigmas cast upon us and upon one of our most respectable religious sects ['Methodist wolves']" but allowed that they were "to minister to the prejudices of Mexico, rather than emanating from a conviction of their truth." He cited the Royal Navy support for Macnamara and Pico's wholesale granting of mission lands in May and June "to British subjects." He put it as fairly as his pro–American feelings would allow. Macnamara was "*so connected with the movement of public vessels and public agents of Great Britain as to raise a strong presumption* that he was secretly countenanced by the British Government. We are constrained to believe that the British commander was fully apprised of Macnamara's objects and that he was there co-operating." It was then that Dix painted with a broader brush, showing vividly how everything pointed to a British conspiracy. The Oregon crisis, the Mosquito Kingdom and the Macnamara project

> were part of a deliberate design to surround us with her colonies and equally to shut us out of the Pacific and its extending commerce. [In California] the drama of the Mosquito coast, the performers only being changed, would have been acted all over again. A California Governor, somewhat above the grade of the King of the Mosquitoes in respectability, but on the same level in subservience, would have been put in the foreground while British subjects would have occupied the country. Thus shut out from the Pacific, our own people would have been met at the Sierra Madre or further east and the tide of emigration and settlement been turned back upon the Atlantic coast.[32]

Gold Discovery

The U.S.-Mexican Peace Treaty had still not been agreed, nor had Frémont's compensation claim been heard, when one of John Sutter's men found "goald" in the new sawmill race at Coloma, on the American River in the Sierra Nevada foothills. This was in January 1848, just north of the Cosumnes River, the proposed northern boundary of the Macnamara tract. Gold was nothing new in California, but this discovery was dramatic, it was in American hands and it coincided with new interest in and new migration to the west coast. As a consequence, the world began to rush into California during 1848 and stampeded in during 1849. California was worked and colonized.

Very quickly, many saw through the gold dream and spotted the agricultural opportunity. They joined the existing newly settled Irish ranchers in the Santa Clara Valley, among them the Murrays, the Murphys, the Fallons, the Whites and the Harts. Martin Murphy, Sr., of Wexford was building his ranchhouse on the road between San José and Monterey when Macnamara landed in California. His son Martin had a grant on the Cosumnes River, the site of a horse-stealing by the Trappers which had prompted the Bear Flag Revolt.

Among the Gold Rush tourists-of-fortune came William Kelly, a London Irish lawyer, formerly of Colooney, County Sligo, whose family business of flour and bleach milling had gone bankrupt, but whose cousins, the Milmos, ran the Bank of Monterrey in Mexico. He had been very highly placed, "a protege of Lord Mulgrave, a favourite of O'Connell and the idol of the humbler classes."[33] Several Santa Clara Valley Irish knew his family from better times and in 1849 he brought letters of introduction. Unlike the swindlers he had met in New York, who "some years in the States" used every "blarney and brass" to draw sympathy "and to pass for modern refugees," the Irish ranchers had no need to pretend. "On some of the happy evenings I spent amongst them, it afforded me a tearful pleasure to witness the strong feelings of sympathy and sorrow they evinced in adverting to the miseries of their suffering brethren at home, 'starving and dying,' as they said, 'on the green fields of poor Erin,' while *they* had enough and to spare in a foreign land." Kelly, for all his Irishness and love of anecdote, made no mention of Macnamara, though they may have talked of him in the Santa Clara Valley. California, he thought, was unfit for agriculture.

The Memory Fades

Isaac Hartmann, a leading lawyer in San Francisco, may have known anti–Semitism, but it did not dilute his acid towards former Governor Pío Pico, whom he described as corrupt, non–English speaking, negroid, dwarfist and Latino. He shared the prejudices of the American establishment and local feeling in San Francisco in 1852, which was ill-disposed towards anything Latino or Irish. Irish gravestones in San Francisco Mission Dolores proclaimed, *May God Forgive My Persecutors* and *Remember Oh Lord Not Our Offences*. "Native" prejudice and greed (that of second generation Protestant arrivals) attacked immigrant corruption and greed (that of first generation Catholic arrivals). Hartmann vented his feelings about Macnamara,

> more bitterly hostile to the American people than any other foreigner who had ever visited California. [Having failed in the land grant, he and Forbes] undertook the more pleasant task of serving themselves. The pen of history has not yet written any account of the subsequent Apostolic Missionary labours of Fr Macnamara and we here lose sight of him.[34]

Those who dealt with Macnamara were the first to forget him. Ex-Governor Pico, who gave him the largest concession in California's Departmental history, barely remembered him ten years later and objected in court to questions about the Macnamara affair. In a later, lengthy memoir of his time in office, Pico made no mention of Macnamara at all. Pico's son-in-law, John Forster of San Diego, who had hidden Pico, Bandini and Argüello from the Americans, together with the Macnamara papers, in his ranch house, added only a little in 1878 when he remembered that Seymour had tried to get to Monterey in time to raise the British flag, "as had been arranged beforehand between the Californian government and British government through an Irish Catholic priest named Macnamara." This in turn may reflect Macnamara's own self-inflating. Forster himself founded a colony on Pico's old ranch of Santa Margarita: Forster City, near San Onofrio, grew to three buildings and a street layout before it was abandoned.[35]

Comandante Castro, who had helped Macnamara transfer the mine into British hands, also had little to say in court save that he once thought the Irishman was important. James and Alexander Forbes documented some of what they knew about Macnamara in court, but in their own papers said and left nothing about him at all. Eusebio Galindo, a magistrate of Santa Clara, into whose family James Forbes had married, told Bancroft's interviewers in 1877 that he remembered Macnamara and the concession "on the Sacramento" [*sic*] to counteract the "Protestant Americans. It is believed by some that Macnamara was an agent in this country of the English who have been accused of having ideas for taking possession of this country."[36] David Spence of Monterey, who met Macnamara more than once and witnessed his empowerment as attorney for the mercury mine in June 1846, made no mention of him, nor did Antonio Osio, another witness of the power of attorney contract in Monterey. Admiral Seymour, a man with a gift for friendship, never referred to him again, even though he read and annotated his 1846 *Private Diary* afresh in 1851.

Those who did speak of Macnamara later had ample time to learn of him on the grapevine. Age, poverty and alcohol also crept up on witnesses and affected their memories. John Forster, for instance, had a serious drink problem. Many, like Pico, were reduced to poverty. Thomas Lancey, a sailor in the sloop USS *Dale* which came to the California coastline in December 1846, wrote about Macnamara from third-hand, and thirty years later. His detail was sometimes bizarre, as when he had Macnamara meeting Pico in 1844 *before* arriving in Mexico City, but he vented cheap spleen on the harmless ghost of Macnamara, who could at least still make the front page of a California newspaper.

The English transport *Palinurus,* instead of taking the good Father to Van Diemen's Land [Tasmania, the British convict settlement], left him at

Mazatlan about December 1846 and in 1847 he went round the Horn in a ship and soon afterwards died.[37]

A fellow Irishman, John Ross Browne, had an opportunity to hear of Macnamara from informed sources, since he was *Congressional Globe* reporter for the California Convention in 1849 at Monterey which included Juan Bandini. He accorded Macnamara only a passing spat. Browne was a surveyor, a Dubliner, known for self-aggrandizing journalism, but also for sharp and accurate surveys. He simply cited Berthold Seeman with HMS *Herald* at San Blas in November 1846,

> Having on board no less a person than the Rev Father Macnamara who was making such a noise about that time in founding his great colony of Irish Catholic refugees in the Tulare valley of the present State of California.[38]

Macnamara would have been more disappointed by the short memories of others. Narciso Botello, second senior member of Pico's Departmental Assembly, who had recommended Macnamara to José Moreno and supported Figueroa in passing the Macnamara project from the Assembly to Pico on July 7th, remembered him only inaccurately, and in doing so accused Pico of the corrupt lining of his family's and friends' pockets, "Don Juan Bandini especially among others," in the last days of Mexican California.

> During that time, an Irish priest, Eugene Macnamara, visited Los Angeles. He came recommended by the Central Government and brought a project to establish in California a colony of Irish Catholics, asking for that purpose a land concession. This business went through the procedure of the Assembly and there was conceded to him a land title in northern California near Cape Mendocino [*sic*]. This was in June and July 1846.[39]

Antonio Coronel had also been in the small assembly chamber in Los Angeles on July 7, 1846 when they approved Bandini's recommendations. Thirty years later, he just remembered that Macnamara came to put an Irish colony in the way of the Americans encroaching into California "and to enable England to protect her subjects." The American invasion had put an end to both colony and protectorate.[40]

The Unkindest Cuts

By the 1870s the State of California was settled and tranquil, its more fortunate surviving pioneers rocking on their verandah chairs in retirement. Others were still scratching a living as they had done when they first arrived, too late for either mines or land. The Irish formed roughly one-tenth of the state's population, mostly in commerce or on the land. Californian Irish had left behind them much of the sectarianism, Catholic and Protestant alike, which so afflicted Europe. The United States Constitution, in refusing to favor one religion against another, underpinned this fresh start. Distance also helped. The Irish clergy who came in the wake of the Irish settlers, for the most part, took this opportunity for a fresh start and to sink Old World differences. A few, however, saw prejudice and conspiracy everywhere. A deep-rooted inferiority complex compelled one immigrant chaplain to see an idealized "Milesian nobility of soul" in every "fine Irish face" he met. Hugh Quigly, a priest of the pre–Famine period, published *The Irish Race in California*, to boost the self-respect of the Irish Catholic migrant. With its green binding embossed with gold harp, it was an Irish version of the commercial "mugshot histories," vanity publications popular in the California counties at the time. Men could puff and re-invent themselves, because they contributed their own account of themselves.

Bancroft wrote of the Irish as "whiskey soaked and ignorance drenched … ever atoning for weakness with infectious humour … hardy and versatile … with a bent for political agitation and for crowding into city suburbs." He attacked Quigly for "painting their wealth and influence in glowing colours." Respect from oneself and from others is a classic immigrant need, after the material concern of basic survival has been met. Quigly set out to meet this need by traveling the counties of California to record everything favorable about the Irish, mainly the Catholic, that he could find. Quigly was erratic, pompous, sentimental and gullible, but even he could not accept the Macnamara Project. It was "apocryphal" or at most, "only true in part," a tale found "in dusty old books."

It did not fit Quigly's world view, in which it was "not likely that the Mexican government which had granted its lands so freely to men who were not Catholic would concern itself about the religion of the immigrants whether they were Protestant, Catholic or atheist. The Mexicans wanted inhabitants for their lands, not enquiries about their religion. More grants of land went to Protestants than to Catholics. Protestant and atheist receive the same liberal treatment [in South America] as if they were the most orthodox Catholics, but if a colony of Catholics applied to any liberal Protestant government would they be as successful? The story of Macnamara and his Irish colony needs confirmation. It has no proof beyond rumour. England was however negotiating for possession of California and an English fleet was on its way to take and keep California, but if England had succeeded she could not have held the country for a month. [Kearney and Stevenson's Irish New York Volunteers] would have made short work of the 'redcoats' had they succeeded in landing in California with a view to conquest."[41]

Quigly was unaware that Mexican religious toleration came late, and only through liberal, anti-clerical governments with ulterior motives, but certainly not under the politically and religiously conservative regimes which backed Macnamara. Quigly's "redcoats" were significant: he had been sent home from Scotland in 1846 for preaching a political sermon in a "redcoat" garrison church. Famously, he reported the Famine in County Clare for *The Tablet* in "Black '47." He was, in fact, a priest of Killaloe diocese, a native of Tulla, less than 20 miles from Ennis, five years younger than Macnamara and near enough a contemporary. (He had also worked as a surveyor's assistant in the military [Ordnance] survey of Ireland, as, apparently, did Jasper O'Farrell, Pico's last surveyor and architect of the layout of San Francisco.)[42]

If Quigly did not quite claim that the Macnamara papers were a forgery, the Californian Franciscan chronicler, Zephryn Engelhardt, did. He accused Frémont outright of having "more to do with the wording of the petition as it exists than Macnamara." He suspected another *Maria Monk* smear forgery, but evidently knew little about Frémont. A decade before Engelhardt wrote, a mellow John Frémont applauded Macnamara's project in his *Memoirs*. "In the interests of his Church, it was a nobly conceived plan; one among the great ideas which affect nations."

Nine

Utopia—No Such Place.
California 1852

The Sacramento and the San Joaquin Valleys are full of
fever, mosquitoes, aridity and ague.—(Special Corre-
spondent in California, *The Honolulu Polynesian,* 11
December 1847)

Peace was finally ratified between Mexico and the United States in
March 1848. California remained an American Territory until statehood in
1850. With the change of law and government, the titles of ownership to
land from Mexican days came under review. California land had once been
given away urgently from a vast surplus, but the new immigration in search
of gold and land brought new problems. Landholders faced determined, often
violent squatters. A Mexican land title was ambivalent, given the anti–Mexican feeling abroad and given the haphazard observance of legal procedure
in Mexican days, especially just prior to the war. Between 1833 and 1843 the
annual number of land grants averaged 53; in 1844 it rose to 122. Another 68
were added in 1845 and 67 in the Mexican six months of 1846. By the end
of the U.S. military occupation of California, Senator Benton's two sons-in-
law, John Frémont and William Carey Jones, had large properties which had
been Mexican grants: Frémont's tract of Las Mariposas sat astride the gold
lode discovered in 1848

Fraudulent or Irregular?

In 1847 Frémont brought to Washington documentary proof of the vast
Macnamara concession and of outright grants made by Pico in the last days
of his governorship, particularly to two British families, the Workmans and

the Reids. He made it clear to the Senate in 1848 that he thought Governor Pico had acted corruptly in disposing of so much, so hurriedly, even after July 7th when Sloat occupied Monterey. There followed considerable Senate discussion of the need to sort out the California land titles and in so doing to tighten the hold on that territory against the foreign claims which Macnamara epitomized. Bancroft dismissed this as a red herring: "the Macnamara bugaboo was buzzing in the Senate's ear," generating fears that the Catholic Church might "present a plausible claim for vast mission tracts," or that "Frémont, Sutter, Vallejo and Larkin might seize all Macnamara had left," or that British individuals might seize what their nation had left.[1] Mexican law was also invoked against Macnamara's concession: it was too large for a Departmental governor's power to concede and its papers were irregularly back-dated. In short, it was fraudulent and illegal.

In 1849, during negotiations for the creation of the new State, Henry Halleck, Secretary for the California Territory, reported to Governor Mason on the anarchy of land ownership. He saw chaos and fraud. Before the year was out, Frémont's brother-in-law, William Carey Jones, a lawyer, also reported on the problem, but to Washington. He took a more relaxed view, which also suited the family's purpose. Irregular procedures approved by custom and usage in Mexican days, he argued, did not amount to fraud; nor were incomplete or technically defective grants necessarily illegal. He cited a Mexican law of December 1833 authorizing "all measures to assure the colonisation and the secularisation of the missions [of California], with power to use the Pious Fund."[2] The departmental governor could grant up to 11 square leagues and contract for larger concessions to *empresarios*: Central Government had to confirm the latter. Mexico had explicitly ordered the governors, Vallejo and Pico among them, to colonize for the defense of the nation. Neither Halleck nor Jones explained that Macnamara's concession had been encouraged by Mexico City, although this was clear from the Macnamara papers held and published in Washington. Macnamara was also acting under extraordinary dictatorial powers assumed constitutionally by General Paredes—but this was not evident from the papers known at the time. The contract had been confirmed afterwards by another Mexican government, still in a state of emergency. The vagueness, lack of paperwork and of due process characterizing most grants was the practice of the day, making for titles technically imperfect, but still legal. They could not be described as fraudulent in intent, and Jones was keen to stress this.

He noted in passing, "the proposed great Macnamara grant *or contract* of which the principal papers are on file in the State Department." Only those papers copied from Macnamara by Pico's secretariat were on file. Without the rest of the really "principal" papers from the file in Mexico City, they did not make legal or chronological sense. Jones did, however, correctly distinguish *a contract*, a concession from which grants could be made, from *a grant* with right of ownership. The Macnamara contract was unique in California, more like Texas concessions than Pico's other California conveyances. The fact that Jones was related to Frémont may further explain why his more liberal report was adopted. Frémont's ten-league grant, Las Mariposas, at the southern end of the gold lode country, was the first property to be confirmed by the new Land Commission. Under the terms imposed by Governor Pico, even had Macnamara come back from the dead to assert his claim, he would have been no threat to Frémont's or to any of the other 14 existing titles to land east of the San Joaquin River from Mexican days. Pico had stipulated that existing third-party rights must be respected and he conceded only public, empty land to Macnamara.[3]

What had been legal title under Mexico was to be recognized by the United States, as agreed in the Peace Treaty.[4] The Macnamara concession may have been pre- or post-dated, but was not thereby illegal. Claimants of land title were ordered to submit evidence of ownership to a California Land Claims Commission within 24 months, 1852-3, the burden of proof resting firmly on the claimants. Three-quarters of the 813 claims lodged were eventually approved, a quarter were declared void, but the expense of coming to tribunal, finding evidence from a laxer age and going on to appeal, reduced many owners to poverty and they had to sell anyway. Had Macnamara appeared among the 813, the issue of Pico's dating the document July 4th would have been argued in Tribunal. The cut-off date of July 7, 1846 laid down by the United States was the victor's arbitrary imposition, a legal fiction, given that the land was not pacified by conquest for some months and that Pico's Departmental Assembly continued to legislate until mid–August. Lawyers for a Macnamara claim before the Land Commission might even have questioned what time of morning on July 7th the Assembly in Los Angeles confirmed the Macnamara petition: was it *before* or *after* Sloat's men ran up the flag at Monterey?

In 1858, during the *U.S. vs. Castillero* case over the New Almaden (formerly Santa Clara) mercury mine, James Forbes put succinctly what so many had felt about the deadline date of July 7, 1846, imposed retrospectively on Mexican land titles: "It was at that period the opinion of foreigners and Mexicans that California would be restored to Mexico."[5] In previous months, other grants had been backdated and *irregular* dating was customary, but there had been no custom of, or perceived need for, *fraudulent* dating in 1846, even after war broke out. In Macnamara's case, Pico signed about five days after the Assembly had approved the grant, but dated his ratification three days before it was approved. It was authentic in spirit, if not by the book. In the empty, informal California of 1846, with communications as bad as ever and paper at a premium, a laxity of procedure was accepted. Pico wrote on common unsealed paper and made no attempt to disguise it. The full text on it may have been an expansion on an agreement already made and signed in précis. Pico knew the minds of his assemblymen, especially Bandini, when he first agreed the contract in principle with Macnamara, both at Santa Barbara on June 24th and in the half-hour conversation by the Los Angeles road on July 1st. Twelve days later, Macnamara obtained a fully composed written agreement with supporting references and figures: it was not a rubber stamp. Pico departed from Bandini's advice where he thought fit. The fact that Macnamara had then to go back to Mexico and get Central Government agreement was secondary: the land was already conceded or contracted legally in principle, and past the crucial primary stage of conveyance. Macnamara would have had a strong case had he claimed in 1852: his due process had in fact begun in May 1845 and the lack of a sketch map was already accepted in many grants. Had the claims commissioners accepted Macnamara's title, already fully confirmed under Mexican law in 1847, only the size and concept of a "colony" would have appeared odd in the new circumstances of a constant inflow of immigrants to California. He would, however, have had only until the end of 1852 to produce colonists, under the terms of the Mexican Government confirmation of 1847. Macnamara's, however, was not among the submissions made, but his name did feature frequently during the long, drawn-out New Almaden (Santa Clara) Mine case. The mine was jinxed. It was enmeshed in a disputed title for the land around it, originally awarded to Commissioner Castillero as a reward by Central Government. The award impinged on the title of a third-party owner and the mine ownership was still in dispute as late as 1873. James Forbes enjoyed little of its proceeds, but it continued to produce until 1976.

Macnamara's "New Ireland"

The Irish Famine was into its second year when Macnamara's colony was confirmed in Mexico City in the spring of 1847. He had until 1852 to put it in place. The London Bondholders' option on lands in lieu of debt repayment expired on October 1, 1847. Gold was found in January 1848 at Coloma, just beyond the northern limit of Macnamara's concession. The state of war with Mexico ran its course until March 1848. The world rushed in before Macnamara's settlers could have arrived, whether by Mexican naval vessels or under their own steam, whether direct from Ireland or, if Macnamara had swallowed his pride, from growing Irish populations in the eastern United States. Only energetic and reasonably comfortable farmers were due to come, with mechanics, doctors, clergy and others in support. Of the many Irish who were drawn by the gold discovery, most had been acclimatized and found confidence back east or in Canada before they came. Few Famine refugees landing in the east could have faced an immediate trek west, the breaking of virgin soil in California and self-defense against a resentful native Indian.

The oven-like climate of the Central Valley would have been a problem in itself: Mark Twain suggested that settlers on the San Joaquin and Sacramento would feel the need for blankets in Hell.

Colonizing projects had to advertise. *The Emigration and Colonial Gazette* throughout 1842 had castigated all things American and advised the emigrant to avoid that "charnel house of humanity." It had approved of and described in detail ventures at San Patricio and on the Red River in Texas, which, like California, was not U.S. territory. Irish colonists were advised to take "a priest of their own nation" wherever they went. *The Emigrant* acknowledged California only in January 1849, where "great numbers of immigrants are flooding from all quarters." A map showed the Rio Sacramento and Rio San Joaquin, along with Lake Bonaventura, better known as Laguna Tulares. The journal continued to promote California, "suddenly planting a nation where we but lately thought solitude was to reign yet for a century," but a warning note was sounded: "If the surface gold should disappear, the settlers must plough it from the soil and hew it from the forest." Until gold was found, "California's chaste attractions went unheeded. Now, all the products of the USA from apples to oranges, potatoes to sugar cane, may be soon produced in the valleys of the San Joaquin and the Sacramento."[6]

Direct appeals to the Irish press from an experienced priest might have brought recruits. The Irish left Ireland in increasing numbers as Famine receded and they fled the west in particular, "emigrants from the remote parts of Clare on their way to Limerick for embarcation, women and children sitting on beds and boxes with swollen eyes and wet cheeks, while with grave and downcast looks men old and young marched slowly by their sides. On the morning of a day arranged for the sailing of emigrant ships, along the roads as far as the eye could see might be seen trains of carts coming in after travelling all night, often in the rain." Evicted tenants made straight for the Limerick road; police morale was undermined by what they saw; Gaelic interpreters were in short supply; Catholic peasants were ashamed to be seen taking meat offered by kind Protestants on a Friday; Scottish troops, a red rag to an Irish population, were provocatively quartered in Ennis.[7]

Travel agents in market towns asked priests to explain details of sailings for their parishioners. Priests in turn initiated projects and split the church. Michael Comyn begged the Famine Relief Commission to develop Doonbeg and district, for people would be "better on the unprofitable wastes of their own native land than compelled to emigrate to some foreign and hostile distant country to swell the ranks of Great Britain's enemies."[8] *The Times*, no friend of the Famine Irish, accused clergy like Comyn of trying to keep their populist power base. Some clergy saw a plot to decimate the Irish; others, particularly those in Limerick, had long favored emigration. In the colonies and the United States, Irish immigration was seen as a Papal plot to take over by invasion, or a dumping of Britain's unwanted. Some churchmen, straining

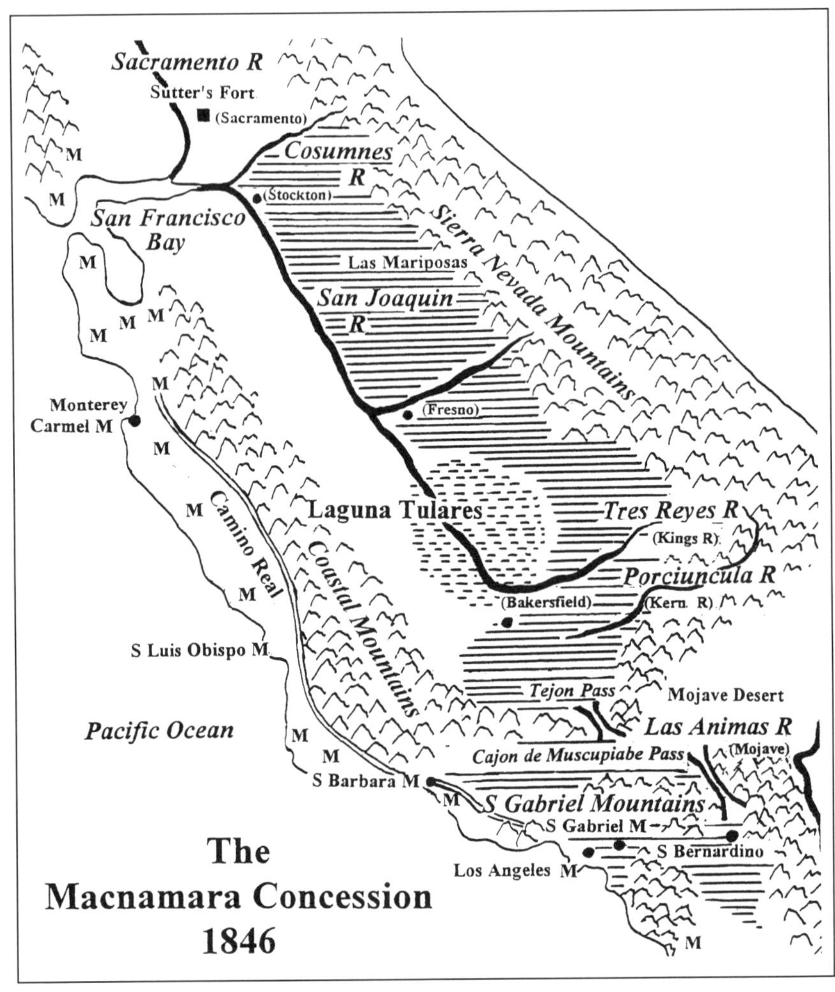

Map of the Macnamara Concession

to make sense of the tragedy, rationalized this Malthusian draining of the young and energetic as "a scattering of the blessings of the Catholic religion over distant lands." A Kenmare parish priest, begged by his people to take them en masse to America, simply could not face it. The Cistercian abbot of Mount Melleray considered moving the abbey to Iowa, and some monks did in fact go. A Wexford priest arranged to take his parish in groups of 300 to Arkansas, but lost control of the first group at Liverpool. A Carlow priest founded the Leinster Emigration Society and circulated local parishes for colonists to New Carlow on the Mississippi. It fell through before Liverpool. By 1850 these priests, eccentric "honorable, honest fanatics," were a dated species and colonies were no longer discussed. Mass individual and family emigration was a fact and the clergy could not explain or prevent the tragedy, only ease it where possible.[9] Any "New Ennis" that Macnamara may have had in mind—a pueblo was always focal point for a colony—would have been swamped with the Gold Rush influx into California, as happened to Montezuma/Sutterville, or might never even have started, like Santa Anna y Farías.

There is no evidence of Macnamara's having returned to Ireland. A single surviving draft flyer was produced for local California consumption only. Zephryn Engelhardt, the Franciscan chronicler, who believed that Frémont had forged the Macnamara papers anyway, also dismissed this publicity draft as a related forgery: it overstated the mineral wealth of California which, Engelhardt thought, was not generally known in 1846. The draft, in Spanish, survived, perhaps as a memento, among Abel Stearns' papers, endorsed "relating to Snr Macnamara." The unusually accurate spelling of the name suggests authenticity. Juan Bandini was Stearns' Peruvian Spanish father-in-law. The flyer was couched in the idiom of spoken Spanish and written by someone who knew the Assembly's approved concession, but it was not Pico's final adjusted version. Directed at a limited, select audience, it assumed that Macnamara had not left for Mexico, but it was certainly written after his meeting with the Assembly. It gave no hint of war between Mexico and the United States, nor of Sloat's having taken Monterey. Everything points to Bandini as its composer, on or shortly after July 7th.

Juan Bandini was as keen a prospector as colonizer. He and others as far away as the British government and the London Bondholders had known for some years the promise of mineral wealth in California, but like good prospectors, played it in a low key. Bandini probably drafted the flyer on July 8, 1846, when he was finishing his correspondence before retiring from public life. In his letter to Macnamara that day, which Admiral Seymour preserved in the back of his diary, Bandini went out of his way to stress the mineral potential of the land and linked the Irish colony directly with extracting that wealth, which may also reflect Macnamara's own changing priorities. The flyer did the same:

> I hasten to inform you of an event of real importance to take place in this country by which we can expect that California will become prosperous and happy. A colony of 10,000 Irish people has requested the Mexican government to be allowed to come to this country to cultivate vacant land under the Mexican laws.
>
> The contractor, Macnamara, an Irish priest, has appeared in front of the Departmental Committee with special recommendations from the Supreme Mexican authorities to find out the extent of wastelands available for colonisation. And this Committee recommends favourably to the Mexican Government so that the Padre *empresario* can return to Mexico to agree with the Mexican Congress the concessions allowed this type of colony. Note the advantages that will occur generally in California, to all the social

classes, given that it is a vast and fertile land as well as a terrain for industries, its minerals already discovered such as silver, gold, copper and mercury. All these raw materials are hidden in the entrails of this virgin earth which will produce whatever man wants to cultivate and will not require laborious industry, but will disgorge from its depths with little labour.

The Mexican government, in order to contain the greed and ambition of the U.S. *del Norte*, needs to promote colonisation and, I believe, as the first step is made for the arrival of an Irish contingent, the government will continue to protect every claim proposed, by way of justified and fair concession. I pass you this important advance notice, above all so as to be prepared just in case someone decides to take the opportunity to profit from the wealth and abundance of this country.[10]

The Valley

Mosquitoes and hostile Indians were the best-known features of the San Joaquin Valley in 1846. It had barely been explored, surveyed or settled. Since 1836, however, 30 ranch grants had been made on either side of the San Joaquin River, speculative outposts in frontier territory. Some grants had to be abandoned. Even Mexican troops stationed east of the river in 1843 had lost horses and equipment to the Indians. When the Land Commission asked former Governor Alvarado in 1852 whether he thought it was "safe or expedient up to July 1846 to occupy a grant of land along the San Joaquin River in consequence of the Indian depredations," he answered unequivocally, "It was not safe or possible." Frémont told the Commission that his ranch, Las Mariposas, was "too dangerous for occupation until nearly the present day" and was still "in constant danger of destruction."

The first Spanish scouts in the interior named the two great rivers of the Central Valley after the Sacrament of bread and wine and after St. Francis of Assisi, patron of the missioners. Legend had a Buenaventura River running direct west through the Sierras to the Pacific, named for a 13th century Franciscan cardinal. It did not exist, but two Sierra torrents which pooled in winter to form the Tulares Lake (at first named Lake Buenaventura) were named La Porciuncula, after a village near Assisi in Italy, and Tres Reyes, after the *magi* at the birth of Christ. Saint Joachim (Joaquin), father of the Virgin Mary, later dislodged Francis as patron of the main river running south to north in the southern Central Valley. Much depended on the church feast-day on or near which a Spanish explorer sighted such landmarks. As late as 1830 the entire San Joaquin Valley was still mapped as virtual wetland and called Los Tulares (Swamp Reed Lands).[11]

The Franciscan missioners planned to extend their coastal chain of missions to an inland loop. A Tulares Valley mission was proposed in 1816, 45–50 leagues east of San Miguel mission, "to take the bird in its nest" and "lead back" the native Indians to Christianity, as if to some Golden Age they had somehow lost. The war against Spain and a shortage of missioners meant the plan was put to the back of churchmen's minds. A further suggestion, that a mission be established at Castaic, Tejon Pass Rancho, was also fruitless, though Castaic and other mission ranches were *asistencias* or unmanned mission outposts, complete with chapels and storehouses. A mission outreach from San Juan Bautista was planned, well east of the San Joaquin River, but nothing came of it, save piled adobe bricks, due to Indian hostility. The farthest inland the missioners established themselves was at San Bernardino, an *asistencia* of Mission San Gabriel. "If the Mexican republic had been bred in peace, California might have had a new chain of missions in the very heart of paganism," Padre Narciso Durán wrote to his community in Mexico City in 1837.[12]

Macnamara never traveled the Camino Viejo, the Old Trail through Central Valley, but kept to the Camino Real or State Trail ("King's Highway" in a colloquial sense) nearer the sea. The ranches and missions there made for convenient staging. Central Valley in June-July was an oven, in sharp contrast to the breezes, fogs and "air conditioning" of the coast. The Valley may have been watered by mountain tributaries and the two great rivers themselves, but the water was not spread out. From the San Joaquin estuary back up to its source, a dry plain extended east to the foothills of the Sierra, away from the banks of the rivers. Towards its southern end, the Valley became a "boggy basin," the Tulares, in extreme winters 800 square miles of wetland and lake. Swamp reeds as high as 20 feet filled areas up to two miles across. The wetlands of the San Joaquin Valley were an ecosystem of riverbank oaks, otter, beaver and wildfowl, a trappers' and hunters' paradise. Malaria and cholera also prevailed and travelers complained of the tarantulas and the mosquitoes.

Summer was the time for exploration and reports made the dry-roast Valley sound an unattractive proposition. The browned wheatgrass of the western foothills of the Coastal Range would make the casual traveler believe the great inland was in fact a desert. Comandante Castro and former governor Alvarado both took lands east of the river, including Las Mariposas, which Frémont later bought. The "Pathfinder" himself reconnoitered the Valley in 1844 from Sutter's Fort to La Porciuncula (Kerns) and Tres Reyes (Kings) rivers, and again in 1845 when he watered near the Laguna Tulares. Macnamara's contract was for vaguely defined, infested, dangerous territory; his colonists would have had to work hard to lay their table in the wilderness.

If all 3,000 families had appeared, there would have been a crisis. If the Central Government's allocation of *eleven times as much* land to each family had been in force, there would have been a disaster. The 3,000 square leagues, 13,284,000 acres or 20,280 square miles contracted were unsurveyed land. South from the River Cosumnes, to beyond the source of the San Joaquin as far south as the southern extremity of the Tulares wetlands beyond Laguna

Tulares itself, then east to the Sierras, even including the nearest foothills with their arable and pasture land, amounted to 12,000 square miles. The wetlands took away nearly 1,000 square miles (150 square leagues, approx. 660,000 acres) and the eleven ranches already granted in the area of the Macnamara concession took up another 790 square miles, (117 square leagues or 518,076 acres). They would also have been thinly spread, not in Edward Wakefield's ideal "villages." A condition had been imposed that settlers' plots must alternate with vacant plots of public land. If this were to be league for league, then the eastern, arable San Joaquin Valley could provide for only a quarter of Macnamara's proposed colonists, or just under 800 families. The vague extension south of the Valley itself, beyond San Gabriel to Cajon Pass and the Mojave River, unless it meant the whole San Bernardino Valley, would not provide much more. Pico knew it, actually stipulating that if there were not enough land, the *empresario* would have to be satisfied with his lot. Macnamara's irritation would have been considerable.

He was also being adroitly used. If the Irish were to settle between the Cosumnes and the Mojave Indian Trail they would have had to be trained in arms and even protected. These prospective farmers would no longer be Irish military veterans of the Napoleonic or Bolívar wars, trained in self-defense and combat. The danger from the Miwok, Yokut, Chumash and Mojave Indians was very real. At the Weber (Stockton) ranch in 1847 the settlers built adjoining houses, village-style, for protection, returning there as if to a static wagon circle after the day's work in their separate fields. Another ranch, well west of the San Joaquin river, built a blockhouse home, with rifle ports along all walls. Bunkhouses were built on several ranches for laborers and *vaqueros*; overseers had a separate home, however small and rough-hewn. Corrals for cattle and fences for crops were a priority. The Indians stole horses and rustled cattle; one ranch fired a cannon every night to frighten them. A small grant in the mouth of the Cajon de Muscupiabe on the Mojave Indian Trail west, made to an Irishman in 1843 in the hope that he would stem the Indian raiders, had to be abandoned. By 1850 the Indians had been rounded up into a reservation near Fresno, and in 1853 into another near New Tejon Pass on a former grant called Tejon. A fort there was manned for five years by U.S. troops.[13]

Parallel Beginnings: Gran Colombia, New Granada and Texas

John Diston Powles of the London Bondholders, who with Robert Wyllie had pressed for the colonization of California, knew about colonies. Had Eugene Macnamara ever had a London backer, it would have to have been Powles. Topo in Gran Colombia was his great failure. The people of Caracas knew Topo was toxic and doomed to fail. At first everything went well. Colonists traveled on well-aired ships, where comforts were planned right down to games for the children and Spanish lessons for the adults on the long voyage. With Scottish Pastor Ross and his doctor assistant went shepherds, shopkeepers, weavers, a blacksmith, a joiner and a gardener. Fourteen families settled on the Topo River and were content; another sixteen settled above them, as far as five miles away from water, but well-drilling equipment ordered from England took eight months to arrive. The first 140 settlers, two-thirds of them children, were housed in a longhouse built by the Company on a height to catch the fresh air. It was 120 feet long, of adobe, glass and tile, with two rooms each for 30 families, with separate entrances, like terraced houses. Later newcomers were due to stay in this transit block while plots were allocated and their homes built. Equipment and tools were stored in military tents. The British consul kept in touch and the talk was of growing indigo, cotton and coffee. By 1827 it had all failed: Topo was only fit for goats.[14] Intendente Ross, responsible for surveys, discipline, tools, crises, staking, stores and stock, burned himself out. He bought food and equipment in Caracas, supervised local labour and spent hours in the saddle. In 1826 they cleared and cultivated 120 acres, but harvested poorly. The settlers dreaded being slaves, common laborers or even bankrupts, and turned down well-meaning offers of work on other ranch estates. They forgot how bad Scotland had been. Ross, not surprisingly, drank seriously and was nicknamed by the Venezuelans, "the sucking priest." His Highland flock also drank. Powles' company, which had been behind the Columbia Immigration Society, disowned its unfortunate offspring and left Topo to the bottle.

Powles and Wyllie failed to stimulate the colonization of California in 1845-1846. "Let not the lesson be lost," Powles warned in 1863, as Chairman of the Committee of South American Bondholders. His address was 11 Austin Friars, in the "little Mexico" of London's financial district. New Granada (about to become "Columbia") had assigned 4.3 million acres of land for debt repayment. Bigger than Jamaica, the land would be worth much more with a population. Supporting witnesses advised that sawmills to clear the forests be a priority (shades of Sutter at Coloma); that cotton, coffee and cocoa be grown; that it was "a corresponding situation and temperature" to Demerara, and that with military protection and proximity to a river or a town, they could employ native labor with little risk. An Irish priest testified, "all that is needed is three or four active-minded gentlemen as officers, acompanied by a mason, carpenter and blacksmith from England. All the rest would be native labour." The estate or plantation was the model in 1863, no longer the commune or the colony. The New Granada government invited them to choose one and a half million acres from the Columbian Sierra Nevada, where the streams created an ideal new farming area. Fifty British families would occupy cheap temporary houses on the foothills, arriving at the sowing season.

Claims would only be confirmed after five years, when everyone was on site; after another five years' acclimatization, the colony would clear the plain for tobacco, cocoa, coffee, sugar and cotton. It was a topography remarkably like the San Joaquin Valley and its Sierra foothills. Ten years would see the first profits to company shareholders.[15]

Irish and other Europeans had long known Texas. In 1804 a priest called Brady contracted for 1,500 families to settle and create a port: nothing happened. In 1825 the Department of Coahuila/Texas appealed for *pobladores*. Four resident Irishmen (Power, Hewetson, McMullen and McGloin) offered themselves as *empresarios*. The first two petitioned land for 400 "hard working, moral and Catholic" families, a quarter of them Mexican, the rest Irish. Two years later permission came through, but for only 200 colonists, of whom half were to be Mexicans. Power returned to Ireland in 1833 to recruit by poster and "personal canvass" in his home county of Wexford. Two hundred and fifty signed up, cattle raisers for a square league of 4,428 acres, arable farmers for 177 acres. Stock was sold off, seed was bagged, tools crated, foodstuff sufficient for a year was salted and barreled. From Wexford they sailed to Liverpool and from there, on two ships, for New Orleans. Storm, sunstroke, sickness and overcrowding ravaged them. They caught cholera in New Orleans and were shipwrecked outside Copano, Texas, before finally arriving at the former mission of Refugio where they found five or six huts, Power's thatched cabin and stakes marking out the projected *pueblo* of Refugio. They built temporary huts from poles, mud and grass, covering the board floors with river sand. They farmed in common as a precaution against Indians and outlaws, but the bitter nights and inferno days got to them. A Mexican commissioner arrived and swore in a *pueblo* council and militia. Nearby, the colony of San Patricio was founded by the other two *empresarios*, McGloin and McMullen, recruiting from County Tipperary.[16]

Macnamara had to have his colony in place by 1852. By then, more Irishmen than he could have imagined, including experienced miners from near Borrisokane, were making California their home. The notion of separate national colonies gave way, appropriately for gold producers, to the metaphor of smelting pots. Europeans had a relatively common background and in California shared a new common language and horizons. The Irish came there in plenty, a constant one-tenth of the population for the two decades after the Gold Rush, but they neither came nor lived in colonies.[17]

The California Irish

They were already there in small numbers before Macnamara appeared, like the Den brothers of Santa Barbara, the Santa Clara Valley Irish and Jasper O'Farrell, Governor Pico's surveyor. They came in with the Stephens-Townsend-Murphy party in 1843 and with the Donner-Breen party in 1846.

They appeared in strength in the Gold Rush. Like all California pioneers, the Irish complained of the mosquitoes, warmed at the sight of crows they could name from home and devised names for the other animals, plants and landmarks which had no name. Their descendants waxed about an Ireland they never saw, but the original California Irish came to forget Ireland. Friend and foe agreed that the Irish tended to miss the opportunities on the land, yet Ireland was a rural nation. While the soil gave the Irish their skills, it was also where their confidence in cash, crops, landlords and in themselves had often collapsed. Many must have shrunk at the thought of extensive land. An unrecorded minority also came from mines in Ireland, ranging from lead and zinc to copper, silver and gold. Silvermines Mountain in Tipperary, brooding just to the south of Macnamara's parish at Borrisokane, and the Goldmines River in Wicklow, were two important centers.

> The gold is obtained only by continual washings. The pick, shovel and trowel do it all. A spot on which to labour is a matter of chance. The gold is found principally along the sides of the stream and sometimes at a depth of many feet under it. The clay is conveyed to a wooden trough into which a stream of rapid water is made to run and the clay is constantly raked. Any gold in the heap will sink to the bottom. The result after half an hour is scarce enough to fill an iron buddle [bowl] which is continually shaken. Every now and then the surface is scraped off by hand and thrown away until the quantity is reduced to as much as will cover the bottom of the bowl. This is examined very carefully and the gold is detected by its bright colour.[18]

This gold was being panned in County Wicklow, south of Dublin, in 1841. Toward the end of the 18th century, in a theme from an Irish comedy, a schoolteacher had secretly supplemented his pay with riverbed gold. His fiancée talked and triggered a ten-week Wicklow gold rush. British troops took over the area and the teacher, understandably, broke with his fiancée. Shortly afterwards in 1798, Irish rebels destroyed the mine workings, but intermittently down to the present day gold has been mined in counties Wicklow, Tipperary and Tyrone. Several hundred "miners" figured in the Wicklow census of 1841, although not by name. Irish miners brought their experience to the gold mines and streams of the Sierra Nevada foothills from these areas and lie buried in El Dorado, Sutter Creek and Jackson.

Although there was no New Ireland ("New" was rare in California place-names), Dublin, Limerick and Murphys, and in the foothills, a score of Irish Towns, Irish Hills, Irish Creeks and Irish Cemeteries made up for it. One historian called them the "uncounted Irish," but while true of the exodus from Ireland, the California Irish were as well counted as any others in the censuses west of the Sierra Nevada from 1850. At times of anti–Irish feeling—in 1852, Macnamara's colonists would have landed amid "lynch" and "shillelagh" law in San Francisco—it helped to be able to disguise a birthplace. "British" was the Irish legal nationality and an Irish name or accent could pass for Scots, Cornish, Welsh or Manx (Isle of Man). It distorted census returns. When the Irish, who were *legally British*, took out United States citizenship, they abjured allegiance to Queen Victoria, swore loyalty to the United States, but remained *ethnically Irish*. A Celtic accent and the roar of wind or water changed names in the 1850 census lists, which were compiled from the saddle. Miners often refused to give details, treating the census as a joke or a government intrusion. It was easier to scribble down a guess and ride on. The Irish "Fitzpatrick" became a German "Fritz Patrick"; "Eamonn" nasalized into "Almond." Census sheets in 1850 recorded "countess," "poet" and "gentleman" alongside Irish daguerrotypists, marble polishers, interpreters and "virtuous women." In 1870, 54,000 Irish-born formed one-tenth of California's total population and, most significantly, 29 percent of the state's foreign-born population. These names cannot be matched with names in the censuses or church registers of Ireland since both were largely destroyed in Dublin during the Anglo-Irish War of 1921. Had they survived, the story of the Irish migration to America would have been cross-matched in detail long ago. Macnamara's "families" were loose descriptions—single bachelor brothers, networks of cousins, mother and daughters. If feet had itched, cities beckoned, mineral *bonanzas* lured or cooler coastal breezes tempted, they could not have been held on the San Joaquin by an intendente (or even an apostolic vicar).

Once they had landed and met the material concern of basic survival, the colonists would have to meet the other need—that of respect. "To be decently buried without undue ostentation" was the last wish of an Irish miner in Sutter County in 1871, "but with proper regard to my station in life." Wealth, fame, land and reinvented identities helped provide this respect. Very few burials of "a native of Ireland" recorded details of home, and fewer noted the pain of exile, although the bulk of the deal headboards have perished. "That I should come so far to die and leave my friends where I was bred," one El Dorado wife did lament on her husband's tomb. "The angel on watch took the wanderer in," wrote another. "Alone and far from his native home," recorded a third. These seem to have been exceptions. The emotions were vented in life, or simply suppressed. Long inscriptions also cost money, even from a fellow–Irishman. Thomas Kerr, who came from Londonderry direct to California in the winter of 1849-50, cried into his diary, "I regret coming. I have shed floods of tears. I have earned comparitively nothing to what my expenses were."

Vanity publishers produced County Histories in which subscribers paid to have their place in history. Origins were recreated out of collective folk memory, but not all self-styled victims of famine or oppression were such. One subscriber claimed to be a Blennerhasset-Chute of Chute Hall, County Kerry; another, one of the landowning Smyths of County Cavan. Both were famous families and such claims, true or false, brought respect. Some claimed, with a patter of Latin, to be graduates of Trinity College, Dublin, but all Catholics, even the beggar on the Dublin streets, picked up Latin from church services. Respectability in print cost $50 and could not be checked. Flattered subscribers made for satisfied customers; copies were even freighted to Europe to impress. In one classic case of padding, when nothing else remained to be said, an emigré's parents back in Ireland "*would also have been* industrious and patriotic Americans *if they had come here*" (author's italics).

They died young, went back east or turned from mining to farming. Gold was a phase and a delusion for most. Farm and mine subsidized each other on the same claim, depending on economic circumstances. "Farmer" looked better than "miner" on the Great Voting Register. Only occasionally were both occupations claimed together. The speech of the Irish was a figure of fun because they thought in "direct" Gaelic while speaking in "roundabout" English. Two languages bred the distinctive Irish humour of the pun. Many, if not themselves Gaelic speakers, had Gaelic speaking parents back home to whom they wrote letters laced with Gaelic phrases they had heard as children.

The "California Letter" became proverbial in Ireland. It was not necessarily from California, but it carried remittance of money, news of land and of opportunity. It confirmed the legends of gold and youth in the west. Ironically, of hundreds of such surviving immigrant letters from America, only four correspondences survive from California itself.[19] Letters from the Sierra Nevada sometimes enclosed gold dust. Others remitted through banker's order and listed networks of relatives and neighbors in the mines and ranches. Official figures put the total amount remitted to Ireland in 1854 alone, from the entire United States, at a record $6.8 million. California earnings helped create this peak. Emigrants also begged money from home to invest in a *bonanza* or to tide them over a bad patch. They spoke of returning home permanently, as if the long journey had been a seasonal trip. Perhaps the truth of a final break with home was too much. They held on to straws and life took over. The single temporary emigrant became a married (occasionally homesick) settler; promises to visit were made, but talk of return faded. The promise changed to a hope of retiring back home; finally they expressed the wish to see the old place one last time before death. Few did. Men died in their eighties with Cunard and White Star brochures beside them.

For all their numbers and Lancasterian schooling, the Irish left relatively few written records. William Clarke left an overland diary (uncovered in a Colusa County barn in 1931). A god-fearing Donegal Presbyterian and teetotaler, he chased away wolves rather than waste bullets, although "they seemed as though they would like to have tasted Irish blood." (Perhaps he was a poor shot who told a good story.) He was a financial success, treating people much as he treated wolves, down to fists and guns in the courthouse. In the end he killed himself. Suicide was not unknown in an emigrant's later years, when early memories loomed clearer and the repressed trauma made itself felt. When a tiny minority chose razor, bullet or poison, the inquest recorded their last words from witnesses or a note, the only time an immigrant's words might be preserved. Christmas, New Year, July 4th and St. Patrick's day in March were times of serious nostalgia.

During the economic depression of the later 1850s, a Hibernian Benevolent Society was formed in Tulomune and Calaveras counties where the Irish population was, in places, as high as 25 percent. (This would have been well inside the Macnamara concession.) The Hibernian Society was a mutual help association, a social focus and allowed a feeling of being in touch with Ireland without actually being so. It recorded no political stance. After the Civil War, a Fenian or Irish Republican Brotherhood was formed in the same communities. It raised money, words and music, but not a single volunteer, for a failed rebellion in Ireland and failed "invasion" of Canada in 1866. Macnamara's colonists would have been little different.

William Kelly, the lawyer from Sligo, was not from a potato patch, but he wrote for those who were:

> I had no position at home, where there is poverty and not a potato to dig. I set out to dig for gold in the hopeful fields of California where the lords and squires are unable to reach. Though there was no rot in the crop nor greedy landlord to watch, and bone and sinew beat the professions, I found the produce was most jealously guarded by agues, fever, scurvies and rheumatisms.[20]

Kelly never saw the San Joaquin, but he knew John Frémont's description of it as timbered, mild and genial, heard John Marsh call it "a very inviting field for emigration," and, like everyone else on the west coast in 1846, had read Lansford Hastings description of "a great extent of fine rich country." He disagreed: it had only "a few highly favoured localities where wheat might be raised if peopled with enterprising settlers from the old country, but I saw no grain and heard only vague missionary traditions of its having been once grown there." The Tulares was fit only for rice, wild horses and a little vine growing. He did acknowledge, however, that Frémont was content with Las Mariposas, especially after gold was found.

Utopia: "No Such Place"

Forty years later, John Frémont wrote his memoirs, a retrospective tying up of the loose ends of a long life. The Las Mariposas ranch, which he lost, and the San Joaquin to the west had evidently kept him reminded of Macnamara, whom he had once met briefly. Agribusiness had cleared and enclosed much of the Valley, the Indian culture had been destroyed, the Tulares wetlands were a fraction of their old size, the southern rivers were being dammed and syphoned for irrigation. Frémont, who once claimed to have saved California from the Macnamara threat, described what Macnamara's Irish *utopia* might have been. He believed that it was a purely church project, a replacement for the Franciscan missions. There was no more talk of British agents or threats. He knew or remembered nothing of Macnamara's interest in mineral wealth. In 1886, Frémont was a wiser, poorer, more transparent and chastened man. He was not a young man under oath, watching his words before a court martial or Senate Committee, fighting for career and reputation. Alibis were no longer needed.

> Under Macnamara's direction the three thousand families would have spread over the whole beautiful valley of the San Joaquin. Farms would have occupied the river lands, and the plains between would have served as cattle ranges; and among the innumerable springs and streams of the foothills and up to the snow of the Sierra would have been happy and prosperous homesteads. Under the guidance of an intelligent and stable authority the groves of grand old oaks and the magnificent pine forests would not have been swept away. With its advantages of climate, soil and abundant streams the whole valley would have presented a picture of agricultural beauty unsurpassed on earth.
>
> The mountain Indians would have been reclaimed and made useful herdsmen and labourers and the abandoned missions along the coast would have been restored on a higher level as centres of productive labour. The Indians would have been held under the steady influence of a firm government and educated to the advantages of civilisation and not left only to the degrading contact with its vices. This is not merely an opinon. It was a reality proved by the successful work of the missions when the country was very remote and the resources were only from within themselves. I realised fully in 1846 what I have been here writing, for when the [Macnamara] colonisation project failed, I wrote from the quiet of the beautiful ruin of the old Carmel Mission to Senator Benton of the events which had brought me to that date and place. "*Carmel Mission July 24th 1846*"carried with it for me, a marked significance; it ended my mission as well as that of Macnamara.

Age and hindsight frayed Frémont's thread of consistency. The letter from Carmel was dated July *25th* and in it, even then in the heat of the moment, he made no mention of Britain, Macnamara or colonization. They had never really been uppermost in his mind and had only come to matter with the need for carefully selected evidence a year or so later. The scheming of an ambitious young man gave way to an old man's generous final tribute to Macnamara.

> We cannot fail to sympathise with the grief of a mind which had conceived a project so far-reaching and which had experienced the shock of overthrow in the moment of its complete success. The time, the thought, the labour of solicitation, the patient endurance with slower or inferior minds—all, had resulted in the blank of absolute failure.[21]

Notes

Preface

1. Hubert Howe Bancroft, *History of California 1848–59*, Vols 1–6, 1888. Vol 5, p 215–223; John Charles Frémont, *Memoirs of My Life*, 1886, Vol 1, p 560.

2. Mary Karam, OP, *Elusive Entrepreneur; Eugene Macnamara's California Land Grant and Colonization Scheme of 1846*, MA Dissertation, University of San Francisco, 1967.

3. Ignatius Murphy, *The Diocese of Killaloe in the Eighteenth-Century*, 1991; *The Diocese of Killaloe, 1800–1850*, 1993; *The Diocese of Killaloe, 1850–1904*, 1995; *A People Starved: Life and Death in West Clare, 1845–51*, 1996.

4. *The Dogtown Territorial Quarterly*, produced since 1990 from Paradise (near what used to be known as Dogtown), Butte County, is the sole remaining independent history periodical in northern California.

Chapter One

1. H.H. Bancroft, *History of California*, 1888, Vol 5, p 215–223; J.C. Frémont, *Memoirs*, 1886, p 560.

2. Mrs. Bankhead to Charles Vaughan, 29 October 1845, refers to "My two Irishmen," her husband, the Minister to Mexico, and Percy Doyle, Chargé d'Affaires. "Minister" was the style adopted by ambassadors, as "Ministers Plenipotentiary." Vaughan Papers, C20/3, All Souls College, Oxford.

3. London Public Record Office (PRO), Foreign Office (FO), 204/88, p 483–484, Despatch 52, 30 May 1845.

4. F.J. Weber, *Writings of Bishop García Diego*, 1976; G.P. Hammond, *The Larkin Papers*, Vols 1–10, 1951–68; Warwickshire Record Office, The Seymour Papers, CO 114A; Archivo General de la Nación, Mexico City, 1845-6, Gobernación, Caja 4, 1846, Expediente El Proyecto Macnamara; The whereabouts of the 1847 Macnamara dossier in the Mexican Archive was still unknown at the time of publication.

5. Colm Cooke, Archivium Hibernicum (Catholic Record Society of Ireland), 35, 1980, *The Modern Irish Missionary Movement*, p 234–246; Santa Barbara Mission Archive, 1034 and 1038, Letters from Patrick Short to Padre Duran, 1836, in which Short reports the Pope's travel plan to Great Britain from authoritative Irish and Roman church sources cited in the U.S. press; Archivium Hibernicum, Dublin Dibcesan Archives 38, 1983, p 66.

6. Seymour Papers (C114A), 374, 17, *Private Diary*, 17 October, 1840.

7. G.L. Rives, *The United States and Mexico*, 1913, Ch 5; L.H. Jenks, *Migration of British Capital to 1875*, 1937; E. Turlington, *Mexico and Her Foreign Creditors*, 1930; B.A. Tennenbaum, "Merchants, Money and Mischief," *The Americas*, 35, 3, 1978-9, p 317–329; H.J. Heath de Bohiges, *British Commercial Houses in Mexico*, Ph.D. Thesis, London School of Economics, 1988; H.J. Heath, "British Merchant Houses in Mexico," *Hispanic American*

Historical Review, 73, 2, May 1993, p 261–290.

8. Patrick Milmo, one of two brothers from County Sligo, was a cousin of William Kelly, a neglected Irish writer on California, 1849. Kelly's background came to light during research for this book: see Chapters 8 & 9 for more on Kelly.

9. H.H. de Bohiges, *op. cit.*, p 160; 269; 275. On the West Indies Royal Mail ships, see T. Bushell, *Royal Mail, 1839–1939*, 1939; R. Baker, *Great Steamers, White and Gold*, 1993.

10. Testimony of José Castro, Castillero vs U.S., New Almaden Mine Case, 29 November 1854, Vol V of Case Pamphlets, Castro Evidence, p 3, Bancroft Library.

11. J.A. Hawgood, "A Proposed Prussian Colonization of California," *Southern California Historical Society Quarterly*, 48, 1966, p 353–368. The papers survive in the Archivo General de la Nación, Mexico City.

12. Mexican Council of Government Response to the Macnamara Project, September 1845, 1845–6, Gobernación Caja 4, 1846, El Proyecto Macnamara, ff 3–9 and verso.

13. Letter, Parrott to Buchanan, August 16, 1845, cited from "Mss archive, Washington" by R.G. Cleland, "Early Sentiment for the Annexation of California," *South Western Historical Quarterly*, 18, January 1915, p 238–239. The letter is not in Vol 8 (Mexico), of U.S. Diplomatic Correspondence, 1831–1860.

14. M. Quaife, *J.K. Polk's Diaries*, 1910, Vol 1, October 24, 1845; C. Sellars, *James K. Polk, Continentalist, 1843–6*, 1956, p 355.

15. T.H. Benton, *Thirty Years View*, 1856, Vol 2, p 693; J.C. Frémont, *Memoirs*, 1886, Vol 1, p 535.

16. Edward Gibbon Wakefield, *England and America, The Art of Colonisation*, 1833, Vol 2, p 243.

17. *Ibid.*, Vol 1, p 56–57.

18. Hans Rheinheimer, *Topo*, 1988; F.G. Dawson, *The First Latin American Debt Crisis*, 1990, p 186–188.

19. Colm Cooke, Archivium Hibernicum, 35, 1980, *The Modern Irish Missionary Movement*, p 234–246.

20. Seymour Papers, 374, 23, *Private Diary*, 1846, entries on unnumbered back pages.

Chapter Two

1. Ignatius Murphy, *Diocese of Killaloe, 1800–1850*, 1995, p 95–98.

2. C. Chevenix Trench, *Grace's Card: Irish Catholic Landlords, 1690–1800*, 1997; J. McCarthy, *Grattan*, 1886, p 44; D.H. Akenson, *Small Differences: Irish Catholics and Protestants, 1815–1921*, 1991. The ban on mixed marriages, for instance, came from Rome only as late as 1908.

3. S.J. Connolly, *Priests and People in Pre-Famine Ireland, 1780–1845*, 1982, p 11; W. Fitzpatrick, *Life and Times of Dr. Doyle, Bishop of Carlow*, 1880, Vol 2, p 5.

4. Brian Merriman, *The Midnight Court*, 1787, translated D. Marcus, 1953.

5. E.T. Gray (adaptation), *Ralahine, An Irish Commune*, 1928; W. Thompson, *The Distribution of Wealth, The New System*, 1824.

6. Mss list (1934) of Killaloe students, Irish College, Paris, Killaloe Diocesan Archive, Ennis; L. Swords, *The Irish French Connection, 1578–1978. The Irish College, Paris*, 1978; R. Hayes, *Biographical Dictionary of the Irish in France*, 1949; P. Boyle, *The Irish College, Paris*, 1901; *Catholic Encyclopedia* (USA), 1910; *National Catholic Encyclopedia* (USA), 1966.

7. W. Fitzpatrick, *Life of Dr. Doyle*, 1880, Vol 1, p 441; Vol 2, p 38, 87.

8. Denzinger-Schonmetzer, Papal Encyclical *Mirari Vos*, August 15, 1832.

9. Archivium Hibernicum, 45, 1990, *Dublin Diocesan Archive*, p 36, 45.

10. H.A. Whelan, *The Picpus Story*, 1964; L. Joré, "Picpus Fathers," *Southern California Historical Society Quarterly*, 48, 1964, p 293; *Catholic Encyclopedia*, 1910, entry "Sandwich Islands"; the Picpus archives are crated in Rome and are inaccessible.

11. Archivium Hibernicum, 37, 1982, *Murray Papers*, p vii, 58.

12. W. Battersby, *The Complete (Irish) Catholic Directory*, 1838; S. Lewis, *A Topographical Dictionary of Ireland*, 1837, to

which Comyn, Birmingham, Walsh and Bishop Clancy's brother were local contributors.

13. H. Weir, *Houses of Clare*, 1986. Balthard House has been demolished.

14. I. Murphy, *A People Starved*, 1996, p 45; HM Commissioners for the Poor, Ireland, First Report, County Clare, 1835; I. Murphy, *Building a Church in 19th Century Ireland*, The Other Clare, Shannon Arch. and Hist. Society, Vol 2, 1977; Charles Lever's best known novel was *Harry Hinton*.

15. Commissioners for the Poor, Co. Clare, Ireland, 1835.

16. T.P. O'Neill, *The Catholic Church and the Relief of the Poor, 1815–45*, Archivium Hibernicum 31, 1973; B. Macnamara, "The Second Reformation," *Irish Theological Quarterly*, 33, 1966, p 39–64.

17. J. Birmingham, *Memoir of Fr. Theobald Mathew*, 1840. The list of clergy involved (p 76, London edition; p 106, U.S. edition) was evidently wrongly typeset from its manuscript original.

18. C. J. Rathmuller, *Frederick Lucas*, 1862; E. Lucas, *Life of Frederick Lucas*, 1886.

19. J. McEvoy, *Carlow College, 1793–1993*, entry for William Clancy; P. Guilday, *Life and Times of John England*, 2 vols, 1927; John Hynes' Diaries and Correspondence, Melbourne Diocesan Archive, Australia; *The Tablet; The Royal Demerara Gazette;* Shorrocks Manuscript, Jesuit Archives, London and Georgetown, Guyana.

20. *The Tablet*, May 15 and 29, 1841.

21. The letter from Bishop Kennedy to Rome concerning Macnamara's offense and suspension could not be found by Ignatius Murphy who searched the Propaganda Fide Archive for any Killaloe item. Patrick Connors SJ in Guyana has seen a copy (since mislaid in Georgetown) and describes it as "vague and bland." "Proven seduction" was quoted from the letter, in Bishop Clancy's brother's poison pen attack on Macnamara and Bishop Hynes in 1844 (see chapter 3). Bishop Clancy, in 1844, gave a copy of Kennedy's letter to the Colony Secretary, Georgetown.

22. *The Tablet*, May 15, 1841, where Clancy described the willingness of Irish volunteers to go to Guiana, with Macnamara uppermost in mind, during a speech

to student priests at Ware, Hertfordshire, April 28.

23. Annals of North Presentation Convent, Cork City, 10 and 17 June, 1841.

24. *The Tablet*, 29 May, 1841.

Chapter Three

(London, Public Record Office [PRO], Colonial Office [CO], 111, Vols 183–229, cover the period, with correspondence, reports and enclosures between Governor Light of British Guiana and the Colonial Office in London.)

1. *The Tablet*, 29 May, 1841; *Royal Demerara Gazette*, 3 July, 1841; U.S. Consul in Guiana, Sol Benjamin, British Library Mss, SPR, Mic. B 22, (144). No passenger lists survive from the period, only selected names shortlisted in *The Tablet* and *Demerara Gazette*.

2. *The Tablet*, 12 March, 1842, letter to Charles Weld, barrister (attorney) of The Temple and a *Tablet* Trustee.

3. London PRO, CO 111, 203, f 371, *Report on the State of Religion in British Guiana*, September 1843.

4. J. Bernau, *Missionary Labours in British Guiana*, 1847, p 5; A. Trollope, *West Indies and the Spanish Main*, 1859, p 167 ff; Barton Premium, *Eight Years in British Guiana*, 1850, p 26.

5. *The Tablet*, 12 March, 1842, second letter to Charles Weld.

6. Georgetown Catholic Archives, Letters Macnamara to Clancy and Clancy to Light, 15 December 1841 (abridged).

7. *The Tablet*, 7 March, 1842.

8. *Ibid.*, 30 April, 1842.

9. *Ibid.*, 4 July, 1842; 3 September, 1842.

10. London PRO, CO 111, 203, f 372, *State of Religion in British Guiana*, September 1843.

11. *Ibid.*, Correspondence, British Guiana, CO, 112, 25 & 26, *passim*.

12. *Ibid.*, CO 111, 185, 25 May, 1842.

13. *Ibid.*, CO 111, 189, 24 June, 1842; CO 111, 191, 22 July, 1842.

14. *Ibid.*, CO 111, 208, f 500, 29 February, 1844, marked *Private and Confidential*.

15. *The Tablet*, 8 July, 1843.

16. W. Ireland, *Demerariana*, 1896, p 52–53 ; B. Premium, *Eight Years in BG*, 1850, p 38–39; H. Dalton, *History of British Guiana*, 1855, p 127, 444–446, 452; *Emigrant and Colonial Gazette*, 1, 22 August, 1848; M. Menenez, *The Portuguese in Guyana*, 1982; B. Moore, *Guyana after Slavery*, Caribb. Stud., 4, 1987.

17. J. Rodway, *History of British Guiana*, 1891, Vol 3, p 102; Shorrocks Mss, p 69–70; see also F. Millroux, *Émigration à la Guyana Anglaise*, 1842; London PRO, CO 111, 229, September 1845, enclosure from Dr Charles Stilwell of London; W. Dupouy, (ed.), *Diary of Sir Robert Ker Porter in Caracas, 1830–41*, 1966; N. Perrazzo, *La Imigración en Venezuela, 1830–50*, 1973; J. Rodway, *Story of Georgetown*, 1920.

18. *Royal Demerara Gazette*, 16 May, 1843; 3 June, 1843.

19. London PRO, CO 111, 203, f 375–6, *State of Religion in BG*, September 1843.

20. John Hynes' Diary, Melbourne Diocesan Archive, 1, 6 and 11 May, 1843.

21. *Ibid.,* 20 August, 1843.

22. *The Tablet,* 26 August, 1843; London PRO, CO 111, 217, f 138 enclosure, printed version of letter from Francis Clancy to Lord Stanley, August 1844, enclosing printed version of original letter sent from Clancy to Hynes in January 1844; Shorrocks Mss, p 76; *The Tablet*, 26 August, 1843; London, PRO CO 111 208, f 495, 29 February, 1844.

23. Macnamara's week in Rome is reconstructed from John Hynes' Diary, Melbourne Diocesan Archive. The Diary for January 1844–May 1845 has been lost.

24. Shorrocks Mss, p 145 and reconstruction from the *Royal Demerara Gazette*.

25. London PRO, CO 111, 208, f 495–7, 29 February, 1844.

26. *Ibid.,* CO 111, 203, f 375, *State of Religion in BG*, September, 1843.

27. Lord Stanley's endorsement on Light's dispatch, 29 February, 1844, see above note 14.

28. *The Tablet*, 18 November, 1843; 31 August, 1844; 26 June, 1844.

29. London PRO, CO 111, 208, f 497.

30. *Ibid.,* CO 111, 209, f 306–9; 217, f 130, ff 498–9.

31. *Ibid.,* 217, f 500, 503.

32. *Ibid.,* 209, f 302, 312, 317, 319, 494; 210, f 64; 211, f 206–8; 208, f 493.

33. John Hynes' Diary, 23 and 30 December, 1843.

34. London PRO, CO 111, 211, f 192 with enclosures, f 326; 212, f 167.

35. *Royal Demerara Gazette,* 3 September, 1844; 20 August, 1844.

36. Shorrocks Mss, p 86–7; London PRO, CO 111, 215, f 524.

37. John Hynes' Correspondence, 12 June, 1844; *The Tablet*, October 1844.

38. *The Tablet*, October, 1844; *Royal Demerara Gazette*, 17 October, 1844.

39. London PRO, CO 111, 217, f 138–9.

Chapter Four

1. For background travel detail in this chapter and elsewhere see F. Calderón de Barca, *Life in Mexico* (Letters), 1843; Lansford W. Hastings, *The Emigrant Guide to Oregon and California*, 1845; M. Orozco y Berra, *Historia de la Cuidad de Mexico*, 1854. Packet ship details from Vera Cruz Consulate papers, London PRO, FO 207 31.

2. H.H. Bohiges, *British Merchant Houses in Mexico*, 1988, London School of Economics Thesis, p 42–3.

3. London PRO, FO 207, 19, f 98, Consular Miscellany, Mexico City.

4. *Ibid.,* FO 204, 89, ff 588–90, Despatch 52 (draft letterbook copies), or 204, 88, ff 483–4 (originals) Bankhead to Aberdeen, 30 May, 1845.

5. W. Fitzpatrick, *Correspondence of Daniel O'Connell*, Vol 1, p 206–210, with J. Sturge, Quaker abolitionist.

6. See Note 4.

7. F. Calderón de Barca, *Life in Mexico*, 1843, p 13.

8. A. Forbes, *California: A History of Upper and Lower California*, 1839, p 310–311, 314, 321.

9. G.L. Rives, *The United States and Mexico*, 1913, especially Ch 21; R.G. Cleland, "Early Sentiment for the Annexation of California," *Southwestern Historical Quarterly*, 18, 1–3, 1914–15; *A History of*

California, 1922, Ch 14; E.D. Adams, "English Interest in California," *American Historical Review*, 14, 4, 1909, p 744–63; L.G. Engelson, "Proposals for Colonization of California by England," *California Historical Society Quarterly*, 18, 2, 1939, p 137–148; S.G. Jackson, "Two Pro-British Plots in Alta California," *Southern California Historical Quarterly*, 15, 2, 1973, p 107–112; "The British and the California Dream, Rumors, Myths and Legends," *Southern California Historical Quarterly*, 57, 3, 1975.

10. On Powles' regret about California as a lost opportunity, see Ch 7 and his *New Granada*, 1863; on the Bondholder loans, see E. Turlington, *Mexico and Its Foreign Creditors*, 1930; C. Fenn, *Compendium of Foreign Funds*, 1837, p 77.

11. R.Thompson, *London Directory*, 1846.

12. Joseph Tasker's annotated copy of Wyllie's *Report* is now in the British Library.

13. Vallejo Papers, Bancroft Library, CB 33: 369. CB 34: 13, 14, 16, 72; also, S. Dakin, *The Lives of William Hartnell*, 1949, esp p 259–70.

14. Vallejo Papers, Bancroft Library, CB 34: 2, 10, 17, 26, 68.

15. R.C. Wyllie, *Mexico, A Report for the South American Bondholders*, in Spanish. Mexico City 1843, in English, London 1844, p 267.

16. *Ibid.*, p 70–74.

17. C. Sellars, *James K Polk, Continentalist, 1843–6*, 1956, p 332.

18. A copy of this petition, Document A/1, was among papers brought to Washington from California in 1847 by John Frémont. They were found packed in trunks at a house in Los Angeles, just as Governor Pico had left them, key documents selected from his Departmental Archive to take on his flight into Mexico. Frémont selected from the trunks the Macnamara papers and several others crucial to his claim that he helped stir up California because of a serious British threat to take it over, but before formal war with Mexico. They were printed in Washington as an appendix to Frémont's California Claims, Senate Committee Report 75 (p 19–21 in the original Spanish and p 77–79 in Wash-

ington translation), 30th Congress, 1st Session, 1848. As copies, they were open to dispute, especially as Frémont's reputation stood to benefit, and he was accused by some of forging an anti–Catholic smear. This can finally be put to rest as the originals of three out of the five papers taken to Washington have now been located in Mexico, Archivo General de la Nación, Gobernación, S/C Caja 4, El Proyecto Macnamara, ff 12–16 and verso, 1846. For the first time, the original papers from Mexico are used here. The petition is in secretarial script, in Spanish, signed by Macnamara but not dated. It is identical to the copy found by Frémont, which in turn would have been a copy made by Pico's secretariat from an authenticated copy carried by Macnamara. Herbert E. Bolton's *Guide to Materials for U.S. History in Mexico Archives* (1913) gives a source reference for Macnamara's documents which is no longer valid. According to M. Karam, OP, *Elusive Entrepreneur* (1967), p 51, n 6, the National Archives Service has no trace of the Frémont manuscript copies in Washington, although the Macnamara papers were the only California papers Frémont left in Washington. The rest he took back and lost en route. (All citations are slightly abridged to reduce both rhetoric and repetition. 1 league was 2.6 miles; 1 square league was 4,428 acres.)

19. *La Voz del Pueblo*, 5 February, 1845.

20. G.L.Reeves, "Mexican Diplomacy on the Eve of War with the United States," *American Historical Review*, 18, 2, 1913; London PRO, FO 204, 89, ff 622–4, 30 July, 1845 (draft original), with Mackintosh's enclosure, ff 625–31; or 204, 88, f 521ff (received copy).

21. Archivo General de la Nación, Mexico City, Gobernación, S/C Caja 4, 1846, El Proyecto Macnamara, ff 10–11 and reverse, in secretarial script and in Spanish, signed after corrections by Macnamara, undated.

22. R. J. Scally, *The End of Hidden Ireland*, 1995, on an exceptional assisted emigration from Crown lands; Kerby A. Miller, *Emigrants and Exiles*, 1985, p 48–50, 195–197, 237, 295.

23. Zephryn Engelhardt, *Missions*

and Missionaries of California, 1896, Vol 4, p 548–549.

24. W. Shepperson, *British Emigration to North America*, 1957, p 135.

25. St. Matthew's Gospel, 7, verse 15.

26. *British Guiana Guidebook*, 1832; S. Lewis, *Topographical Dictionary of Ireland*, 1837; *The Tablet*, 15 May, 1841.

27. *The Tablet*, 1 June, 1844.

28. Samuel Morse, *Imminent Dangers of Foreign Immigration*, 1835, p 8–10.

29. C.M. Drury, "Protestant Beginnings in California," *California Historical Society Quarterly*, 26, 1947, p 154–165.

30. C. A. Milner et al., *History of the American West*, 1994, p 368–369.

31. H. H. Bancroft, *History of California*, Vol 3, p 259–290; C. Hutchison, *Frontier Settlement in Mexican California*, 1967; also A. Osio, *Memoirs*, Chapter 7, p 126–132.

32. *La Reforma*, notably 22 January and 10–15 February, 1846.

Chapter Five

1. José Ramírez, December 1845, collected correspondence in *Mexico During the War with the U.S.*, University of Missouri Studies, Vol 23, 1, 1950, p 15; Archivo General de la Nación, Mexico City, Publications Vol 15, 1925, Diplomatic Correspondence, *Lord Aberdeen, Texas y California*, Murphy to Foreign Minister, 1 January, 1846.

2. All Souls College, Oxford, Vaughan Papers, Bankhead Correspondence, C 20/3, Mrs B. to Chas Vaughan, 29 October, 1845.

3. H.H. Bancroft, *History of California* (1884–90), Vol 4, p 523–529; British Museum Add Mss 43170, p 24, Bankhead to Aberdeen, marked *Private*, 30 July 1845, Letterbook précis; *La Voz del Pueblo*, 4 June, 1845.

4. London PRO, FO 204, 88, ff 520–1, Despatch 74, Bankhead to Aberdeen, 30 July, 1845; Archivo General de la Nación, *Lord Aberdeen, Texas y California*, 1925.

5. U.S. Diplomatic Correspondence, Vol 8, Mexico 1831–1848, Wm Parrott to Jas Buchanan, Secretary of State, 5 August, 1845.

6. Among published Frémont Claim Papers, 30th Congress, 1st Session, Senate Report 75, 1848, Document D, Spanish version dated 11 August, 1845, with Washington translation. The original is not in the Macnamara dossier of 1846 in Mexico City, but would have been carried by Macnamara like a passport. The Frémont version was the copy made by Pico's secretariat. See Chapter 4, Note 18.

7. State Department "manuscript archive" letter, not printed in U.S. Diplomatic Correspondence, Vol 8, Mexico, but cited by R.G. Cleland in "Early Sentiment for the Annexation of California," *South Western Historical Quarterly*, Vol 18, 1915, No 3, p 238.

8. M. Cole (ed.), *Pío Pico's Historical Narrative*, 1973, p 122.

9. G.P. Hammond, *The Larkin Papers*, Vol 3, Stearns to Larkin, 19 June 1845.

10. F. J. Weber, *Writings of Bishop García Diego*, 1976, p 174 & 180. Letters to Híjar, 8 August, and to Herrera, 27 September, 1845.

11. Hammond, Vol 4, Pico's Proclamation of the Santa Barbara *Junta*, 13 May 1846.

12. Hammond, Vol 4, Larkin to Editor *New York Sun*, 31 May, 1845.

13. Hammond, Vol 5, from Marsh, 7 July 1845; from Stearns, 19 June, 1845; from Jones, 10 June, 1845.

14. Hammond, Vol 5, from Jones, 10 June, 1845.

15. Hammond, Vol 5, Larkin to Bandini, 10 July, 1845.

16. Hammond, Vol 4, from Jones, 21 September, 1845; from McKinley, 23 January, 1846; Hartweg Correspondence, Royal Horticultural Society, RHS Linley Library, London, H. to London Horticultural Society from Queretaro, 21 December, 1845. Hartweg refers to Herrera's attempt to disperse the army for fear of a coup. Orders were given in November but Paredes refused to obey. R.S. Ripley, *War with Mexico*, 1849, p 66–67.

17. Hartweg's Journal, RHS, Linley Library, London, 2 July, 1846.

18. All Souls College, Vaughan

Papers, Bankhead to Vaughan, C20/4, 29 December, 1845; C20/1, 29 October, 1844; C20/5, 29 May, 1846.

19. All Souls College, Oxford, Vaughan Papers, Doyle to brother John, Doyle Correspondence 2.

20. J. Hussey, "Origin of the Gillespie Mission," *California Historical Society Quarterly*, 19, 1940, p 43–53.

21. G.L. Rives, "Mexican Diplomacy on the Eve of war with the U.S.," *American Historical Review*, 1913; Archivo General de la Nación, Publications Vol 15, 1925, *Lord Aberdeen, Texas y California.*

22. London PRO, FO 207, 19, British Consular Records, Mexico City.

23. Polk authorized Slidell to pay $20 million for San Francisco or $25 million for the addition of Monterey; $40 million was available to settle the transfer of all desired land. After the War, Mexico was given just $15 million, most of which was taken by British creditors and currency dealers, with Mackintosh as principal agent. By 1850, California had produced gold vastly exceeding any purchase price previously discussed.

24. Parentheses denote words from the report which Lanzas crossed out in his draft letter and omitted completely from the final copy to Macnamara. Corrected draft, Archivo General de la Nación, Gobernación, Caja 4 1846, El Proyecto Macnamara, f 17. Final Copy, printed in English and Spanish, Document C, among the Frémont Claim Papers published in Washington, 30th Congress, 1st Session, Senate Report 75, p 22 & 79, 1848. See Chapter 4 n 18.

25. Archivo General de la Nación, Mexico City, Gobernación, Caja 4 1846, El Proyecto Macnamara, ff 18–19 & vv. Written and signed in English by Macnamara. Government translation into Spanish added to dossier.

26. Hammond Vol 6, 1846, Larkin to Buchanan, 18 June, 1846; see also Larkin's letter to Stearns, written from Monterey on 14 June, Stearns Collection, SG Box 40, the Huntington Library, San Marino.

27. Hammond Vol 5, 1846, Larkin to Buchanan, 19 August, 1846.

28. Archivo General de la Nación,

Mexico City, Gobernación, Caja 4 1846, El Proyecto Macnamara, ff 3–9 & vv.

29. This must be a reference to the Joseph Lancaster (Lancasterian) system of education, religiously neutral and adopted in Ireland's National Schools, but not in England where "National Schools" were a Protestant Church of England institution. Latin American countries such as Mexico and Gran Colombia adopted the system and Lancaster himself spent much time in Latin America as an educational consultant. The Consul in Mexico City handled his finances.

30. British Library Add Mss 43170, 26; London PRO, FO 204, 91, f 453, Bankhead to Aberdeen, May 1846, where Bankhead reminded Aberdeen of "a colonisation plan to secure that fine country" which he mentioned in a dispatch of 30 July, 1845. Presumably he refers to the Mackintosh plan, fully detailed in that letter, not the Macnamara plan which had been outlined in a previous dispatch of May and only mentioned in passing in the July dispatch.

31. U.S. Diplomatic Correspondence, Vol 8, Mexico, 3651 and footnote letters; 3650 and footnote; Parrott to Buchanan, 2 September, 1845.

32. Hammond, Vol 4 , Larkin to Jacob Leese, February 1846; M.Wale, (ed.), *Journals of Francis Parkman*, 1947, entries for May 1846; W. Jakobs, (ed.), *Letters of Francis Parkman*, Vol 1, p 38 & note, 1964.

33. Abraham Nasatir, "French Consulate in California," *California Historical Society Quarterly*, 1933, 12, p 35–50—Paris Foreign Office source, Political Correspondence, Mexico, Vol 33 (Paris), fol 281–4, 29 April, 1846, Chapeau, Mexico City, to Guizot, Paris; fol 323–4, 13 May, 1846, Gerault, to Mexico City from Mazatlán.

34. London PRO, FO 203, 19, Mexican Consular Records; Seymour Papers, 418, 2, f 166ff, Seymour to Bankhead, 26 April, 1846; f 245, Seymour to Ellenborough, 13 June, 1846.

35. F. Walpole, *Four Years in the Pacific*, 1849, p 181; Lansford W. Hastings, *The Emigrants Guide to Oregon and California*, 1845, p 138–9.

36. U.S. Diplomatic Correspondence,

Vol 8, Mexico, Black to Buchanan, 21 April, 1846.

37. Alban Gilliam, brother of U.S. Consul in Monterrey, Mexico, *Travels in Mexico 1843–4*, 1847, p 63. I am grateful to Hugh Fenning OP, Archivist of the Irish Dominicans, for the background to John Urquhart, OP.

38. Deposition of J. Forbes, U.S. vs Castillero, Case No 420, San Francisco, July 1858, p 88, Exhibit 181, Letter from J. Forbes to Alexander Forbes, 28 June, 1848.

Chapter Six

1. Berthold Seeman, *Voyage of HMS Herald*, 1853, Vol 1, p 122–125, November 1846.

2. John Hynes' Diary and Correspondence, Melbourne Diocesan Archive. Entries for January 1844–May 1845 are missing from the Diary, the period when Macnamara was suspended and moving on to Mexico.

3. Archives of the Jesuit Provinces of Maryland and of New York.

4. John Hynes' letters to nephew, James Goold.

5. John Hynes' Diary, extracts from May 1845 onwards.

6. *Ibid.*, April 16 and August 1846.

7. Cork Cathedral is a stone's throw from Hynes' Dominican house. A marker in the corner of the Cathedral car park indicates Clancy's grave. Hynes recorded on 28 July, 1847, "News of the unfortunate Dr Clancy's death."

8. Annals of Presentation Convent, Midleton, Cork, 27 January, 1848.

9. F.J. Weber, *Writings of Bp García Diego*, 1976, Letter to the clergy, Santa Barbara, 20 April, 1846; also Introduction, p 21.

10. Seymour Papers, 374, 23, *Private Diary*, 1846, 26 April.

11. London PRO, FO 5, 461, f 56, Seymour to Aberdeen, 6 March, 1845, Payeta, Peru; Seymour Papers, 418, 3, from Aberdeen, 13 June, 1846.

12. *Ibid.*, 418, 2, f 166ff, Seymour to Bankhead from Mazatlan, 26 April; 374, 23, *Private Diary*, 2 May.

13. *Ibid.*, f 186ff, to Bankhead, from Mazatlan, May 6.

14. Hartweg Correspondence, Royal Horticultural Society, Linley Library, London, April 8 to LHS; also Hartweg Journal, *passim*, March and April 1846.

15. Seymour Papers, 418, 2, f 196, Seymour to Bankhead; London PRO, ADM 52, 2713, Logbook, HMS *Juno;* Also Seymour Papers, 374, 23, *Private Diary*, 18 April, 1846.

16. Seymour Papers, 374, 23, *Private Diary*, 11 May, 1846; 418, 2, f 207, letter to Sloat, 11 May; 412, Commander-in-Chief's Journal, 12 May, 1846; 418, 2, f 201, to Alexander Forbes, 6 May.

17. Hartweg Correspondence, RHS Linley Library.

18. London PRO, ADM 38, 8416, Ships Muster Rolls, HMS *Juno.*

19. Seymour Papers, 418, 2, f 245, to Ellenborough, 13 May.

20. Berthold Seeman, *Voyage of HMS Herald*, 1853, Vol 2, March 1849, p 158.

21. London PRO, 5, 462, f 95–115, Blake's letters to Seymour, July 1846.

22. Testimony of José Castro, 29 November, 1854, Castillero vs U.S., New Almaden Mine, Case Pamphlets, Vol 5, Bancroft Library.

23. F.J. Weber, *Writings of Bp García Diego*, 1976, Letters 190, 191, 192; M.J. Geiger, *Franciscan Missionaries in Hispanic California*, 1969, p 164, 249ff; J.R. Browne, "Down in the Cinnabar Mines," *Harper's New Monthly*, October 1863.

24. Exhibit in SF District Court, U.S. vs Castillero, New Almaden Mine, Transcript Vol 4, p 2692, with Spanish original.

25. *Ibid.*, p 2637–9, with Spanish original.

26. Stearns Papers, SG Box 40, Huntington Library, San Marino, omitted from Hammond, *Larkin Correspondence.*

27. H. Hague and D.J. Langum, *Thomas O. Larkin*, 1990, p 37.

28. London PRO, FO 204, 88, f 484, Despatch No 52, Bankhead to Aberdeen, 30 May, 1844.

29. *Ibid.*, CO 384, 78, f 223; CO 386, 41; CO 384, 79, f 4–5; 80, f 77, 82; 82, f 81, 138; 41, f 214.

30. Hammond, Vol 5, Larkin to Buchanan from Los Angeles, 19 August, 1846.

31. Vallejo Papers, Bancroft Library, CB 34, 14, 17 March, 1844.

32. London PRO, FO 5, 461, f 213, 2 June, 1846, Powles to Aberdeen.

33. J.D. Powles, *New Granada, Its Internal Promise*, 1863, p 31.

34. Larkin did mention the Bishop's death in a letter on June 18. Hammond, Vol 5.

35. The *facultas* or permit to administer sacraments was registered in the diocesan *Libro Primero di Gobierno* at Santa Barbara and signed by Rubio as Vicar Administrator after García Diego's and Narciso Durán's deaths. The original is in the Archive of Los Angeles Archdiocese. Cited by Karam, p 6.

36. On Patrick Short—see H. Whelan, *Picpus Story*, 1964, p 7, 53, 121; Sta. Barbara Mission Archive, letters 1034 and 1038, Short to Padre Durán, 1836.

37. Larkin preserved Pico's Proclamation, 13 May and Castro's vivid response, 8 June, Hammond, Vol 4.

38. London, PRO, FO 5, 462, ff 99–115, three letters written by Blake to Seymour in July 1846. On board *Juno* Forbes explained to Blake that Lansford Hastings' *Emigrants Guide to California and Oregon*, 1845, had triggered interest in migration from the east. Hastings made much of California's untapped mineral wealth. Macnamara almost certainly knew the book.

39. Testimony of J. Forbes, 30 June, 1858, U.S. vs Castillero, New Almaden Mine, Case Pamphlets, Vol 5, p 7–8.

40. London PRO, ADM 53, 2713, Logbook, HMS *Juno*.

41. For the letter from Pico to J. Forbes, see E.A. Wiltsee, "British Vice Consul in California and the Events of 1846," *California Historical Society Quarterly*, 10, 2, 1931, p 114–115. Document F of the Frémont Claims Papers, published for Senate Committee Report 75, 30th Congress, 1st Session, 1848, refers to a note from Pico about the Macnamara scheme to the Assembly dated 24 June, discussed on 6 July by the Assembly before being passed to Bandini who reported back to an extraordinary session on the following day: Legislative Record, Vol 4, f 363, Bancroft Collection, Bancroft Library. The originals of the California Department Assembly records were destroyed in the San Francisco earthquake of 1906. Pico Testimony, U.S. vs Castillero, New Almaden Mine, 22 October, 1859, Transcript Vol 4, p 2539— Pico was under doctor's orders in 1859 and his evidence may have reflected his condition. He was unhappy about being questioned on Macnamara and events of 1846, a low point in his life. He thought he first saw Macnamara *before June* in Los Angeles, then later on the road "at the end of June or start of July." He "*probably* became well-acquainted with him." The date of his signing the Macnamara Contract was 4 July, later described as "fraudulent" during the California land disputes, though it was never tested in court. Bancroft and others thought he may have signed it in mid–July and backdated. Macnamara was in Monterey by 16 July with the signed copy, which may have been completed at Santa Margarita, Pico's ranch on the road between Santa Barbara and Monterey where Pico stopped, 12–13 July, and met José Castro for a reconciliation in the face of the common enemy. It is also possible he *pre*-signed blank sheets, knowing the mind of his Assemblymen. It was an accepted practice. James Forbes' evidence only adds to the confusion since he had Macnamara leaving Santa Barbara for Los Angeles on 3 July, *after* Pico's interviews with Blake on HMS *Juno*. Forbes was frequently careless about detail and dates.

42. Document D of the Frémont Claim papers published in Washington dated 1 July 1848. See previous note. The Stearns Collection, SG Box 42, Huntington Library, San Marino, has a "contemporary copy," but dated 2 July, in secretarial script, unsigned. It may have been Bandini's copy.

43. Bandini Mss, Bancroft Library, CB 79, Pico to Bandini, 23 June; 84, Lataillad to Bandini, 2 July.

Chapter Seven

1. Seymour Papers, 417, 1, f 306 ff, Misc. Letterbook, to Forbes from Monterey, 17 July and to son Francis in London from Monterey, 19 July.

2. Seymour Papers, 374, 23, *Private Diary*, 1846, 13 June.

3. *Ibid.*, 418, 2, f 246ff, to Bankhead, 14 June; to Horace Simpson MP, 15 June; to Ellenborough, 15 June; A. Gordon, *Lord Aberdeen*, 1905 p 183, 4.

4. *Ibid.*, 374, 23, *Private Diary* 1846, May-July, *passim*.

5. W.M. Wood, *Wanderings in California*, 1849; T.H. Benton, *Thirty Years View*, 1856, Vol 2, p 652.

6. Frémont Claims papers, Document F, in Spanish and English, Washington, 1848; Bandini's Committee judgment as agreed by the Assembly of Mexican California, 7 July, 1846, Legislative Record, Vol 4, f 364–368; Bandini Mss, Bancroft Library, CB 68, 87, with Bandini's comments.

7. Legislative Record, Vol 4 (originals ff 20–24), f 365. Bancroft Library.

8. W.D. Putney, *et al.*, "San Salvador, a New Mexican Settlement in Mexican California," *Southern California Historical Society Quarterly*, 59, 4, 1977.

9. Bandini Mss, Bancroft Library, CB 68, 81, Letter, 3 June.

10. *Ibid.*, 86, note, 7 July; R.H. Becker, *Diseños of California Ranches*, 1964.

11. Copy in Stearns Collection, Huntington Library, San Marino, SG Box 42. See Ch.9, note 10.

12. Bandini Mss, Bancroft Library, CB 68, 88, to César Lataillad.

13. Seymour Papers, 374, 23, *Private Diary*, 1846, back blank pages.

14. Hammond, Vol 5, Stearns to Larkin 8 July, 1846, which may have been carried north by Macnamara.

15. J.C. Frémont, *Memoirs of My Life*, 1886, p 560, also citing Rodman Price, formerly of USS *Cyane*.

16. Frémont Claims papers, Document E, Pico Concession, Washington, 1848; E.Cole (ed.), *Pico's Historical Narrative*, 1973, p 130ff.

17. Frémont Claims papers, Document E, Pico Concession, Washington, 1848.

18. J. Moreno, *Documentos para la Historia di California*, Bancroft Library, CD 17–18, 38ff: Macnamara may have carried this letter north to Secretary Moreno who was presumably with Pico's retinue on the road.

19. Evidence, 20 October, 1859, U.S. vs Castillero, New Almaden Mine, Transcript, Vol 4, p 2538ff.

20. Hammond, Vol 5, Larkin to Stearns, 10 July, 1846.

21. Seymour Papers, 374, 23, *Private Diary*, 1846, 12 and 16 July.

22. London National Maritime Museum, Captain H. Kellet's Letterbook, 1841–50, to Seymour, 21 January, 1847; W.D. Phelps, *Fore and Aft*, 1871, p 295; F.B. Rogers (ed.), *Navy Surgeon in California*, 1857, p 54–5, and note; J.C. Frémont, *Memoirs*, 1886, Vol 1, p 532.

23. W. Colton, *Three Years in California*, 1851, p 297–305; Seymour Papers, 374, 23, *Private Diary*; F. Walpole, *Four Years in the Pacific*, 1850, p 204; Rodman Price of USS *Cyane* cited in Frémont *Memoirs*, 1886, Vol. I p 542; Sloat's report is cited in *U.S. Mexican War Documents*, Vol I, 1846, p 641 and 667.

24. Seymour Papers, 417, 1, f 306, Misc Letterbook, to J. Forbes from Seymour, 17 July; London PRO, ADM 52, 2713, Logbook HMS *Juno*; FO 5, 462, ff 99–115, Letters from Blake to Seymour, 5, 17 and 30 of July, 1846.

25. Hartweg's Journal, RHS, Linley Library, London 2 July; Seymour Papers, 374, 23, *Private Diary*; London PRO, ADM 53, 2278, Logbook HMS *Collingwood*.

26. Seymour Papers, 417, 1, Misc Letterbook, to son Francis, 19 July.

27. Hammond, Vol 5, Larkin to Buchanan, 19 and 23 August.

28. H.H. Bancroft, *History of California*, Vol 5, p 214, note; Seymour Papers, 374, 23, *Private Diary*, 1846; F. Walpole, *Four Years in Pacific*, 1850, p 251; W. Colton, *Three Years in California*, 1851, p 305; J.C. Frémont *Memoirs*, 1886, Vol 1, p 532–563.

29. Seymour Papers, 417, 1, Misc Letterbook, letters to Pico and Forbes; 374, 23, Private Diary, July-August 1846 and back blank pages; E.A. Wiltsee, "The British Vice Consul in California and the Events of 1846," *California Historical Society Quarterly*, 10, 2, 1931, p 98–128; *Illustrated London News*, 8 November, 1845, p 299–301, on life aboard HMS *Collingwood*; Seymour Papers, 416, 1, f 307ff, Admiral's

Letterbook, 28 August, 1846, Report on California to Admiralty from Honolulu.

30. A. Nasatir, "French Consulate in California," *California Historical Society Quarterly*, 12, 1933, p 35–50, citing Ministry of Foreign Affairs, Paris, Box Monterey, Dossier 21, from Gasquet, 1 August, 1846, from Monterey, received in Paris 4 May, 1847; J.C. Frémont, *Memoirs,* 1886, Vol. I p 545–547, 554.

31. London PRO, FO 5, 460, f 129–35, 26 April from London.

32. U.S. Diplomatic Correspondence, 1831–60, Vol 7, Great Britain, Despatch 44, 18 May, 1846.

33. London PRO, FO 5, 461, 2 June, 1846; U.S. Diplomatic Correspondence, 1831–60, Vol 7, Great Britain, Despatch, 18 June, 1846.

34. London PRO, FO 5 461, f 166–8, Henry Parish to Aberdeen, 14 July, 1846.

35. F. Walpole, *Four Years in the Pacific,* 1850, Vol 2, p 221.

36. *Ibid.,* p 249. Fr Louis Yim, archivist of the Honolulu Catholic Diocese, searched for reference to Macnamara in church records and found nothing; the Picpus records in Rome are inaccessible, packed away awaiting a permanent home: information courtesy the Rev. L. de Reyes, archivist.

37. J.D Raeside, "The Journals of Dr Wyllie, a Minor Hawaiian Mystery," *Hawaiian Journal of History*, 18, 1984, p 87–95.

38. London PRO, FO 331, 11, f 267, Miller to Addington, Consular Section, 9 December, 1846; f 315, March 1847; Seymour Papers, 695, 4, to son Francis, 3 September, 1846; London PRO, FO 331, 11, f 260, 262, Miller to Addington, 26 October, 26 November, 1846.

39. *Ibid.,* f 246–7, Miller to Aberdeen, 28 September, 1846.

40. Kingdom of Sandwich Islands Foreign Office Letterbook, No 11, p 163; San Francisco's *Bulletin,* 17 July, 1858, printed Macnamara's 1846 letter in full after it was required as evidence from J. Forbes, July 1858, Case 420, District Court, San Francisco, U.S. vs Castillero, New Almaden Mine. Forbes thought the letter came "in November 1846, probably by trading vessel."

41. M. Wale (ed.), *Journals of Francis Parkman,* 1947, entries May-June 1846; W. Jakobs (ed.), *Letters of Francis Parkman,* 1964, Vol 1 p 38; Vol 2, p 236–237.

42. London National Maritime Museum, Captain H. Kellet Letterbook, 1841–50, Letter to A. Forbes, 16 November, 1846; London PRO, ADM 53 1919, Logbook, HMS *Herald;* Berthold Seeman, *Voyage of HMS Herald,* 1853, Vol 1, p 122–5.

43. U.S. vs Castillero, New Almaden Mine, Transcript Vol 2, p 540, letter of J. Forbes to A. Forbes, 22 September 1846; PRO, London, FO 50, 201 ff 124–9.

44. Berthold Seeman, *Voyage of HMS Herald,* 1853, Vol 1, p 125.

Chapter Eight

1. London PRO, FO 50, 115, f 91, Despatch 80, A Forbes to Bankhead, November 28, 1846; J. Forbes evidence, Case 366, U.S. vs Castillero, 1857, New Almaden Mine, Transcript p 433ff.

2. *Ibid.,* p 485–487.

3. *Ibid.,* p 541–542.

4. J. Forbes evidence, Case 420, U.S. vs Castillero, July 1858, New Alamaden Mine, Transcript, p 88, Exhibit 181, Letter from Sta Clara, 18 June, 1848.

5. *Ibid.,* p 88–90, above letter cited in testimony.

6. A. Peachey, *U.S. vs Castillero*, p 36, 45, 51, 139ff, 170–180, a defense attorney's view.

7. *Ibid.,* p 45–63, *passim,* including letters from Negrete to Forbes, 16 December, 1846, and Castillero to Negrete, 16 December, 1846, to record to A. Forbes "that my island of Santa Cruz as well as the quicksilver mine may also appear as an English possession."

8. Report of Senate Committee 75, 30th Congress, 1st Session 1848, p 46–9.

9. U.S. Diplomatic Correspondence, 1831–1860, Vol 7, Great Britain, Despatch 4 January, 1847.

10. I. Murphy, *Life and Death in West Clare,* 1996, p 45.

11. London PRO, FO 203, 91, Palmerston to Bankhead, 30 June, 1847.

12. W. Kelly, *A Stroll Through the*

Diggings of California, 1852, 2 Vols; *Life in Victoria, Australia*, 1859; K.A. Miller. *Emigrants and Exiles*, 1990; D.H. Akenson, *The Irish Diaspora: A Primer*, 1993; C. Woodham Smith, *The Great Hunger*, 1962; R. Scally, *The End of Hidden Ireland*, 1995.

13. *Diario del Gobierno*, 30 November, 1846.

14. G. Thompson, *Puebla*, Ph D Thesis, Oxford University, 1977, p 199 ff.

15. Gómez-Farías Papers, University of Texas at Austin Library, 1826, p 56–62, 18–24 September, 1846.

16. M. Quaife (ed.), *J.K. Polk, Diaries*, 1910, 14 October, 1846.

17. M. Hogan, *The Irish Soldiers of Mexico*, 1997, p 99; R.R. Miller, *Shamrock and Sword*, 1989; London PRO, FO 203, 88, f 155, 165, records $100 Mexican aid to 17 deserters, paid through the British Consulate in 1846; also $50 each in cash to 34 men in 1848 in lieu of land grants.

18. José Francisco Ramírez, Mexican Foreign Minister, writing to the Governor of Durango, 25 April, 1847, from collected correspondence in *Mexico During the War with the U.S.*, University of Missouri Studies, 23, 1, 1950, p 127. Ramírez had property in California. It is impossible to correlate the various schemes for and attempts at enticement of U.S. deserters.

19. H. Wise, *Los Gringos*, 1849, p 249; W. Callcott, *Church and State in Mexico 1820–57*, 1926, p 156; J. Smith, *The War with Mexico*, 1919, Vol 2, p 221.

20. U.S. Diplomatic Correspondence, Vol 8, Mexico, N. Trist, 25 October, 1847.

21. R.R. Miller (ed.), *Letters of Ralph Kirkman*, p 21, to his wife from Puebla, 1 June, 1847; J. Smith, *War with Mexico*, 1919, Vol 2, p 81.

22. R. Anderson, *An Artillery Officer in the Mexican War*, 1911, letters to his wife, p 80, 314.

23. J. Kenly, *Memoirs*, 1873, p 300, 381.

24. J. Baldwin, Testimony in Frémont Claims, Senate Committee Report 75, 1848, p 47–48; H.E. Bolton, *Guide to Materials for U.S. History in the Principal Archives of Mexico*, 1913, located the documents in Legajo 8 and 9 of the documentary group Fomento (Dirección de Fomento de Colonización), 1847, Archivo General de la Nación. However, Mexican archivists, while insisting that Bolton's reference is now out of date, could not locate the 1847 papers at the time of publication of this book. A detailed, but hostile report of the confirmation was carried in the Honolulu *Polynesian*, 11 August, 1847, and copied verbatim in Samuel Brannan's *San Francisco Californian*, 29 September, 1847.

25. Petition for Compensation to Senate Committee on Military Affairs, Report No 75, 1848.

26. C. Upham, *Life of Frémont*, 1856, p 229, 235, 241.

27. T.H. Benton, *Thirty Years View*, 1856, Vol 2, p 691.

28. London PRO, FO 207, 19, Mexican Consular Miscellany, showing several Irish "doctors" in Mexico.

29. J. Velasco, *Noticias Estadisticas del Estado de Sonora*, 1850, p 306–310.

30. J. Forbes evidence, Case 366, U.S. vs Castillero, New Almaden Mine, 30 June, 1848, Transcript, p 489.

31. U.S. Diplomatic Correspondence, Vol 8, Mexico, Doc 3752, O'Reilly to Jas Buchanan, 15 February, 1848.

32. *Congressional Globe*, 29 March 1848.

33. J. O'Rorke, *History of Sligo*, 1892, p 247; W. Kelly, *A Stroll* etc., 1852, Vol 2, p 231–2.

34. Isaac Hartmann, *Brief in Mission Cases*, 1852, p 63–65, Bancroft Pamphlets on New Almaden, Vol 3.

35. Bancroft Mss 68, 99c, ff 63–5, J. Forster, *Memoir*, 1878.

36. Bancroft Mss CD 172, E. Galindo, *A Puntes para la Historia de California*, 1877.

37. *San José Pioneer*, 17 May, 1879.

38. J. R. Browne, *Sketch of the Settlement and Exploration of Lower California*, 1869, p 45.

39. Bancroft Mss, CD 49, f 134, N. Botello, *Anales del Sur*, 1875.

40. Bancroft Mss, CD 61, f 69, A. Coronel, *Cosas de California*, 1877.

41. H. Quigly, *The Irish Race in California*, 1878, p 216–219; Z. Engelhardt, *Missions and Missionaries of California*, 1896, Vol 4, p 549, note.

42. G.P. Mawn, *Jasper O'Farrell, Surveyor*, 1970, MA Thesis, University of San

Francisco. I am grateful to Janice Valderama of Petaluma, a direct descendant of O'Farrell, for her hospitality and for prompting me to explore the surveyor's Irish background. The (Military) Ordnance Survey of the time seems to be the only way he could have received his experience, basically as a temporary casual worker, like Quigly, who worked in County Wicklow.

Chapter Nine

1. H.H. Bancroft, *History of California*, 1888, Vol 6, p 530ff, 540.

2. H. Halleck, *Report*, 1 March, 1849, Senate Executive Document 17, 31st Congress, 1st Session; W.C. Jones, *Report*, 9 March 1850, Document 18, p 14.

3. *Ibid.*, Jones, p 24, 29; Legislative Record, Vol 4, 7 July, 1846 Article 2, Bancroft Library.

4. G. del Castillo, *Treaty of Guadeloupe Hidalgo*, 1990, p 72–77.

5. J. Forbes Evidence, Case 420, U.S. vs Castillero, July 1858, Transcript p 6.

6. *Emigration and Colonial Gazette*, 8 January and 21 May, 1842; *The Emigrant*, Vol 25, January 1849.

7. S. T. Hall, *Life and Death in Ireland 1849*, 1850.

8. I. Murphy, *A People Starved: Life and Death in West Clare, 1845–51*, p 18.

9. O. McDonagh, "The Irish Catholic Clergy and Emigration During the Great Famine," *Irish Historical Studies*, September 1947, 5, No 20, p 287–303.

10. Stearns Collection, the Huntington, San Marino, SG Box 42, two pages, endorsed, unsigned and undated.

11. E.G. Gudde, *California Place Names*, 1949; I am indebted to John Robinson, historical adviser to *The Dogtown Territorial Quarterly*, for identifying the Las Animas River as the Mojave.

12. G.W. Beattie, "An Inland Chain of Missions in California," *Southern California Historical Society Quarterly*, 14, 1929.

13. W. Smith, *Garden of the Sun*, 1939, esp Ch 5.; G. Haslam, *The Other California*, 1990; D. Hornbeck, *California Profiles*, 1983.

14. H. Rheinheimer, *Topo*, 1988. See also Chapter 1.

15. J.D. Powles, *New Granada*, 1863; C. Richardson, *J.D. Powles*, 1854.

16. L.P. Graf, "Colonizing Projects South of the Nueces," 1820–45, *South Western Historical Quarterly*, 50, 1947, p 431–448; R. Roche, *The Texas Irish*, 1975; M. Henderson, "Minor Empresario Contracts for Texas," 1824–34, *South Western Historical Quarterly*, 31, 4, 1928, p 295–324.

17. J. King and M. Fitzgerald, *The Uncounted Irish*, 1990; Louis Bisceglia, uncompleted work files on the Calaveras Irish and Mss, *Irish Identity in the Mother Lode*, Irish Studies Program, University of California at San Jose; P. Blessing, *West Among Strangers*, 1977, Ph. D. Thesis, UCLA, concentrating on the Irish in Sacramento and Los Angeles, 1850–58; R. and F. Rohrbacher, "The Fenian Brotherhood in Northern California," *The Dogtown Territorial*, 27 & 28, 1996; J. Fox, "Researching the Gold Rush Irish," preliminary findings, *DTQ*, 30, 1997.

18. A.C. Hall, *Ireland*, 1841, 2 Vols. Hall's father, Colonel F. Hall, was a mining pioneer in Ireland and members of the family may have joined in the rush to the mineral bonanzas in California and elsewhere.

19. McGiffert (Co. Down) of El Dorado and Sacramento, 1851–3, and Gamble (Co. Down) of Placer and Calaveras, 1850–55, letters in private hands, Northern Ireland; Williamson (Co. Armagh) of Placerville and Monterey, 1850–53, Northern Ireland Public Record Office; Hurley (Co. Cork) of California and Nevada States, 1870–1938, Cork Archive. The Hurley brothers were this writer's great-uncles. Professor K. Miller, University of Missouri, Colombia, kindly gave me the rest of the above information.

20. W. Kelly, *A Stroll Through the Diggings*, 1852, final words of Vol 2; Lansford Hastings, *The Emigrant Guide to Oregon and California*, 1845.

21. J.C. Frémont, *Memoirs of My Life*, 1886, Vol 1, p 545–547, 553–554.

Index